D1190480

The Lost Paratroopers of Normandy

The fateful days and weeks surrounding 6 June 1944 have been extensively documented in histories of the Second World War, but less attention has been paid to the tremendous impact of these events on the populations nearby. *The Lost Paratroopers of Normandy* tells the inspiring yet heartbreaking story of ordinary people who did extraordinary things in defense of liberty and freedom. On D-Day, when transport planes dropped paratroopers from the 82nd and 101st Airborne Divisions hopelessly off-target into marshy waters in northwestern France, the 900 villagers of Graignes welcomed them with open arms. These villagers – predominantly women – provided food, gathered intelligence, and navigated the floods to retrieve the paratroopers' equipment at great risk to themselves. When the attack by German forces on 11 June forced the overwhelmed paratroopers to withdraw, many made it to safety thanks to the help and resistance of the villagers. In this moving book, historian Stephen G. Rabe, son of one of the paratroopers, meticulously documents the forgotten lives of those who participated in this integral part of D-Day history.

Stephen G. Rabe is the Ashbel Smith Professor in History (emeritus) at the University of Texas at Dallas. He is a veteran of the US Marine Corps. *The Lost Paratroopers of Normandy* is his thirteenth book.

The Lost Paratroopers of Normandy

A Story of Resistance, Courage, and Solidarity in a French Village

Stephen G. Rabe

CAMBRIDGE
UNIVERSITY PRESS

CAMBRIDGE
UNIVERSITY PRESS

Shaftesbury Road, Cambridge CB2 8EA, United Kingdom

One Liberty Plaza, 20th Floor, New York, NY 10006, USA

477 Williamstown Road, Port Melbourne, VIC 3207, Australia

314–321, 3rd Floor, Plot 3, Splendor Forum, Jasola District Centre, New Delhi – 110025, India

103 Penang Road, #05–06/07, Visioncrest Commercial, Singapore 238467

Cambridge University Press is part of Cambridge University Press & Assessment, a department of the University of Cambridge.

We share the University's mission to contribute to society through the pursuit of education, learning and research at the highest international levels of excellence.

www.cambridge.org
Information on this title: www.cambridge.org/9781009206372
DOI: 10.1017/9781009206389

First published 2023 (version 3, March 2023)

Printed in the United Kingdom by TJ Books Limited, Padstow Cornwall, March 2023

A catalogue record for this publication is available from the British Library

ISBN 978-1-009-20637-2 Hardback

Grandson Ethan Emil
Born 12 February 2021
Named after his great-grandfather, S/Sgt. Rene Emil Rabe

The heroic collaboration of US paratroopers and the people of Graignes, Normandy in June 1944 made Ethan's life possible.

CONTENTS

FIGURES

MAPS

INTRODUCTION

This is a story to remember. It is not a well-known story. At 2:38 a.m., on 6 June 1944, a date to be forever known as "D-Day," nine C-47 transport planes dropped 143 paratroopers from the 82nd Airborne Division near the village of Graignes in Normandy, France. This was not where the paratroopers were supposed to be. They were about thirty-five kilometers away from their drop zone. Many landed in marshy water, the *marais* of the Cotentin Peninsula. A few became entangled in their parachutes and drowned. Another C-47 dropped a contingent of paratroopers from the 101st Airborne Division near Graignes. They, too, were hopelessly off target. A glider plane attached to the 101st, with two pilots, two enlisted men, and equipment, slammed into the marshes. The wet, confused paratroopers made their way to Graignes. The village was visible from the *marais*, because it was on a hill. The troopers could also see the steeple of the village's remarkable twelfth-century Romanesque church.

By the end of D-Day, the commanding officer had ordered that the paratroopers would defend Graignes and wait for the Allied invasion forces to reach them. The officer's decision was facilitated by the enthusiasm of the villagers. On their own initiative, villagers had taken their boats into the flooded areas to retrieve the bundles of equipment that had been dropped in distinctive blue parachutes. The paratroopers now had radios, machine guns, mortars, and ammunition. With visions of first communion, confirmation, and wedding dresses in their heads, girls and young women gathered up the unused white silk reserve parachutes. On 7 June, the men in the village assembled in the church, and, with the encouragement of the mayor and priest, voted unanimously to support their unexpected guests. Villagers, including Albert Mauger, the leader of the local Resistance, carried out reconnaissance missions in the surrounding areas for the paratroopers. Germaine Boursier, the owner of the local café, organized women in a round-the-clock effort to cook for the paratroopers. Women drove their horse-drawn wagons into villages occupied by German troops and surreptitiously purchased bread and food. Children brought meals to the paratroopers ensconced in their foxholes.

Until 10 June, the paratroopers and the 900 people of Graignes enjoyed a semblance of peace. The US men offered their chocolate and chewing gum to the children. The children taught the soldiers Norman songs. Plans were made to stay in touch in the postwar world. Hope for liberation arose when two infantrymen who had landed at Omaha Beach, some twenty-five miles from Graignes, wandered into the village on 9 June. But the troopers had destroyed a bridge to their north and twice clashed with German troops. The Americans knew on 10 June that a *Waffen-SS* division had entered the area.

The battle for Graignes began on the morning of 11 June, when villagers and troopers of the Roman Catholic faith were attending Sunday mass. The well-prepared US forces routed the German invaders. But in the afternoon and then in the late evening, a battalion of the 17th *SS Panzergrenadier* Division launched assaults and pounded the village with artillery fire. The church suffered heavy damage. The paratroopers began to take casualties, with more than twenty dying of battlefield wounds. By the end of Sunday, the paratroopers were shooting off their red flares of distress and preparing to withdraw from Graignes. The *SS* invaders had at least a five-to-one numerical advantage, and the US mortars did not have the range to hit the German artillery. Most important, the paratroopers had run out of ammunition. One frustrated machine gunner took to hurling pieces of slate from a roof at the advancing *SS* men.

What happened after the withdrawal order proved even more haunting. Nineteen US uniformed men stayed behind. They included a medical doctor, medics, and the wounded. The *SS* men murdered them all. Their war crimes included bayonetting badly wounded men and pushing them into a pond. Nine other men suffered similarly hideous fates at the hands of the Nazis. They were forced to dig their own graves and then were shot in the back of the head. Two officers, one of whom was the doctor, were interrogated and then executed. The Nazi rampage was not limited to uniformed personnel. The SS murdered the village priest, his religious associate, and two elderly housekeepers. Their crime was that they had ministered to the wounded soldiers. German troops subsequently torched the village. Of the 200 structures in the town, all but two were either destroyed or damaged by fire or artillery bombardment.

In the midst of unspeakable horror and depravity, the people of Graignes remained defiant. The SS men rounded up forty-four villagers and tried to intimidate them into identifying collaborators. No one broke. Indeed, the resistance continued. Individuals hid fleeing soldiers in their homes. Approximately ninety Americans made it to the regional center of Carentan, thirteen kilometers from Graignes, by the evening of Tuesday, 13 June. US forces had just liberated the strategically vital town. During their difficult journey through the *marais*, the paratroopers received guidance and food from country folk.

Two extraordinary young women, nineteen and twelve years of age, saved twenty-one paratroopers. They led fleeing men to the loft of the family barn, some three kilometers from Graignes. For three nights, the girls and their parents concealed the men and shared their meager rations with them. Looking for Americans, German soldiers actually entered the barn but did not investigate the loft. Discovery of the paratroopers would have inevitably led to the execution of the family. Germans typically shot male resisters and dispatched female resisters to Germany to be beheaded. On the night of Thursday, 15 June, the twenty-one paratroopers made it to Carentan. Their hosts arranged for a guide and a large, flat boat to navigate the marshes and canals.

The farm family and the people of Graignes would soon themselves be refugees. The Germans ordered an evacuation of the village and the region. Villagers could not return until the middle of July, when US forces liberated Graignes. On 22 July 1944, a US priest and a French priest celebrated mass in Graignes to commemorate the military and civilian victims. Postwar celebrations included weddings, where the heroines of Graignes took their marital vows in gowns made from white parachute silk. The D-Day "silk from the sky" had become a tangible symbol of liberation and the enduring nature of the Franco-American alliance.[1] The village would not, however, be fully restored until the mid 1950s. The grand church could not be saved. One arch was preserved as a memorial to the soldiers and civilians who had died defending Graignes and France.

Figure I.1 Here are two of the many intrepid females who lived in the village of Graignes, Normandy on 6 June 1944, or "D-Day." They are sisters. Behind them is their brother Jean Claude Rigault, who was an infant in 1944. To the right is Odette Rigault Lelavechef, a self-described "soldier" of the French Resistance. She was nineteen years old in 1944. Odette passed in October 2018 at the age of ninety-three. The younger sister, Marthe Rigault His, was twelve years old in 1944. In 2021, Marthe remains as lively as ever, cooking enormous feasts for visitors from America and painting scenes from the family home for the children and grandchildren of the US paratroopers she knew in 1944. The two women recounted their story innumerable times. But, in Marthe's words, "we always live and feel it." Photograph courtesy of the Rigault family.

What happened at Graignes was historically significant. The battles of 11–12 June had slowed the progress of the 17th *SS Panzergrenadier* Division. Their primary mission was to recapture

Figure I.2 The "silk from the sky" wedding of Odette Rigault and her older sister, Marie Jean in 1945. The third person to the right of Marie Jean is Marthe Rigault, sitting next to her little brother, Jean Claude. Gustave and Madame Rigault are standing behind Marthe. Courtesy of Marthe Rigault His.

Carentan, the port town which lay between Utah and Omaha Beaches. German control of Carentan would prevent the US invaders from joining forces. The defenders of Graignes had delayed the attack on Carentan by at least a day, giving the 101st time to consolidate its hold on Carentan. They had also bloodied and wearied the *SS* attackers of Graignes, the 1st Battalion of the 37th Regiment. That very same battalion led the 17th *SS Panzergrenadier* Division attack on Carentan on 13 June and reached some of Carentan's outlying streets. The 101st Division held on, however, and, by the end of the day, tanks of the 2nd Armored Division had forced the Germans into retreat. Carentan remained liberated.

By helping to save the lives of well over 100 paratroopers, the bulk of whom were members of Headquarters Company, 3rd Battalion, 507th Regiment of the 82nd Airborne, the people of Graignes contributed to Allied victory. These survivors of Graignes participated in future combat in Normandy in June and July 1944, in the Battle of the Bulge in Belgium in the winter of 1944–1945, and in a combat jump over the Rhine River on 24 March 1945. The paratroopers then waged war in the Rhineland area, before Germany finally surrendered on 8 May 1945. The paratroopers also freed thousands of Eastern European slave laborers toiling in German factories. In their individual ways, the defenders of Graignes, many of whom were repeatedly wounded during their eleven months of combat, contributed to the defeat of Nazi Germany and the liberation of Western Europe.

The memory of D-Day looms large in the popular imagination. As Olivier Wieviorka, a French scholar, has noted, the invasion of Normandy "unquestionably ranks among the greatest events in human history."[2] The stakes could not have been higher. The forces of liberation embarked on a journey to defeat and eliminate the murderous, genocidal, imperialist regime that was Nazi Germany. That odious Nazi regime slaughtered Professor Wieviorka's Jewish grandparents. One would spend a very long time trying to master the ever-expanding literature on the invasion and the liberation of France. Films like *The Longest Day* (1962) and *Saving Private Ryan* (1998) are considered cinematic classics. The quintessential American movie hero, John Wayne, played the role of an officer in the 82nd Airborne in *The Longest Day*. President Ronald Reagan gave a memorable speech in 1984, when he became the first US president to attend in Normandy a commemoration of D-Day. The president hailed the "boys of Pointe du Hoc," the American Rangers who scaled the cliffs of Omaha Beach. The Rangers, who suffered appalling losses, had, in Reagan's words, "fought for humanity."[3]

What happened at Graignes is part of the storied history of D-Day and its aftermath. But what happened at Graignes was also distinctive. It is a case where an entire locale rose in defense of the Allied troops. To be sure, individual Normans and Resistance members aided the Allies. French partisans began carrying out sabotage missions against the 17th *SS Panzergrenadier* Division, as the division made its way from the interior of France toward Graignes and Carentan in the immediate days after the invasion. Other French towns and villages, such as Oradour-sur-Glane, suffered foul war crimes at the hands of *SS* units. Nonetheless, what prompted an entire village to act spontaneously to protect men that they and their descendants continue to refer to as "the liberators" or "our paratroopers" deserves analysis. Despite losing friends and relatives, their village, and, for a time, their way of life, the people of Graignes never regretted their commitment. At a twentieth anniversary service in 1964, the village priest drew an analogy between the *paras* floating down toward Graignes and God sending his only son, Jesus, to earth.[4]

The people of Graignes also do not fit the standard characterization of French partisans under German occupation. Those who pledged allegiance to the French Resistance tended to be politically active, urban people who disproportionately identified with leftist groups like the Socialist and Communist parties. Graignes was a rural village. People worked with their famed Norman cows and the butter, cheese, and milk byproducts and on orchards that produced the fruit for distilling Normandy's sublime Calvados brandy. The French Department of *Manche*, where Graignes was situated, tended to vote for political conservatives, not political leftists. Women, both young and old, played principal roles in defending their *paras* and the village. This was a notable development in a country that, as late as 1944, still denied French women the right to vote. Histories of D-Day and its aftermath traditionally focus on men, not the adventures and contributions of Norman women and girls to liberation.

The war crimes that the Nazi soldiers committed at Graignes against civilian and military personnel have not been thoroughly assessed. One high-ranking enlisted man in the 17th *SS Panzergrenadier* Division was found guilty in 1947 by a US military tribunal for overseeing, on 17 June 1944, the execution of US soldiers in a village a few kilometers away from Graignes. US military investigators interviewed the villagers of Graignes, including the mayor, in 1947 about the execution of the nineteen paratroopers. The decision was made, however, not to pursue justice, as the *SS* men that had perpetrated war crimes had vanished into eternity. During the summer of 1944, Allied forces destroyed the over 900 men of the 1st Battalion of the 37th Regiment of the 17th *SS Panzergrenadier* Division. Finally, what also needs highlighting and remembering was the steadfastness of the doctor and the medics, who stayed with the wounded paratroopers in Graignes and were murdered for their loyalty to the ideals of medicine.

Graignes in Historical Writing

The people of Normandy and France are familiar with the story of Graignes. For a variety of reasons, the story is less well known in the United States. In 1948, France awarded the village the *Croix de Guerre*, with silver star. The next year, US Ambassador to France David K. E. Bruce attended a ceremony to establish a Franco-American memorial in the ruins of the church. General Dwight D. Eisenhower had previously issued commendations to villagers who had rescued paratroopers. In the ensuing years, the village held memorial services to mark notable anniversaries of the dramatic days in June 1944. But in the postwar years, the villagers had to focus on rebuilding their village and their lives. European and US economic aid assisted the rebuilding of Normandy and Graignes.

For nearly four decades, contact between villagers and the surviving paratroopers was infrequent. The Rigault family, who had hid paratroopers in the barn, did not know the fate of the men. The family had lost the paper signed by the twenty-one paratroopers commending them to US authorities in the hurried rush to evacuate their home in late June 1944. For their part, the paratroopers were not fully aware of the death and destruction that SS troops had inflicted on Graignes. Between the middle of June 1944 and May 1945, the paratroopers concentrated on staying alive in Normandy, the Battle of the Bulge, the jump over the Rhine River, and the concluding, dangerous house-to-house fighting in the Rhineland region. Some of the paratroopers also pulled occupation duty in Berlin in the second half of 1945. When they returned to the United States, the veterans wanted to forget the economic hardships of the Great Depression and the combat traumas they had experienced. They wanted a spouse, family, work, and a middle-class life. By the mid 1950s, most veterans had achieved this in an America that was growing and prosperous. Corporal Homer H. Poss, who left high school to enlist and at the age of nineteen was one of the youngest paratroopers in Graignes, served as mayor of his town of Highland, Illinois. Staff Sergeant Fredric Boyle returned to his wife Charla, set up housekeeping, and attended Palmer Chiropractic School in Davenport, Iowa. Dr. Boyle and his wife had four children. He also served as mayor of Keosauqua, Iowa. The veterans of Graignes did occasionally reminisce at barbecues in Stamford, Connecticut hosted by Technician Fifth Grade (T/5) Edward T. "Eddie" Page. Page had hidden in the Rigault barn with his buddy, Staff Sergeant (S/Sgt.) Rene E. Rabe. Rabe related how a "farm family" had hid him and others in a barn and provided them with a meal of cabbage with melting butter, when they were ravenously hungry. Page told his wife, Betty, that if he ever returned to Europe, Graignes would be his first stop.

The fortieth anniversary of D-Day in 1984 seemed to motivate the veterans to think about Graignes. President Reagan had given his inspiring speech. Veterans of the 82nd and 101st Divisions, then in their sixties, initiated an annual ritual by jumping once again out of C-47s over Normandy on 6 June. The "experienced" paratroopers had white hair or no hair but seemed as fit and fearless as ever. American citizens saw on television visual images of the stunning but sad rows of Christian crosses and Stars of David at the American Cemetery in Colleville-sur-Mer, which is near Omaha Beach. Division and recrimination had characterized public debate in the 1960s and 1970s over the Vietnam War. D-Day seemed worth remembering as a time of national purpose and unity. Renowned television journalist Tom Brokaw kept the positive feelings flowing with his popular book *The Greatest Generation* (1998).[5]

The veterans of Graignes began to act individually and collectively. The large, extended family of Private (Pvt.) Arnold J. Martinez of Colorado, who had died at Graignes, began an extensive writing campaign to the Department of Defense trying to determine the circumstances of his death. In 1944, Martinez's parents had initially been informed that their son was missing in action. Later in the year, they received another telegram saying that Arnold had been killed in action, but with no further explanation. Arnold's younger brother, Samuel Martinez, Jr. would subsequently receive financial backing from his employer, Coors Brewing, in his quest to honor his brother. In the 1980s, veterans, who were approaching retirement, now had the time and money to travel to Europe. Some paratroopers approached the idea hesitantly, because they believed they had let the villagers of Graignes down, when they retreated in the dark hours between 11 and 12 June. To their relief, they discovered that villagers annually commemorated their "heroism" and "bowed in sorrow" for those who had sacrificed their lives "for the liberty of our people."[6] Veterans began to bring their families to meet the people that had aided them in Graignes. Most important, two career military officers, Colonel Francis E. Naughton and Lt. Colonel Earcle R. "Pip" Reed, gathered information and lobbied the Department of the Army to recognize the heroism of the people of Graignes. Both men had been junior officers in 1944 and had helped lead the withdrawal from Graignes to Carentan. On 6 July 1986, in a grand ceremony, Secretary of the Army John O. Marsh, Jr. awarded eleven Distinguished Service Medals, several of them posthumously, to the people of Graignes. The medals are the highest award that the Department of Defense can award to a civilian. Five US veterans of Graignes and the brother of Pvt. Martinez attended the ceremony.

The story of Graignes thereafter entered public consciousness. Gary N. Fox's *Graignes: The Franco-American Memorial* (1990) offered a useful summary. Having attended reunions of the 507th Regiment, Fox wrote from the perspective of the veterans. Fox's book was published by a small press and had limited distribution.[7] Two chroniclers of the 507th Regiment, Dominique François and Martin K. A. Morgan, tried to publicize the history of Graignes. François, who lives in Normandy, has a special connection to D-Day. His grandparents, who lived on the coast of the Cotentin Peninsula, were unfortunate victims of Allied bombing on 5 June 1944. The German defenders had built a large bunker near their village. The couple's three sons survived the bombing, and US soldiers initially cared for François's father and two uncles. François has written *La bataille de Graignes: Les paras perdus, 5–12 Juin 1944* (*The Battle of Graignes: The Lost Paratroopers, 5–12 June*) (2012), which includes testimonies by French citizens.[8] François also assisted Colonel Naughton in establishing a memorial to the 507th Regiment in Amfreville, the village where the regiment, including the defenders of Graignes, were supposed to land.

Martin Morgan, who has worked with the National Geographic Society, has led battlefield tours around the world. Both his history of the 507th Regiment in Normandy, *Down to Earth* (2004), and his photographic history of D-Day (2014) have sections on Graignes.[9] Morgan's approach has been to give equal weight to the memories of the paratroopers and those of the villagers. Morgan has also served as an authority for two television broadcasts, *D-Day: Down to Earth, Return of the 507th* (2004) by the Public Broadcasting System and *D-Day: The Secret Massacre* (2004) by the History Channel. François has also aided a compelling visual presentation, *Papa Said: We Should Never Forget* (2009) produced by Georgia Public Broadcasting. The twenty-four-minute story focuses on twelve-year-old Marthe Rigault and pointedly asks young people in America if they would be as brave as Marthe was in defending liberty. François's wife, Gaelle, played Madame Rigault and Denis Small, the long-time mayor of Graignes and a historian of the village, played the father, Gustave Rigault. The historical recreation garnered significant recognition, including an Emmy Award.[10]

Despite these artistic and literary endeavors, the story of Graignes remains generally unknown and incomplete. As Martin Morgan lamented at the end of 2018, "despite my best efforts though, the story of Graignes has still not reached a broad audience, nor has it been popularized to any meaningful level."[11] A new look at Graignes is justified, because significant new evidence has become available. In the early twenty-first century, historical societies and universities in states such as Minnesota, Tennessee, and Wisconsin began projects to interview aging veterans. In part, these archivists and librarians were reacting to the "greatest generation" phenomenon. Research in the military records of the veterans of Graignes has always been difficult, because a massive fire at the National Personnel Records Center in St. Louis in 1973 destroyed 80 percent of individual service records of those who served in the Army. But some records, such as those of Private First-Class (Pfc.) Harold J. Premo, survived replete with burn and water marks.

Properly telling the story of Graignes also highlights developments in scholarship on US foreign relations. Scholars have increasingly employed innovative approaches to international history, such as "decentering" the United States as a foreign-policy actor and analyzing the roles of ordinary people in the making of international history.[12] This study is grounded in documentary evidence not just from the United States but also from France and Germany. In the case of Graignes, non elite actors, the paratroopers and the villagers, made choices that affected the conduct of US foreign and military policy, the liberation of France, and the defeat of Germany. The women of Graignes were among those who made critical decisions and exercised power. The story of Graignes teaches us that a "local" event can tell us much about "global" history.

A complete understanding of Graignes also demands analysis of the roles and memories of French citizens and German soldiers. French archivists and librarians, such as in the Norman city of Caen, collected the memories of older Normans about D-Day and the subsequent warfare in Normandy. The interviews included testimonies by villagers from Graignes. As historian Mary Louise Roberts demonstrated in *D-Day through French Eyes* (2014), the joy of liberation was always tempered by the reality that nearly 20,000 Normans lost their lives in the fighting in 1944.[13] After a long period of silence, the French have also been asking hard questions about official and private collaboration with the German occupiers from 1940 to 1944. The long-running television series *Un village français* (*A French Village*) (2009–2017) explored the compromises that citizens made with the Germans during the occupation. The seventy-two-part series proved dramatically compelling and drew a large audience in France for seven years. In the twenty-first century, the government has declassified records that revealed painful incidents and uncomfortable secrets about French life under occupation. Ronald C. Rosbottom of Amherst College made good use of occupation records to write *Sudden Courage* (2019), his stirring telling of French adolescent resistance to Nazi tyranny.[14]

Probing the actions and rationales of the 17th *SS Panzergrenadier* Division at Graignes is a scholarly challenge. For seventy-five years, *SS* officers and their civilian acolytes have been trying to cover up the division's war crimes. Massimiliano Afiero, a prolific Italian chronicler of the Axis powers, goes as far as to assert in his coffee-table-style illustrated history of the 17th *SS Panzergrenadier* Division that "throughout its history, the division was never involved in any war crimes or in any war crimes against civilians, as witness of its character as a strictly military unit."[15] Afiero and other chroniclers of the division conveniently ignore in their books the assault on Graignes on 11–12 June. But the Germans kept precise, comprehensive records of their military activities. Using German archival sources facilitates an understanding of the course of events in Graignes and further demonstrates how historical actors and their enthusiasts will try to shape an understanding of an atrocious history for future generations.

In preparing this study, the author has had singular access to the military veterans of Graignes. As a budding young historian, I soaked up the conversations that I heard my father, S/Sgt. Rabe, have with other veterans in our neighborhoods in Connecticut. I further listened in to the anecdotes that he and his colleagues told at Eddie Page's reunions. I now realize that some of these tales were about Graignes. I naturally spent most of my time at reunions with the other children. In the past few years, I have renewed my relationship with them and they have provided me with valuable written resources about their fathers. Many of these childhood friends had already traveled to Graignes and met the French heroines of Graignes. As an academic historian, I told myself that I would tell the story of Graignes. But for more than four decades, my scholarship focused on the history of US foreign relations with Latin America. It would have been preferable to conduct in-depth interviews both with the paratroopers and with the villagers, almost all of whom have sadly long since passed.

This study proceeds in a chronological fashion. To provide context, the first three chapters look at the preparation and training of the US paratroopers, the organization of the 17th SS *Panzergrenadier* Division, and the character of life in France and Graignes under German occupation. In these opening chapters, readers are introduced to the background and lives of individual paratroopers, villagers, and SS officers. The opening section also focuses on the influence of a US military officer who was not in Graignes, Major General James M. Gavin, the Associate Commander of the 82nd Airborne. General Gavin put his imprint, in terms of physical fitness and mental agility, on the men of the Headquarters Company of the 3rd Battalion of the 507th Regiment.

The fourth through seventh chapters detail the intense scenes – the landing, the battle, and the escape from Graignes. These chapters emphasize the interactions between the villagers and the paratroopers and the central roles that the villagers played in the drama. Documentary materials provide insight into the three attacks that German military units launched against Graignes. The story is continued through July 1944. The villagers faced hardship, hunger, and death as refugees. The paratroopers who survived Graignes would spend another month in Normandy and would engage in hard combat. After their failure at Carentan, the SS soldiers who attacked Graignes and executed the wounded would be engaged in costly, futile combat in June and July 1944, trying to forestall the liberation of France.

The final chapter surveys postwar developments. The villagers worked on rebuilding Graignes and establishing their village's honored place in French history. The young US veterans of Graignes returned to America and started creating their civilian lives. Many veterans had, however, suffered grievous wounds, and all had to work through their respective traumas. Four decades would pass before they would return to Graignes, both mentally and physically. The handful of SS soldiers who survived World War II undoubtedly had their physical and psychological issues. But they never had to defend publicly their execution of priests, wounded soldiers, and medical staff in Graignes.

1 PARATROOPER

The young men of Headquarters Company, 3rd Battalion, 507th Regiment of the 82nd Airborne Division who landed near the village of Graignes, Normandy in the early morning of 6 June 1944 embodied a cross-section of their society that grew up in the United States in the Great Depression of the 1930s. As had their parents, the paratroopers had experienced hard times that limited their education and job prospects. But these ordinary men had become pioneers. The idea of airborne assaults behind enemy lines was a new and challenging concept in US military science. The men had also undergone a regimen of physical training that set them apart from other uniformed personnel. Their beloved leader, James N. Gavin, the youngest general in the US military, embodied the background and aspirations of the men he commanded. The product of a hard-scrabble life, Gavin defined for his men what it meant to be a paratrooper.

Airborne

Human beings have long fancied flying or floating through the sky. In Greek mythology, Icarus tried to escape the island of Crete with wings of feathers and wax designed by his father, the master craftsman Daedalus. The hubris of Icarus led to his failure and demise, and prompted the everlasting warning about "flying too close to the sun." The genius of the Italian Renaissance, Leonardo da Vinci, sketched in his notebook something that looked like a parachute, a tent of linen that was thirty-six feet wide and thirty-six feet deep. Da Vinci predicted that with his device a man "will be able to throw himself down from any great height without sustaining any injury." Indeed, in 1887, a large crowd assembled at Golden Gate Park in San Francisco to cheer Thomas Scott Baldwin, who successfully jumped from a hot-air balloon tethered at 5,000 feet. Baldwin and his brother, Samuel, designed the parachute.[1]

Military implications quickly became associated with the concept of jumping from something in the sky and landing safely. In 1783, the Montgolfier brothers demonstrated the efficacy of hot air balloons to the delight of King Louis XVI and Queen Marie Antoinette. The first "test pilots" were a sheep, a duck, and a rooster. Benjamin Franklin, who was serving as the first US Minister to France, subsequently foresaw the day when "ten thousand men descending from the clouds" could do "an infinite deal of mischief before a force could be brought together to repel them." More than a century later, another American in France, Colonel William L. "Billy" Mitchell, attached some concrete plans to Franklin's vision. Mitchell, who commanded US air forces in France in 1918, recommended to General John J. "Black Jack" Pershing on 17 October 1918 that the United States could shorten the war against Germany by launching an airborne assault on the city of Metz. The troopers would then attack German forces from the rear. Major Mitchell predicted that he would soon have large enough airplanes to accomplish the mission.[2] The war ended, however, less than a month later.

US military planners did not follow up Mitchell's ideas on paratroopers or his larger belief in air power. Twelve US Marines did a demonstration jump in 1927 in Anacostia, which is part of Washington, D.C. But until 1940, the US military did not have a parachute unit. Other global powers led the way. The Soviet Union began developing parachute forces in 1929 and by 1933 had created twenty-nine parachute battalions. On 30 November 1939, at the outset of Soviet aggression against Finland known as the "Winter War," a small detachment of Soviet paratroopers dropped in northern Finland. Soviet military officials never, however, relied on airborne assaults and by 1943 had given up on the idea, judging that the dropping of paratroopers raised too many logistical challenges.[3]

Nazi Germany, led by *Oberst* (Colonel) Kurt Student, a protégé of *Reichsmarschall* Hermann Göring, assembled eleven parachute divisions by the end of World War II. *Oberst* Student established a parachute training school at Stendhal, west of Berlin. The paratrooper branch of the *Luftwaffe*, known as *Fallschirmjäger*, participated in 1940 in the invasions of Norway, Holland, and Belgium. Most notably, a German parachute infantry division successfully attacked the island of Crete in May 1941. Thereafter, German generals, upon the orders of Führer Adolf Hitler, deployed the *Fallschirmjäger* solely as ground-based infantry units. Hitler heaped praise and medals on the Nazi conquerors of Crete. The Führer apparently thought, however, that the costs of conquest were high, with casualties at 33 percent and 200 airplanes destroyed. Hitler further reasoned that parachute assaults depended on the element of surprise, which would no longer be possible during a time of general war.[4]

In one of the ironies of history, US military planners drew different lessons from the Nazi airborne assaults on European countries and the invasion of Crete. The Crete operation had been conducted entirely from the air, with parachute drops, glider-plane landings, and air-landed forces. Captain James M. Gavin, a young instructor at West Point, judged the German parachute drops, "bringing parachute troops and glider troops to the battlefield in masses," a "promising" development in military science. Gavin analyzed the German invasion orders, copies of which he obtained from the War Department.[5]

High-ranking officers agreed with Captain Gavin's assessment. In April 1940, Major William "Bill" Lee, often dubbed the "father of the US Airborne," received permission to organize a "test platoon" of paratroopers. Major Lee developed an intensive eight-week training course at Ft. Benning, Georgia based on training models for British Commandos and US Rangers. The experimental nature of the training was highlighted by the use of football helmets by troopers to protect against crash landings. In September 1940, a mass jump of Lee's platoon of approximately fifty men suitably impressed Chief of Staff General George C. Marshall. Marshall authorized the expansion of the platoon into a battalion. Thereafter, as the lessons of Crete took hold, the US military created three additional parachute battalions in 1941. Captain Gavin escaped from the classroom, graduated from jump school at Ft. Benning, and took command of a new parachute battalion. Gavin also wrote Field Manual (FM) 31–30, "Tactics and Techniques of Airborne Troops."[6]

The Japanese attack on Pearl Harbor on 7 December 1941 and Nazi Germany's declaration of war against the United States four days later accelerated the development of airborne capabilities. The 82nd

Infantry Division would be designated an airborne division in August 1942. The division had been activated a few months previously. The 82nd Division had fought with distinction as an infantry unit in France during World War I. The division had created the "AA" or "All American" shoulder patch in red, white, and blue to celebrate that it had soldiers from all forty-eight states. Sergeant Alvin C. York became the most celebrated of the division's soldiers, winning the Congressional Medal of Honor. At the conclusion of World War I, the War Department deactivated the 82nd.[7] In mid 1942, General Mathew Ridgway, who graduated from West Point in 1917, assumed command of the division. Gavin, now Colonel Gavin, brought his parachute infantry regiment, the 505th, to the 82nd in early 1943.

From the outset, those who volunteered to jump out of "perfectly good airplanes" learned they were "special" members of the US armed forces. That designation proved to be a double-edged sword for those who served as parachutists in the 82nd Airborne. Lee, Ridgway, and especially Gavin imparted their visions on what it was to be "special." The paratroopers wore their chestnut-brown, custom-designed jump boots at all times, even when wearing dress uniforms. They bloused their pants over their boots. On their overseas cap, they wore a cloth patch depicting a white parachute on a blue field. When a soldier graduated from jump school at Ft. Benning, he was awarded a unique badge of "silver parachute wings." Their combat uniforms appeared "baggy," with oversized pockets in their blouses and pants to carry what they needed when they hit the ground. Famed war correspondent Martha Gellhorn, who reported on the 82nd in Europe, felt overwhelmed in the paratroopers' presence, noting "each man wears his soiled and baggy clothing as if it had been designed for him alone and was not Army issue at all."[8] As a scholar of the 82nd observed, the men had their "totems."[9]

The special status also meant higher pay. Jump pay for paratroopers was $50 extra a month and $100 extra a month for officers. In the context of prevailing civilian and military wages, this was a king's ransom. A private in the US Army earned about $21 a month and then had $1.25 deducted to pay for laundry expenses. Paratroopers training in England in 1944 for D-Day earned more than a mid-ranking British officer. John Hinchliff, who had grown up poor in Minnesota and sadly recalled being mocked at school for wearing second-hand clothing, found the extra $50 most attractive. John W. "Jack" Dunn, a medic who jumped with the 82nd, rued his life of hard poverty in Milwaukee. Bob Bearden, who had become a sergeant in the Texas National Guard and earned $80 a month, thought a monthly salary of $130 would be "a lot." Bearden further dreamed that his romantic life would improve, thinking that young women "would go crazy for parachute wings."[10]

Lee, Ridgway, and Gavin wanted intelligent, athletic volunteers, described as "men of the highest order" that "never faltered or failed."[11] Gavin reasoned, an analysis that was supported by experience, that paratroopers dropped behind enemy lines inevitably would be scattered. They would fight as small units, without central command. Enlisted men would need to show initiative, think for themselves, and show an independent streak, even as they accepted military commands. In order to qualify for the paratroopers, an enlisted man was required to score high on the standardized examination, the Army General Classification Test (AGCT). Although many recruits lacked four years of high school, they often achieved test results high enough to qualify for officers' candidate school. Having enlisted personnel that had the mental capabilities of their officers helped create a unique military structure. Homer Jones, who was a platoon leader in Normandy and would achieve the rank of Lt. Colonel as a career military man, recalled that in the 82nd "the normal walls between officers and enlisted men broke down. I often finished marches carrying a mortar or machine gun."[12]

Whereas astute observers might quickly glean the native intellectual abilities of paratroopers, their first impression would be of their overwhelming physical presence. Paratroopers appeared and moved like athletes ready to compete in the Olympics. From the outset, jump training at Ft. Benning was characterized by its "sheer physical brutality." General Ridgway wanted each trooper "to be as finely trained as a champion boxer." General Gavin would have made physical training challenging for legendary champions like Joe Louis or Jesse Owens. Gavin once took his paratroopers on a night march of twenty-three miles. The men conducted field exercises for the entire day. At 9:00 p.m., the troops were granted two hours of sleep. They then hiked back to camp that night by a different route. They had covered more than fifty miles. Any man who complained or fell out of formation would no longer be a paratrooper. Such a regimen, Ridgway and Gavin agreed, produced "a special kind of animal."[13]

Recruiters judged that young men who had participated in athletics in high school or college might best be able to complete the training. Lt. Frank Naughton and Sgt. Hinchliff had both been boxers. Homer Poss of Illinois had competed in track and field. The Roman Catholic Chaplain, Father and Captain John Verret, played football and hockey in high school in Burlington, Vermont. Private Robert R. Miller, a medic who died at Graignes, was considered "one of the best baseball catchers ever" at Boyertown High School in Pennsylvania.[14] The 82nd Division had officers who had attained "All-American" accolades in football at various universities. Ben Schwartzwalder was a center and captain of his football team at West Virginia University. Captain Schwartzwalder coached the 507th Regiment's football team and performed splendidly in action, garnering the Silver Star, the Bronze Star, and the Purple Heart. Schwartzwalder was the head football coach at Syracuse University from 1949 to 1973. Ernie Davis, the first African-American to win the Heisman Trophy, and Jim Brown, one of the greatest professional football players ever, played for Coach Schwartzwalder.

Recruiters took a subtle approach in making their sales pitch for joining the paratroopers. The recruiters were handpicked, or, in Gavin's words, "very alert, sharp-looking guys." The recruiters would spend a day at a training base before talking to men. They would be seen at the Non-Commissioned Officers (NCO) Club and at the commissary or PX. Their totems – the jump boots, the wings, the airborne patch – would create a buzz. When meeting with potential recruits they would show off their gymnastic abilities by doing a series of exercises, such as tumbles. They wanted to challenge the men and show off the "élan" of a paratrooper.[15] Reverse psychology was also applied. James P. James of Wisconsin recalled that a recruiter displayed a matchbox designed to look like a coffin and asked: "Who wants to join the paratroopers or go home in one of these?" Commanders at training bases understood that recruiters were overwhelming their trainees. Officers at Ft. Warren, near Cheyenne, Wyoming tried to talk Kurt Gabel out of becoming a paratrooper, reminding him "of the gravity of choice." Gabel, who was a German-Jewish émigré, was in the Battle of the Bulge and jumped over the Rhine River. Rene E. Rabe did basic training at Ft. Wolters in Mineral Wells, Texas. His commanding officer used scatological language, trying to warn him about the harshness of training at Ft. Benning.[16]

Jump training proved as arduous as advertised. Less than 50 percent of the recruits – officers and enlisted men – completed the training course within the designated four-week period. James Megellas, who claimed the title of "the most decorated officer in the 82nd Airborne," remembered that only twenty-seven of the eighty-six officers in his class finished jump school.[17] The first week consisted of running and calisthenics, followed over the next two weeks with lessons on folding chutes and practice jumping from 250-foot towers. Instruction on hand-to-hand fighting was also included. Five-mile runs before breakfast were routine and twenty-five pushups had to be done for every mistake. Recruits were encouraged to do one-handed pushups. All movement was "double-time." Edward M. Isbell from the Blue Ridge Mountains of North Carolina recalled that during the first days of training aching men had to help each other out of bed. Isbell added that "the drill instructors were merciless," trying "to make it so tough that men would ask for a transfer." Drill instructors also played with the minds of the recruits, alternately employing shame and praise. Men who quit had to undergo the humiliation of packing their bags in front of others. The drill instructors assured those who endured, however, that a single paratrooper was superior to five soldiers. A sign on the shed where parachutes were packed read: "Through these portals pass America's finest troops. Pack well, and jump again."[18]

During the final week of training, recruits were required to complete five jumps, including usually a night jump, in order to secure their parachute wings. Officers estimated that 98 percent of the recruits had never been in an airplane before their first jump. The initial jump might be at 1,200 feet altitude and the last at 800 feet. John Hinchliff laughingly remembered about his first jump that he felt the opening shock "and I looked up at that canopy and I said, 'God damn.'" Ed Isbell "looked up to see this beautiful white canopy of silk that meant life itself." Many troopers admitted to being nervous about their subsequent jumps, perhaps now comprehending what could go wrong. Colonel Mark J. Alexander, a battalion commander in the 82nd, witnessed a training accident, with a C-47 suddenly losing altitude and hitting and killing three men floating to earth. Ambulances normally waited on the ground ready to collect those who broke ankles and dislocated knees. The landing shock was the equivalent of jumping from a fifteen-foot-high platform. On his fourth training jump, Hinchliff landed on top of an ambulance, injuring his tailbone. Against medical advice, his buddies carried him out of the hospital so he could make his all-important fifth qualifying jump. General Gavin made over fifty jumps, suffering a fracture in his spinal cord on one of his four combat jumps. In civilian life, Gavin would suffer pain from the accumulated toll of the opening and landing shocks.[19]

Figure 1.1 A paratrooper carries out a practice jump during World War II. The paratrooper is in excellent position – upright and having turned his body away from the airplane. His parachute is beginning to deploy. Note the bundles of equipment with parachutes underneath the airplane. Rene E. Rabe photograph.

Airborne soldiers came to perceive their profession as an indispensable duty, not a privilege or pleasure. S/Sgt. Frederic Boyle made twenty-five jumps, including two combat jumps with Poss and Rabe. He told his family he was frightened every time.[20] Bob Bearden concurred with Boyle, noting that "I never made a parachute jump that I liked." The men took sustenance, however, from the "esprit de corps" that characterized paratrooper life. Gavin reinforced this by trying "to impress upon them what outstanding individual soldiers they were." He explained that "we wanted to do everything we could to enhance their pride." Bearden found out that civilians had bought into the image of paratroopers as "supermen." When he returned home in September 1942 after jump school, citizens in Dallas, Texas immediately noticed his jump boots. As he explained, "it was this national infatuation and adoration along with fifty dollars a month jump pay that kept me and the rest of the new breed of soldier jumping."[21]

James M. Gavin

Matthew Ridgway commanded the 82nd Division during the invasion of Normandy. Brigadier General Gavin was the assistant commander of the division. To his credit, Ridgway, who was forty-nine years of age, jumped on D-Day and remarkably had one of the most accurate and softest landings of the more than 6,000 men in the division who jumped. He landed in a gentle cow pasture, near the target zone of Amfreville, Normandy. Ridgway had not graduated from Ft. Benning. The Normandy jump was only his fifth jump. Ridgway initially planned to arrive later on a glider plane but decided he needed to be in Normandy at the outset of the mission. Whereas Ridgway was strong and skillful, he is usually not identified with the 82nd in Normandy. Paratroopers minced no words in identifying General Gavin as their commander. Veterans would later focus on singing Gavin's praises, not Ridgway's.[22] General Gavin was in charge of the training of the three parachute infantry regiments, the 505th, 507th, and 508th, who jumped on 6 June 1944. Gavin not only put his imprint on those regiments but also defined what it meant to be a paratrooper.

James M. Gavin led a life of hardship and striving right out of a novel by Charles Dickens. Gavin was born on 22 March 1907 in Brooklyn, New York to a single mother. The pregnant Katherine Ryan had emigrated from County Clare, Ireland. Unmarried pregnant women faced shame, ridicule, and hardship in the conservative Catholic country. Sometime after his birth, Ryan placed her baby in the Angel Guard Home, an orphanage run by the Catholic Diocese of Brooklyn. Martin and Mary Gavin, a couple who lived in the anthracite coal-mining region of Pennsylvania, adopted the two-year-old James. Mary Gavin was an abusive, violent alcoholic. Her husband often considered leaving her. Their adopted son was a dedicated student in grammar school, who especially loved studying history. His parents forced Gavin to leave school after completing eighth grade, insisting that he supplement the family income. The teenaged Gavin peddled newspapers, pumped gasoline, and sold shoes. He read history books at night in the local library. At the age of seventeen, he ran away from home to his birthplace, New York City.

Gavin's grim, unhappy life took a positive turn. On 1 April 1924, Gavin enlisted in the US Army. A helpful recruiter arranged for a surrogate father to sign the underaged Gavin's enlistment papers. Gavin had told the recruiter he was an orphan. The Army became Gavin's family, although Gavin dutifully sent half of his $21 monthly pay to his adoptive parents. He was initially assigned to the US military base in Panama for training and rose rapidly to the rank of corporal. His superiors recognized his ambition and intelligence, and encouraged him to take the entrance examination for West Point. Nighttime study helped him master the math and science subjects he had missed in high school. With his appointment to West Point in 1925, Gavin had become a "mustang," an enlisted soldier who matriculated to the military academy. Gavin graduated from West Point in 1929, finishing in the top third of his class. Gavin studied at night in the latrines, compensating for his lack of formal education. He took notes and wrote mathematical formulas on pieces of toilet paper.[23]

Over the next ten years, Gavin had routine military assignments and progressed slowly in the peacetime Army. In 1939, he was promoted to captain. Upon graduation from West Point, Gavin had married Irma M. "Peggy" Baulsir from Washington, D.C. Baulsir had experienced a prosperous, stable upbringing. The couple had one child, Barbara, born in 1933. Gavin adored his daughter, whom he called "Babe," writing 209 letters to her while in Europe. A mere five days after landing in Normandy, Gavin wrote to his daughter, reassuring her that he had been "shot at but not shot." Barbara Gavin Fauntleroy reminisced that Gavin wrote so often "because he wanted her to have the security and love he did not have in his youth."[24]

Gavin wrote only once to his wife, and that was about divorce. The marriage had broken down before World War II. Peggy Gavin did not enjoy the life of a military spouse. Gavin confessed to his diary in 1940 that he had become "sexually indifferent" to his wife.[25] The couple stayed married during the war, because it made life easier for Peggy and Barbara. But Gavin no longer thought he was married and became sexually adventurous in Europe. He often called on Valerie Porter in London, took up with Martha Gellhorn, the estranged third wife of writer Ernest Hemingway, and had a brief affair with the famed German actress Marlene Dietrich. During his command in occupied Berlin in the second half of 1945, Gavin arranged for Dietrich's mother to escape the Soviet-controlled sector of Berlin. Except perhaps for Gellhorn, Gavin was not emotionally involved with his lovers. Just before the outbreak of the Battle of the Bulge, Gavin visited Valerie Porter. His diary entry read: "Had a wonderful time. Just what I needed."[26] Gavin divorced his wife in 1947 and married Jeanne Emert Duncan of Knoxville, Tennessee in 1948. She was sixteen years younger than Gavin. Like her new husband, Jeanne Gavin brought a daughter to the marriage, and the two of them produced three more daughters. They remained married for more than four decades.

Gavin recognized that paratrooper duty was a young man's game and seized his opportunity, although he was comparatively old, thirty-four years of age, when he completed jump school. His stature grew with his field manuals on paratrooper warfare and his innovations in training. He led his 505th regiment in airborne assaults into Sicily in July 1943 and near Salerno, Italy in September, 1943. For his service in Sicily, he received the Distinguished Service Cross for valor and a Purple Heart for the wound he suffered to his leg. By the end of 1943, he had attained the rank of brigadier general. He had risen in rank from captain to general in less than five years. When he assumed full command of the 82nd Airborne after Normandy and was promoted to major general, he became, at age thirty-seven, the youngest general to command a division since the Civil War. Tall, slim, fit, and handsome, Gavin seemed to have emerged from central casting in Hollywood. His reputation did not suffer from the worshipful reports that Martha Gellhorn, who had a wide audience, sent about him and his paratroopers in Europe. As Gellhorn gushed: "From the general on down, they are all extraordinary characters and each one's story is worth telling, for men who jump out of airplanes onto hostile territory do not have dull lives."[27]

Gavin's biographers summarized their subject by noting his commitment to a "Spartan" life, characterized by heavy manual labor, long-distance marches, and a simple diet. Above all, Gavin believed "in the virtue of physical toughness."[28] Routine training involved a daily run of four or five miles, followed by long sessions of calisthenics. Once a week, paratroopers took a twenty- to thirty-mile forced march, with the warning "if you fall out, you ship out." A restless Gavin would go for a run in the afternoons, informing an aide: "Son, let's go for a run." After a field training exercise, he would lead his paratroopers in a jog back to camp. Gavin focused on grinding down junior leaders, reasoning that weary men made mistakes and those who commanded small fighting units had to learn how to cope with the "fatigue factor." Gavin turned an especially critical eye toward his high-ranking officers. He demanded the replacement of Colonel Herbert Batcheller, the commander of the 505th Regiment, when he learned that Batcheller had skipped a training exercise so he could be with the Irish woman whom he loved. Gavin could care less that Batcheller, a married man, was unfaithful. Not participating in training with your men was, however, a mortal sin. Colonel George V. "Zip" Millett, Jr., the commander of the 507th Regiment, was a family friend. Millett's sin was that he was "overweight" and "not in shape" and lacked "the leadership and dedication to professional soldiering."[29] General Ridgway rejected Gavin's request that he be replaced. A few days after landing in Normandy, Millett was captured by the Germans and sat out the rest of the war as a prisoner of war (POW). Perhaps sarcastically, Gavin informed his daughter in a 21 June 1944 letter that everyone was fine, but "Zip probably likes cabbage soup and black bread."[30]

The emphasis on physical toughness fit into Gavin's straightforward perception of war in Europe. The Allied forces would be victorious, when his paratroopers killed German soldiers as quickly as possible. He once characterized paratroopers "as cold-blooded killers." In a 12 June 1944 letter from Normandy to Barbara he judged the performance of the paratroopers, most of whom were "green" to combat, as "nothing short of remarkable." He added that "I believe that the violence and savagery of their combat technique is without parallel in our military history. The Germans fear them now and give them lots of elbow room."[31] Gavin understood that dropping behind enemy lines would inevitably lead to high casualties. Just before the Normandy invasion, he recorded in his diary the observation that "it is regrettable that so many of them have to get lost, but it is a tough business, and they all figure that parachutists have nine lives."[32] Gavin tried, however, to limit the exposure of paratroopers. His writings emphasized that paratroopers were assault troops. They should be assigned specific, limited missions and be withdrawn once they fulfilled their mission. Paratroopers normally fought without air support, powerful artillery, or tanks. T/5 Eddie Page recalled that he and his colleagues believed that they would spend about a week in Normandy and then be withdrawn.[33] Indeed, the 82nd Airborne Division fulfilled its assigned missions by 13 June. But their ferocity and skill had caught the attention of high-ranking officers. Gavin's superiors, like General Omar Bradley, ordered paratroopers into action because regular infantry units often advanced too slowly. Paratrooper units, whether they be the 82nd, the 101st, or the 17th Airborne, repeatedly "passed through" heavily armed infantry units and took on the enemy. As such, the Headquarters Company that Page was a member of not only defended Graignes, but also engaged in bloody hedgerow fighting in Normandy, and then, in early July, charged up Hill 95, near the village of La Haye-du-Puits. One week had turned into thirty-three days of combat. Page's 507th regiment left Normandy with a staggering 61 percent casualty rate. Traditional military doctrine called for units to be withdrawn after suffering 25 percent casualties.[34]

General Gavin tried to keep his paratroopers out of the battle for La Haye-du-Puits but was overruled by General Ridgway, who thought that the "fighting spirit" of the weakened 507th "was still unimpaired."[35] Gavin had, of course, nurtured that mental and physical toughness. He had also built up their confidence. He told his paratroopers that "they were the most capable guys on earth." A squad of paratroopers was worth as much as a platoon of other soldiers. Gavin further explained that "we wanted these guys to find out there is nothing too good for them; no bed too soft, no food too good, no conditions too good for them." In turn, Gavin expected that paratroopers would accomplish all missions on the battlefield, no matter what the cost.[36] As he told his daughter on D-Day minus 1, the paratroopers were "highly idealistic, gallant, and courageous to a fault. They will take losses to do anything." Overcoming the fear and danger of jumping out of airplanes had transformed the men "in that it exacts out of participants peculiar qualities of courage."[37]

Paratroopers imbibed Gavin's military philosophy, because he was not just offering the standard motivational talk of a football coach. Gavin famously informed a junior officer: "Lieutenant, in this outfit you will jump first and eat last."[38] During training, Gavin met with enlisted men to inquire about their food, mail, and equipment, always urging paratroopers to carry extra pairs of socks. He complained to his diary when he discovered in England that his regimental commanders lived in fine homes, whereas the enlisted men lived in tent camps. As he wrote, "I don't like the mud and rain any more than anyone else, but neither do the troops. Someone is losing their sense of values, maybe their perspective."[39] Officers in the 82nd Airborne, including Gavin, always were the first out of the C-47s. Enlisted men jumped knowing that their commander was already on the ground facing the peril that awaited them. Tom Graham, an intelligence specialist, jumped from the same plane as Gavin over Normandy. Once on the ground, Graham wondered if he could move with cramps in his legs induced by nervous tension. Seeing Gavin moving inspired Graham to get on his feet. Sergeant John McNally of the 508th Regiment elaborated on Graham's experience: "Imagine the terrific morale factor of the simple, stark facts: the General jumps first! If there is a mistake in picking the drop zone, the General is the first to pay the penalty."[40]

Gavin further inspired paratroopers by engaging in combat. Gavin shouldered an M1 Garand rifle. When he jumped into Normandy, he carried 156 rounds of ammunition, four grenades, a pistol, and a knife "in case I had to fight my way through enemy territory, which once I did."[41] Paratroopers saw their general firing his rifle at the enemy. He was acting like a lieutenant leading a platoon. Stories are legion of paratroopers challenging someone approaching their perimeter and becoming aghast when they realized they had aimed at Gavin. The general, sometimes with an aide, conducted reconnaissance on enemy positions. The general added to his legend by introducing himself as "Jim Gavin" to the sentries. Two paratroopers

Figure 1.2 Paratroopers in the 82nd Airborne often saw Major General James M. Gavin as he is presented here, walking alone, conducting reconnaissance, and with a weapon in his hand. General Gavin was the ultimate paratrooper. US Army Photograph.

of the 505th Regiment shared the story of Gavin asking permission to jump into their foxhole in Normandy to escape the rain. The general offered a packet of coffee, which the men brewed. He also took his turn on watch from the foxhole. In the postwar years, veterans unsurprisingly toasted Gavin as the "best commander in the US Army," the "most respected" officer, and "our hero." Gavin frequented reunions, and, when he entered any room or hall, the old veterans would give him a standing ovation.[42]

To be sure, negative, anti-social behavior emerged from the aggressive nature of training. Paratroopers were brawlers and womanizers. Most paratroopers were young, single, looked great in their jump boots, and had plenty of money to spend on European women. As one historian noted, under Gavin "the 82nd had striven to be the best dressed – or at least the 'smartest' unit on any battlefield or in any barroom."[43] The upright General Ridgway once lamented to his trusted aide, General Ralph "Doc" Eaton, "Doc, our people are getting mixed up sexually with British women." Eaton responded: "Right, Matt, we're probably the only two virgins left in the 82nd."[44] Memoirs by paratroopers, like Bob Bearden and John Hinchliff, are filled with accounts of brawls. Ridgway and Gavin agreed that, especially after their feats in Normandy, paratroopers maintained that it was "their God-given right to go around punching other soldiers in the nose."[45] None of this troubled Gavin. In retirement, Gavin related that he told troopers if they needed a blanket, "kill a German and take his." If they wanted a truck, "take a German truck." Soon Gavin discovered that his men were stealing trucks from US infantry divisions. Gavin rationalized that "it was better to learn to tolerate a certain amount of misbehavior but have guys who were really capable fighters and confident and proud." If his paratroopers tore up a town, Gavin would abjure judicial punishment for the miscreants and take his men on a forced march in full-gear.[46]

Headquarters Company

The men who defended Graignes imbibed General Gavin's philosophy of being tough, confident, and proud. The paratroopers who constituted Headquarters Company of the 3rd Battalion of the 507th Regiment had largely unremarkable backgrounds. As Gavin told his daughter, paratroopers came "just from farm, home, school."[47] For the most part, the paratroopers and their families had experienced the hard times of the Great Depression of the 1930s. As was the case with the orphaned Gavin, their education and their career goals had been stymied by poverty and family tragedies. But, as demonstrated by their test scores, they were highly intelligent young men who craved respect and professional attainment. Becoming a paratrooper helped fulfill those ambitions. An analysis of the pre-war lives of some of the officers and enlisted men underscores the themes of their desire for standing and success and their triumph over adversity.

Young men and women in the United States emerged from the Great Depression with physical and mental disabilities. With German, Italian, and Japanese aggression and conquest running rampant, the US government began to bolster the country's military readiness by establishing conscription with the Selective Training and Service Act of 16 September 1940. Local draft boards began conscripting men between the ages of twenty-one and thirty-five for twelve months of service. The age group would be subsequently expanded to between eighteen and thirty-seven years, and uniformed personnel would be required to serve for the duration of the war. The history of World War II conscription revealed the deep traumas the nation had suffered in the 1930s. As President Harry S. Truman pointed out, on 19 November 1945, in his message to Congress on the health status of the nation, the draft had "forcibly" highlighted national health issues "in terms of which all of us can understand." Between 1940 and 1945, five million men, 30 percent of the total examined, were rejected as unfit for military service for physical and mental reasons. Prior to Pearl Harbor, 52.8 percent of men examined were found to be unfit. Under pressure to increase numbers, draft boards relaxed educational and physical standards. A conscript would be judged eligible for military service if he had as little as four years of grammar school. The key physical deficiencies included poor feet, defective teeth and eyes, and "musculo-skeletal" issues. Many problems could be traced back to nutritional deficiencies such as a lack of calcium and protein. Public health scientists, who examined draft records from World War I, found that there had been a noticeable decline in the health of young men in the United States.[48] Eddie Page, a life-long resident of Stamford, Connecticut, knew he would be rejected for military service because of the quality of his teeth. He sought the aid of a local dentist, Dr. Fodiman, pledging that he would pay the doctor for the dental work when he returned from the war.[49]

By definition, paratroopers had escaped some of the ravages of the Great Depression. They had to be physically strong to endure the rigors of jump school and General Gavin's training exercises. Nonetheless, the vast majority of the 143 men from the 82nd Airborne who jumped near Graignes on D-Day had faced hard times in their early civilian years. Captain Leroy David Brummitt was second in command at Graignes. After the presumed death, on the night of 11–12 June, of the commanding officer, Major Charles D. Johnston of Knoxville, Tennessee, Brummitt assumed command of the defenders of Graignes and organized their escape from the village. Dave Brummitt (1916–2002) was born in Excelsior Springs, Missouri, a spa town known for its therapeutic mineral springs. In postwar life, he declined to tell his children much about his youth other than to suggest it was "a very unhappy time." His working-class father died when he was about eleven years of age, and he was raised with care by his paternal grandmother, Susan. Brummitt graduated from high school in 1934 and achieved a couple years of college. Unlike most paratroopers, Brummitt did not participate in organized sports. As a young man, he was passionate about the dramatic arts, working in the theater industry. He earned little money, and preached to his three children the values of thrift in the postwar years.[50]

Dave Brummitt enlisted as a private in the Army in June 1941. He was selected for officer training in April 1942. He had some college, and he undoubtedly scored high on the standardized test. Most of the thirteen officers from the 82nd and 101st at Graignes did not have college degrees. Major Johnston, who graduated from the University of Tennessee, was unusual in that respect. The army accepted for officer training enlisted men like Lowell Maxwell, Frank Naughton, and Earcle Reed, who had graduated from high school and had some college. The three lieutenants helped defend Graignes. Even attaining that high school degree could be a struggle. Brummitt's close friend in the 3rd Battalion, Lt. John W. Marr of Missouri, took six years to attain his high-school diploma. Marr had to enter the coal mines to help his rural family of nine children survive the Dust Bowl drought of the 1930s. The determined Lt. Marr graduated from high school at the age of twenty.[51]

Upon being commissioned a 2nd Lieutenant, Brummitt volunteered for jump school and earned his parachute wings in August 1942. He rose to the rank of Captain in the newly formed 507th Regiment and became the 3rd Battalion's S-3 Officer in charge of operational planning. His family believed that their father joined the paratroopers because he had a life-long desire to be the best and to associate with the best. He also enjoyed being physically fit. In 1943, while training in Alliance, Nebraska, he met his future wife, Mary O'Connor. Captain Brummitt carried a photo of Mary in his wallet throughout the war.[52]

Captain Abraham "Bud" Sophian, Jr. (1915–1944), a medical doctor and battalion surgeon, stood out among the paratroopers at Graignes. He came from a privileged, upper-middle-class background. Sophian's parents were of Russian Jewish heritage. Sophian's father emigrated as a child with his parents from Kiev, Russia in 1890, fleeing religious persecution. Abraham Sophian, Sr. entered Cornell Medical College in New York City at the age of eighteen years and became a star medical researcher. He authored an influential study on cerebral meningitis. Dr. Sophian spent his career in Kansas City, practicing medicine and continuing his medical research. He had the financial resources to send Bud Sophian to boarding school – Phillips Academy in Andover, Massachusetts. Both President George H. W. Bush and President George W. Bush attended Phillips Academy. At the academy, Sophian played golf and football, and earned a letter in varsity wrestling. Sophian moved on to prestigious Stanford University and then Cornell Medical. At Stanford, Sophian played on the golf team. He also associated with Hollywood celebrities, including the famous star Clark Gable. Upon graduating from Cornell in June 1941, Sophian married Dorothy Murphy Keck, a nurse and a Roman Catholic. The Sophian family tried hard to assimilate into the dominant culture. Sophian's sister attended a private school sponsored by Roman Catholic nuns.

Dr. Sophian was inducted into the Army on 17 August 1942 as a 1st Lieutenant. He had hoped to start his medical residency at Mt. Sinai in Cleveland, Ohio. Instead, the Army assigned him to Camp Barkley, near Abilene, Texas, for military medical training. In the summer of 1943, Sophian volunteered for jump school. His biographers noted that he was athletic and adventurous. He may have also found the additional $100 a month in jump pay attractive. Dorothy Sophian had become pregnant and gave birth in November 1943. Captain Sophian never held his child. It was unusual for recruiters to accept a married man with a pregnant wife for jump school. But the paratroopers needed doctors.[53] At Graignes, Dr. Sophian supervised seven other paratroopers who had military medical training either with the 82nd or 101st Divisions. An eighth paratrooper, Pvt. Robert W. Britton of New Jersey, who was a medic, died on the first day, 6 June. Of the nine men, including Dr. Sophian, who had military medical training, only one would survive Graignes.

Lt. Francis "Frank" Naughton (1918–2015), who came from rural Illinois, not only survived Graignes but also became a career military officer, retiring with the rank of colonel. Thereafter, Naughton earned a law degree and served as a Magistrate Judge in Gwinnett County, Georgia. Naughton's career path was as remarkable as that of General Gavin. At the age of two, he lost his mother, who succumbed to tuberculosis. Two unmarried aunts raised Naughton and his brother, Tom. His father lost their farm in the 1930s. Naughton, who took up the sport of boxing, attended the University of Illinois for a semester. He considered it "paradise." He could not, however, sustain his education because of a lack of money. Thereafter, he did the classic 1930s thing, hopping on a boxcar, "riding the rails," seeing the country, and fruitlessly searching for meaningful employment. He enlisted in the Army as a private on 4 August 1941 and then volunteered for jump school. He coveted the extra $50. That money doubled when, in 1942, the Army selected the jump-qualified Naughton for officer training. He received his bronze 2nd Lieutenant bars on 28 July 1942.[54]

Dave Brummitt, Frank Naughton, and Lt. Colonel Earcle "Pip" Reed (1919–1998) were three officers at Graignes who devoted their lives to the US military in the postwar period. Like General Gavin, they had enlisted as privates and achieved high-ranking status. The Army unsurprisingly kept on combat-experienced paratroopers who had ambition, intelligence, and talent. But the relationship was symbiotic. The young officers had wanted a university education. The Army supported Gavin with an appointment to West Point. In the postwar period, the Army sent young officers to school. Naughton spent a year studying at the Army War College in Carlisle, Pennsylvania. Brummitt finished his university education through the University of Maryland extension services, attended the War College in Carlisle, and while there achieved his M.A. degree in international relations under the auspices of George Washington University. Officers who knew misfortune and hard times and had started as privates perhaps had insight into the personal struggles of enlisted personnel.

Empathy and understanding would be required of any officer handling the irrepressible Sgt. John Joseph Hinchliff, the enlisted leader of the machine-gun teams. By his own admission, Hinchliff repeatedly lost and regained his sergeant's stripes. He had a fondness for brawling with men in uniform who had the misfortune not to be paratroopers. Hinchliff (1921–2020) was born in Park Rapids, Minnesota, which is near Lake Itasca, the source of the Mississippi River. His grandmother, a devout Roman Catholic, raised Hinchliff. His mother had been unmarried and, after giving birth, lived in Minneapolis and played a minimal role in Hinchliff's life. Hinchliff was subjected to bullying by older children, who mocked his second-hand clothing and his poverty. His grandmother found a solution that foreshadowed the lovable Christmas movie *The Bells of St. Mary* (1945). She found prize-fighters who could teach her grandson how to box, and he became a local hero for taking down the town's nasty boys. In the film, the good Sister Mary Benedict (Ingrid Bergman) gave the bullied young "Eddie" lessons in the art of self-defense she had gleaned from a book. Despite several near brushes with death, including at Graignes, Hinchliff emerged from World War II physically intact. He ascribed this to his habit of praying constantly, as advised by his grandmother. Hinchliff has never mentioned whether his grandmother would have approved of his wartime brawling.

Hinchliff enlisted in the Minnesota National Guard in 1937 at the age of sixteen. He lied that he was seventeen, and his grandmother signed the enlistment papers. He prized the $15 he received every three months, and he liked training at the rifle range. The Minnesota National Guard was federalized in February 1941, and Hinchliff and his unit were shipped to California for coastal defense. In June 1942, he volunteered for jump school, figuring that the extra $50 combined with his $52 in sergeant's pay would amount to a princely sum. He knew he had made the right decision when he arrived at Ft. Benning in July, noting that "we were duly impressed with the personnel in the airborne troops compared to what I had been used to." On 1 January 1943, in a civil ceremony in Georgia, he married Muriel, who was nineteen years of age and from Minnesota. His commanding officers at Ft. Benning disapproved, not wanting their paratroopers to be married or have children. Muriel Hinchliff, who in the postwar period served on the Minneapolis City Council, immediately became pregnant. To please his grandmother, the couple repeated their marriage vows before a Catholic priest near the training base in Alliance, Nebraska. Hinchliff had the joy of holding his daughter for a couple of months before shipping out to Europe.[55] In the vocabulary of World War II, Hinchliff's daughter was a "bye, bye, baby," a means for those about to enter harm's way to preserve the genetic code.[56]

The inseparable Rene E. Rabe (1923–1982) and Homer Poss (1925–2005) were key members of the two 81 mm mortar teams that defended Graignes. As teenagers, both men enlisted in February 1943, trained in Texas, graduated from jump school together, and then were assigned to the 507th Regiment. Poss and Rabe joined the mortar platoon, because they were strong, powerful young men who could handle a mortar. Each of the three major components of an 81 mm mortar weighed about 45 pounds. A mortar shell weighed approximately 7 pounds. Poss and Rabe fired their mortar shells at Graignes, in Normandy, at the Battle of the Bulge, and in the Rhineland area. They jumped from the same C-47 airplane into Normandy and over the Rhine River. Only enemy fire could separate them. On 28 March 1945, four days after jumping over the Rhine, Rabe's face was splattered with shell fragments from a German mortar round.[57] It may have been part of the same mortar round fragments of which lodged in Poss's head, knocking him unconscious. He woke up in a military hospital in Holland.

Like other men in the Headquarters Company, Rabe and Poss had challenging early lives. Rabe's parents, Emil J. Rabe from Hamburg, Germany and Maria Jeanne Radoux from Liège, Belgium, emigrated to the Canadian Prairies. Emil, who arrived in Canada in 1890 as a teenager, worked for a time on his Uncle William's homestead ranch in Manitoba and in a lumber camp in northern Saskatchewan before acquiring accounting/bookkeeping skills. He became a Canadian citizen in 1895 so that he could visit his parents in Hamburg and not be subjected to Germany's mandatory military conscription. In 1912, at the age of thirty-seven, he married Maria Jeanne, who was eighteen years younger than Emil. They had four children in Saskatchewan, with Rene being the youngest. The family emigrated to the United States in 1924, and built a seemingly secure lifestyle in Westchester County, New York. The family was weathering the Great Depression. Dire poverty and family collapse ensued, however, when Emil suddenly died in 1938. Maria had been a homemaker, and had no work skills for the paid labor force. Rene, a young teenager, thereafter drifted, failing to complete high school and working at jobs without futures. His application to join the Navy was rejected because he was not a US citizen. The Selective Service, however, drafted immigrants. The $50 extra a month in jump pay was a powerful incentive, for he was constantly worried about his mother's financial status and sent money home throughout the war.[58] Becoming a paratrooper also restored the self-purpose he had lost when his father died. He earned four promotions, rising from private to staff sergeant and the enlisted leader of the mortar platoon. The day after escaping from Graignes, he received a battlefield promotion for his ability with his 81 mm mortar.[59]

Homer Poss grew up in Lebanon, Illinois, not far from St. Louis, Missouri. He was the eldest of four boys who came in rapid succession. Tragedy struck, when the youngest child, Gordon, stepped on a nail and died in 1939 from the infection. Homer lived in a two-parent household, but his parents, albeit loving, were not vocationally successful. Patriotism infused the Poss brothers. Homer's brother, Tom, served in the Marine Corps in the South Pacific during the war and his other brother, Duane, served in the Army during the Korean War. Homer left high school, persuading his mother to sign his enlistment papers when he was seventeen. He was outraged by the Japanese attack on Pearl Harbor. He feared that the war would be over before he could participate. As he explained in

Figure 1.3 This photograph of mortar men includes Arnold Martinez and Homer Poss, who are kneeling. Standing behind are Rene Rabe (in a sweater) and Joseph Ferguson (wearing a cap). It is May 1944 in England. Rene E. Rabe photograph.

later life, "I wanted to get my licks in, too." Poss was well-built, had an athletic body, and looked sharp in his service uniform. The women of Europe would take notice of Corporal Poss. Poss would return to the United States with ambition and drive. He would eventually become city manager and then mayor of Highland, Illinois. There are memorials in Highland to his military and civilian service.[60]

Poss and Rabe were close to Eddie Page (1922–1998), the paratrooper, along with Frank Naughton, most responsible for keeping the memory of Graignes alive and the veterans of Headquarters Company together. He hosted reunions of veterans at his Stamford home and would be recognized in 1992 as the "507th Paratrooper of the Year," only the third paratrooper to receive the accolade. He was fond of celebrating each day with the cry of "Airborne." The Page family fared well in the 1930s, until the father, Edward T. Page, Sr., an insurance salesman with Metropolitan Life, died while Eddie was in high school. Young Edward promised his father he would take care of his mother, and he did. Eddie, who did not play competitive sports, dropped out of high-school. He volunteered for the paratroopers "for the adventure and the money." While at jump school in Georgia, he met his future wife, Betty King, from Atlanta. He would write 198 letters to her during the war. When he and Betty had the time and money to travel to Europe in 1990, he told his wife: "I don't care where we go, but I have to go to Graignes."[61]

The US military during World War II practiced racial segregation. There were no African-Americans in the 82nd Airborne. Generals Ridgway and Gavin opposed racial discrimination, and acted immediately when clashes broke out in England in March 1944 between paratroopers who had just arrived on the island and African-American troops who had been stationed there. In the postwar period, Gavin would facilitate the integration of the US armed forces.[62] Black soldiers were recruited to become paratroopers and formed the 555th Parachute Infantry Battalion, nicknamed the "Triple Nickles." The battalion did not serve overseas but did give heroic service in the Pacific Northwest. In the winter of 1944–1945, Japanese forces launched thousands of "balloon bombs," which contained incendiary devices, toward the US West Coast. Some of the bombs started forest fires in California, Idaho, and Oregon. The "Triple Nickles," who were based in Pendleton, Oregon and Chico, California, fought the fires, and, in some cases, parachuted into burning areas.[63] That the United States practiced segregation during a war against racist Nazi Germany has led historians to question whether Tom Brokaw's "Greatest Generation" sobriquet is appropriate.

Hispanic/Latino men – Pvt. Jesus Casas (1924–1944), Pvt. Carlos J. Hurtado (1924–2008), and Pvt. Arnold J. Martinez (1921–1944) – were proud paratroopers in Headquarters Company. Their enlistment records classified them as "white," which was a racist way of saying they were not African-American. Whatever their phenotype or skin color, Casas, Hurtado, and Martinez, like other paratroopers, knew hard times. Casas, a medic who jumped with Captain Sophian, grew up in the Los Angeles region of California. His parents were born in Mexico. The entire family labored in California's agricultural fields. He did not attend high school. Like other medical personnel, Pvt. Casas died at Graignes. Hurtado was born in Texas, but his family moved to Los Angeles. When he enlisted, Hurtado was working in the kitchen of a hotel or restaurant. He had finished one year of high school. Hurtado, who enjoyed a long life, was a popular member of the company who attended reunions and returned to Graignes. He was one of the paratroopers that hid in the Rigault family barn. Veterans merrily told stories of Pvt. Hurtado's penchant for landing in trees with his parachute.[64]

Pvt. Arnold Martinez came from a remarkable extended family that first emigrated from Spain to Florida and then homesteaded in Colorado. Arnold was one of the eldest in a family of twelve children. As part of family tradition, Martinez men joined the US military. Arnold's younger brothers, Gilbert and Jim, served in Korea, and Elias served in the Coast Guard and was assigned to guard the waters off Hyannis Port when President John F. Kennedy vacationed there. During World War II, six of Arnold's cousins were fighting on various fronts. Arnold enlisted three weeks after Pearl Harbor. In December 1941, he lived in Denver, where he had moved because he did not like rural life. He became a mortar man with Headquarters Company. Though short in stature compared with veritable giants in the mortar teams, like Arthur "Rip" Granlund and William P. "Willie" Coates, Martinez had a strong frame. He jumped into Normandy from the same C-47 with his buddies, Homer Poss and Rene Rabe. Martinez did not survive Graignes. His remains rest in the American Cemetery in Normandy, near Omaha Beach. One of Arnold's cousins, Pfc. Ernest "Chili" Martinez, died later in 1944 during the Italian campaign and rests in the American Cemetery in Florence.[65]

Native Americans also fought at Graignes. S/Sgt. Stephen E. Liberty, who was born in 1916, came from Sanders County in northwestern Montana and was listed as a "Native American" on his enlistment card. He had a grammar school education and had worked in Montana's mines. Liberty, a mortar man, survived Normandy, the Battle of the Bulge, the jump over the Rhine River, and the subsequent fighting in Germany. After the war, Liberty worked again in the mining industry near Butte, Montana. Lt. Irwin J. Morales was another Native American who arrived in Graignes. Morales steered, along with his co-pilot Thomas Ahmad, a glider plane with the 101st Airborne Division on D-Day. His glider plopped into a swamp seven miles south of Carentan and twelve miles from the intended landing zone. The glider carried a jeep and two additional soldiers of the 101st. Morales, Ahmad, and two enlisted men made their way to Graignes. In postwar life, Morales attended college, sampled several occupations, and eventually settled on nine acres of land on an Indian reservation in Arizona.[66]

Patterns can be discerned in the early histories of the defenders of Graignes. The Headquarters Company did its part in upholding the 82nd Airborne Division as "All American." Company members came from all regions, with the populous industrial states of the Northeast – New York, Pennsylvania, and Illinois – and California contributing the most paratroopers. Except for Captain Sophian, the paratroopers and their parents had struggled in the 1930s. Financial hardship and stunted educational growth characterized life in the United States. Only a handful of enlisted personnel had completed high school, and many had attended only grammar school. A significant number of men in Headquarters Company had also lost parents during their formative years. Pvt. Marion Hatton, Jr. of the Appalachian region of Kentucky, one of the most impoverished areas of the United States, readily fit into those categories of privation. Hatton, who became a mortar man, finished 8th grade. His widowed mother finished 2nd grade. Hatton's older sister was a waitress. Prior to enlisting, Hatton worked as an unskilled laborer on a road construction project financed by the federal government. How such experiences helped formulate decisions to volunteer for jump school cannot be precisely determined. Most men admitted that they coveted the extra $50 a month. Perhaps also they were searching for something bigger in their lives. Frank Naughton's time "riding the rails" might serve as symbol of that quest. What is certain is that the paratroopers were by definition healthy, innately intelligent, and generally aware they had embarked on a perilous journey. The nonagenarian John Hinchliff jocularly responded to a question of whether recruiters hinted that paratrooper duty was dangerous: "Well, they did mention we have to jump out of airplanes."[67]

Basic training and jump school had not fully prepared the paratroopers of Headquarters Company for the jump into Normandy. Hard, James Gavin-style training awaited them in Nebraska, Northern Ireland, and England. They also had to endure a slow, sickening, and uncertain voyage across the Atlantic Ocean. The training would equip them with the skill and fortitude to carry out their mission of liberation for the people of Western Europe. Life in Northern Ireland and England would also foreshadow their bonding with the villagers of Graignes.

2 OVERSEAS

It was a long, arduous journey to the *marais* of Normandy and the village of Graignes for the young men who served in Headquarters Company, 3rd Battalion of the 507th Regiment. Thirteen weeks of basic training in military bases throughout the United States had been followed by jump school in Georgia. Once they were assigned to the 507th, the new paratroopers trained in Louisiana, Nebraska, South Dakota, Northern Ireland, and England. They traveled by train, ship, and ultimately by C-47 airplanes, covering perhaps 5,000 miles. They spent at least a year, and, in some cases, up to two years, preparing for their first combat jump. They had become superbly conditioned, confident, and able infantrymen. They also had begun to learn to appreciate the cultures of Europeans allied with the United States.

The Long Journey

The US Army activated the 507th Parachute Infantry Regiment on 20 July 1942. The Army simultaneously ordered Colonel George V. "Bud" Millett to be regimental commander. Colonel Millett graduated from the US Military Academy at West Point in 1929, the same year James M. Gavin graduated from the academy. The nucleus of the cadre of the new regiment came from the 504th regiment, with additions from the 502nd and 503rd. Over the next two years, the regiment gradually built up its military strength.[1] In the earliest hours of D-Day, 2,004 men of the 507th regiment headed for Normandy from Fulbeck and Barkston Heath airfields in England.

The 507th trained at Ft. Benning for twenty-two weeks. It conducted its first comprehensive maneuvers, beginning on 6 March 1943, in Louisiana at Barksdale Field, near the Sabine River. The regiment then moved to an airfield base in Alliance, Box Butte County, in northwestern Nebraska, arriving on 23 March 1943. The regiment would train for eight months in what was known as the "sand hills" region of Nebraska. The paratroopers did not know where they would be deployed for combat. Training in the sand hills suggested a deployment to North Africa and desert warfare. The Axis powers surrendered, however, to the Allies in Tunisia in May 1943. The paratroopers also spoke about seeing action in the Pacific against the Empire of Japan. Service records, such as that of Pvt. Harold J. Premo of upstate New York, demonstrate men took courses on "malaria prevention and discipline."[2] Malaria could be found in European locales, like Sicily, but was more widespread in the Pacific.

The 507th developed in a variety of ways while stationed at Alliance. The numbers grew as men graduated from jump school at Ft. Benning. Privates Homer Poss and Rene Rabe, for example, were transferred from Georgia to Nebraska on 21 July 1943. The regiment also began to identify its enlisted leaders, like Sgt. Benton Broussard (1922–1944) of Headquarters Company. Broussard, who enlisted in May 1941, was with the 507th from its inception. Broussard grew up in a Cajun family in the Atchafalaya Basin of Louisiana. As was common among rural folk, Broussard's first language was French. He began to learn English in middle school.[3] Sgt. Broussard jumped from the same C-47 with Poss and Rabe on D-Day. He shocked the Rigault family, when he knocked on their door at about 6:00 a.m. and announced in an accent that was similar to the Norman accent: "Open up, we are your friends, the Tommies."[4] Another trooper who spoke some French, Rene Rabe, received the first of his four promotions to private first class on 1 November 1943. Rabe's mother came from French-speaking Belgium.

While at Alliance, the regiment drilled, conducted infantry maneuvers, and jumped. As described by mortar man Bob Bearden from Texas, the training was challenging, replete with long marches with full field packs and weapons and frequent injunctions to advance in "double-time."[5] Colonel Millett took pride in his regiment's performance and rewarded his men with a twelve-day bivouac at Custer State Park in the Black Hills of South Dakota. South Dakota's oldest state park is a major tourist area today, with a beautiful lake, rolling hills, and roaming buffalo. Beyond practice jumps around Alliance, the troopers raised national pride, stimulated blood-donation drives, and encouraged the sale of war bonds by doing demonstration jumps around rodeos and urban areas like Omaha and Denver. More than 100,000 citizens reportedly witnessed the demonstration jump near Denver. Accidents inevitably happened, with troopers being seriously injured or killed. One trooper hit a live wire and was electrocuted. Bearden and Fred Boyle of Iowa had reason to fret over these "practice" jumps.

Colonel Millett tried to keep his paratroopers, when not training, busy in such a remote place. His men engaged in competitive sports – swimming, boxing, wrestling, even rodeo. Homer Poss ran track. First Lt. Elmer F. Farnham, who led Poss and Rabe's 81 mm mortar platoon, excelled at diving and wrestling. The regiment's basketball team competed against and defeated college hoop teams. Captain Ben Schwartzwalder coached the football team. General Gavin would later look askance at the colonel's promotion of athletics. Despite his best efforts to keep everyone occupied, Millett had to deal with misbehavior, especially after payday. Bearden calculated that 20 percent of H Company was in jail one weekend in September for excessive drinking, carousing, and brawling. The company was confined to base for a week as punishment for their hijinks.[6]

Some troopers were surprised when they learned in November that they would be heading east rather than to perhaps San Francisco for deployment overseas. In the preceding months, men of Headquarters Company, like Rabe and Lt. Frank Naughton, had received two weeks of furlough. It was national policy, as announced by First Lady Eleanor Roosevelt, to give military personnel some freedom before shipping out. The thought was, of course, that many men and women would not make it back to the United States. As the time approached to leave Alliance, Colonel Millett threatened to shave personally the head of any man who was caught absent without leave (AWOL).[7] The troopers had recently taken to shaving their heads as a form of group solidarity.

The railroad cars left Nebraska for the embarkation site, Camp Shanks, in Orangetown, New York, about twenty miles northwest of New York City, on 20 November 1943. The trip took about four days, with the administrators in Headquarters Company reporting in one company morning report that the morale was "bad" but the food was "excellent."[8] The troopers had about a two-week stay at Camp Shanks, before boarding a ship bound for the European Theater of Operations on 5 December 1943. Preparations at Camp Shanks included participating in what must have been a less than comforting "abandon ship" drill.

Headquarters Company personnel had the opportunity to sample life in New York City for a day or two, while at Camp Shanks. Sgt. Edward R. Barnes from Philadelphia compared the clubs and bars of the Big Apple to those of his native city. Pvt. Thomas Travers and Pfc. Michael Kempa grew up in New York City and could visit their families. Travers would die at Graignes. Rene Rabe's mother had moved to New York City. He called on his mother and his girlfriend, Genevieve R. Dreher, who lived on the west side of Manhattan, near Central Park. The Rabe–Dreher families typified the total commitment that millions of US families made to the war effort. Rabe's older brother August served as truck driver in the 26th Infantry Division and, like Rene, was repeatedly promoted, achieving the rank of Master Sergeant. August Rabe's 26th Division liberated the concentration camp at Gusen, Austria. Genevieve's older brothers, William and George Dreher, deployed to the Pacific. William, who was in the Army, served in Saipan, and George served on the USS *Hydrus*, an attack cargo ship. William Dreher, who was married to Rita, would not first see his daughter Lois until 1945, when she was nearly three years old. Baby brother Richard Dreher, who was born in 1934, won a contest sponsored by the *Saturday Evening Post* for being able to identify enemy aircraft. He was ready if German or Japanese aircraft flew over New York City! Genevieve worked long hours during the war at the telephone company, maintaining national communications.

While at Camp Shanks, the men of Headquarters Company were also required to watch segments of Frank Capra's *Why We Fight* (1942–1945) series.[9] The War Department sponsored Capra's seven-part documentary film. The purpose was to explain to US soldiers and the public the reasons for the US involvement in a global war and to persuade skeptics of the necessity of military action. The War Department selected one of the country's most famous directors, Frank Capra, for the assignment. Capra had won two Academy Awards, including "best director" for *Mr. Smith Goes to Washington* (1939) with Jimmy Stewart. In contemporary life, Capra is best remembered for directing Stewart and Donna Reed in *It's a Wonderful Life* (1946), the glorious Christmas film that depicts life in the United States from the 1920s through World War II and the triumphant return of heroic veterans. Capra sought to match the terrifying Nazi propaganda film *The Triumph of the Will* (1935), directed by the celebrated German director Leni Riefenstahl. Capra spliced into his films Axis propaganda footage to help make his point about the evil inherent in Nazi Germany, Fascist Italy, and Imperialist Japan. But he also worked within American film traditions. Especially in the opening segment, *Prelude to War* (1942), Adolf Hitler, Benito Mussolini, and Emperor Hirohito are portrayed as gangsters that had to be stopped. In real life, Americans had Al Capone and John Dillinger to fear, and on film they could loathe actor James Cagney, with his curled lip and taunts like "come out, you dirty, yellow-bellied rat."

What impact the films had on the paratroopers in Headquarters Company cannot be precisely determined. The distinguished French historian Olivier Wieviorka has noted that the D-Day invaders from the United States were not fanatics and had little knowledge of geopolitical or ideological issues. Wieviorka opined that US soldiers fought for each other, for their personal honor, and to return home.[10] What is notable about the memoirs and contemporary documents produced by the paratroopers, whether by General Gavin or a lowly private, is that they rarely referred to Nazism or the annihilation of Jewish people and other non-Aryan people. They sometimes labeled the enemy the Germans, but, more commonly, called them the "Krauts." The Krauts had to be defeated, because they destroyed democracies and occupied other countries. As John W. Dower has pointed out in his award-winning study *War without Mercy: Race and Power in the Pacific War* (1986), both Japanese and US combatants perceived each other as racially inferior, as "beasts," and routinely engaged in savage, atrocious acts.[11] To be sure, the experiences in Graignes, the charge up Hill 95 in Normandy, the Battle of the Bulge, the jump over the Rhine River, and the liberation of Eastern European and Russian slave laborers in the Ruhr Valley hardened the views of the paratroopers of Headquarters Company about the "Krauts." Nonetheless, Eddie Page perhaps best summarized the views of his buddies when he repeated the advice he received from a combat-experienced platoon sergeant in the 82nd Airborne just before D-Day. The sergeant said: "Don't try to be a hero. Do your job and watch out for your own ass."[12]

So as not to alert any enemy spies, the men had previously removed their paratrooper insignias before boarding RMS *Strathnaver* for the voyage to Liverpool, England. The *Strathnaver*, which had gone into service in 1931, was a passenger and mail ship that routinely sailed from London to Bombay and Australia via the Suez Canal. The luxurious ship carried 498 first-class and 668 touring-class passengers. The British government requisitioned the *Strathnaver* as a troop transport ship in 1939 and redesigned it to carry 5,000 troops. After the 507th Regiment boarded on 5 December, the *Strathnaver* left Fort Hamilton in Brooklyn, sailed up the East Coast, and, after three days, joined a convoy for the trip across the North Atlantic, docking at Liverpool early on the morning of 16 December. Crossing the North Atlantic in December would normally be a memorable experience. For the first two days, calm seas and bright weather reigned. On the third day out it began to rain, on the sixth day a terrible storm hit. Seasickness predictably beset the paratroopers. The troopers also wondered if they had boarded the *Titanic*. Another ship hit the stern of the *Strathnaver*. It began to take on water. US destroyers circled the *Strathnaver*, fearing a German U-boat attack. As described by Sgt. John Hinchliff, "she just wallowed in those huge waves. If you were standing on deck by the rail – and it looked like she was going to roll all the way over sometimes because of the way it was wallowing and those huge waves."[13] The *Strathnaver* eventually managed to turn on its pumps, and the convoy proceeded.

North Atlantic storms, an accident on the high seas, and sea-sickness would leave a life-long impression on most passengers. But, from the perspective of the paratroopers, the living conditions ranked as the greatest ignominy. Sixty years after the experience, the paratroopers were still ranting about it. The officers berthed in cabins on decks A and B, above the waterline. They had windows and ventilation. The enlisted personnel were sent into the ship's hold, levels F and H of the *Strathnaver*. There was no ventilation, and the men could feel but not see the sea that surrounded them. They pondered their fate, if a torpedo hit the *Strathnaver*. The troopers ate and slept on or beneath picnic tables. They could smell themselves and the overflowing latrines. The daily cuisine was greasy mutton with a few Indian spices. T/5 Bob Davis of Vermont, who played in the regimental dance band, remembered descending into "this dark unventilated hell, with a stench of unfamiliar eastern cuisine seeping from the galleys." The experience caused Davis to turn literary, noting he felt like "a mentally and physically ravaged piece of subhuman flesh trapped in a seagoing Black Hole of Calcutta." Another trooper used a religious allusion in judging that being "cast into the bowels of the ship" was "as close to purgatory as you could get."[14]

Figure 2.1 The *Strathnaver* brought the paratroopers of the 507th Regiment to Liverpool, England in late 1943. In its pre-war luxury days, the *Strathnaver* carried passengers and the royal mail to India and Australia. During the war, the ship's portholes were all sealed and blacked out, except for decks A and B, where officers resided. The enlisted men were deep in the unhealthy bowels of the ship. UK Government photograph.

From their lofty perches, the regimental officers eventually realized that their men were living in a "floating pigsty" and a "snake pit." They arranged for two daily fire drills so that men could get some fresh air on deck. Colonel Millett approved the use of emergency food stocks to improve diets, and he looked the other way, when his troopers began to raid galleys at night. T/5 Davis was rescued by his fellow paratrooper from Vermont, Captain John Verret, the 3rd Battalion chaplain. The Catholic priest dubbed Davis, a Protestant, his "altar boy" and let him sleep in the bathtub of his cabin. The cabin had three portholes that could be opened. Nonetheless, Davis did not let go of his bad memories. As the 507th regiment began to disembark in Liverpool at 5:00 p.m. on 16 December, Davis noted that, "not unlike dehydrated rats, scurrying from a sinking ship, we eagerly escaped the *Strathnaver*."[15]

The paratroopers had one final scare aboard ship. One paratrooper had come down with spinal meningitis, and the worry was that the entire regiment would be quarantined on the ship for two weeks. But Captain Abraham Sophian and other medical officers successfully isolated the man.[16] Their travels were not yet over, however, because England lacked suitable living and training facilities for paratroopers.

The regiment immediately boarded a train for Greenock, Scotland and then boarded the Liberty ship *Susan B. Anthony* for the short voyage to Belfast, Northern Ireland. Finally, on 17 December, the paratroopers boarded another train for the two-hour train trip to Portrush. In a little less than a month, the 507th Regiment had moved over 4,000 miles from the sand hills of western Nebraska to the stunning Antrim Coast of Northern Ireland.

Training for D-Day

The paratroopers of the 507th Regiment might have felt that a Higher Power had rewarded them for their time in "purgatory" on the *Strathnaver*. The resort town of Portrush is one of the loveliest spots on the face of the earth. The town has a famous golf course, belonging to The Royal Portrush Golf Club, a links course that has been the venue for British Opens. Captain Sophian, the golfing doctor from Stanford University, played the course and shot a most respectable score of seventy-eight.[17] The ruins of Dunluce Castle, a fortress built in or about 1500, rest on dramatic cliffs overlooking the Antrim coast. The kitchen of the castle allegedly fell into the Irish Sea. Most famously, the Giant's Causeway, a World Heritage Site, is near Portrush. The Causeway consists of 40,000 interlocking basalt columns. Most of the stones are perfect hexagons that disappear into the sea and reemerge on land in Scotland. The geological wonder was created by ancient volcanic eruptions, or perhaps it is the result of the work of the legendary giant *Fionn mac Cumhaill* (Finn MacCool), who, it is said, laid down stepping-stones for the walk from Ireland to Scotland.

Portrush intoxicates not just with beauty and wonder. "Smiles broadened" when the paratroopers of the 507th noticed upon arrival that there was a pub on every corner of the resort town. Nearby to Portrush is the Old Bushmills Distillery, purveyors of the finest Irish whiskey. The paratroopers would bring empty quart bottles to Bushmills and the distillers, grateful for the US entry into the war, would fill the bottle for the nominal price of $1.80. Colonel Millett reactivated the regimental dance band. Bob Davis, who played second tenor saxophone, remembered that "the whole town of Portrush was like a club." Another trooper rejoiced: "We marched, cursed, danced our way in and out of dance halls, pubs, and some local places during our stay in Ireland. We had a hell of a good time."[18]

Arriving at the onset of winter in Portrush ironically made life better for the regiment. The paratroopers moved into the quarters that tourists occupied during fair seasons. High-ranking regimental officers stayed in a hotel complete with a bar and a bartender. Lt. Frank Naughton and other officers lived in a small guesthouse called "Lisnavarna." Homer Poss and his colleagues in the mortar platoon lived in a hotel. Other men lived in "bed and breakfast" homes maintained by Irish ladies. Some troopers had views of the Giant's Causeway. On the waterfront, bathhouses and public showers were available to the troopers. The 507th Regiment had it far better than the other 13,000 US troops who were stationed in Northern Ireland in the winter of 1943–1944. Paratroopers in other regiments bunked in Nissen Huts made of prefabricated steel. As the historian of the 82nd Airborne's stay in Northern Ireland remarked, "not only was Portrush beautiful, as a billet, it was about as good as it gets."[19]

To be sure, not all was perfect in Portrush. At any time of the year, Irish weather can be fickle, with hard, cold rain followed by glorious sunshine. In the winter, days are short, with daylight from 9:00 a.m. to 4:00 p.m. Northern Ireland also observed a strict "black-out." Men floundered around the streets in the dark, searching for their favorite pub. Irish guards patrolled the coast at night, on alert for German U-boats surfacing to recharge their batteries. During the day, training consisted of twenty-five-mile marches and endless running, at times through rain, fog, and snow. Dr. Sophian and his medics kept busy tending to battered feet.[20] Northern Ireland had only a small firing range at Magilligan Point, twelve miles west of Portrush. The rolling, lush fields of Northern Ireland were planted to the maximum for the war effort. The paratroopers could not jump or carry out extensive military maneuvers. But, for the enjoyment of the people of Portrush, the 507th marched in a large-scale parade once a month on a Saturday morning.[21]

The people of Northern Ireland remembered the paratroopers' brief stay in their country not just for the parades but also for the close interactions that developed. The stay in Portrush foreshadowed the Headquarters Company's experience in Graignes, Normandy in June 1944. General Gavin, who was stationed in London, but made frequent inspection trips to Northern Ireland, observed to his daughter that, "although the weather may be inhospitable, the people are not. They appear to be quite kind and thoughtful to American soldiers, although I can easily understand how they might resent the good rations, etc., of the Americans compared to this war-rationed bit."[22] The paratroopers of the 507th indeed noticed that rationing made life hard for the Irish. Raider R. "Ray" Nelson, who was born in Norway, grew up in the Chicago region, and became a noted sculptor, recalled that the people were deprived and that food, candy, soap, and cigarettes were in short supply. He and his colleagues "tried to share rations with Irish people, when they could." This sharing might include fresh fruit, tobacco, and a most welcome donation of sugar. When out on exercises, hungry troopers occasionally foraged on Irish farms, taking chickens and eggs. Supply personnel reimbursed the farmers in full, understanding that the hard-pressed farmers might exaggerate their losses a wee bit.[23]

Christmas Day, 1943 proved an unforgettable day for the paratroopers and the children of Portrush, ages five to fourteen. Troopers each picked out a child to entertain during the day. Because the regiment had not yet been paid since leaving New York, one company commander promised a loan of $10 to any trooper who participated in the celebration. Troopers hoarded their allotments of candy, apples, and oranges. The party was held in Orange Hall, with over 500 children arriving in relays. Hot cocoa and doughnuts were served. Santa Claus handed out presents of candy, chewing gum, and fruit. Many of the children had never before eaten an orange. The regimental band and nurses from the American Red Cross played music. The highlight of the day was when children piled into makeshift sleighs, also known as jeeps, and were zipped around town, with children and paratroopers laughing and singing. In the early twenty-first century, author John P. McCann interviewed older citizens of Portrush, who told him that Christmas in 1943 was a remarkable event in their lives. Troopers similarly recalled that the celebration "filled a large void in my life." As Ed Isbell noted, "we were only kids away from home during Christmas time, and they shared their love and understanding with us."[24] For the 507th Regiment and the survivors of Graignes from Headquarters Company, the next Christmas would also be memorable, but for a different reason. On 25 December 1944, they entered combat at the Battle of the Bulge.

Beyond entertaining children, the paratroopers also courted Irish women. Whether it be in Northern Ireland, England, France, or occupied Germany, paratroopers immediately noticed there were many single, unattached young women in Europe. Able, fit, young men from

Northern Ireland were elsewhere, serving in military units of the United Kingdom. When they traveled to Belfast, on weekend passes, the troopers found even more women, for young, single women from the Republic of Ireland crossed the border to work in the city's war factories and shipyards. The famous lament of British military men – "overpaid, oversexed and over here" – especially applied to paratroopers, who received their first overseas pay in British currency on 10 January 1944. They had the money to invite Irish women whom they met in the blacked-out streets of Portrush or Belfast to a pub for a drink. The relative wealth of paratroopers was such that they signed and pinned to pub walls 10-shilling notes ($2).[25] A Portrush native could only sigh and think how much beer or ale could be bought with that note.

Some contemporary scholars, such as Mary Louise Roberts in *What Soldiers Do* (2013), have looked critically at the wartime relationships between soldiers and European women. Roberts dwells on the obvious when she notes that the liberating soldiers had more power than European women and that they often objectified European women, especially French women, as "easy and libidinous and beautiful."[26] US military authorities understood that the troops could alienate Europeans by their behavior. While in Northern Ireland, the men of the 507th Regiment sat through a class on "Sexual Morality."[27] There are enough accounts of shenanigans by paratroopers stationed in Northern Ireland to suggest that the class did not make much of an impression on the men. And medics assigned to the 82nd Airborne have testified that they were kept busy treating sexually transmitted diseases throughout the war.[28] Although, by contemporary standards, much can be found that is problematic about the paratroopers' relationships with European women, there are qualifying issues to put against judgmental attitudes. Young men and women died by the tens of millions during World War II. Young women and men felt compelled to cram a life's experiences into a few weeks or months, whether one was a nurse, a war industries worker subjected to German aerial bombardment, or a paratrooper. Combat veteran Clint Riddle of Tennessee, who was in a glider regiment attached to the 82nd, typified this attitude when he told his family that he had an English girlfriend. He wrote that "I know we are going back into the combat zone, so I am going to have a good time while I am still alive."[29] In any case, paratroopers married nurses, women of the American Red Cross, and Irish, English, French, and

German women. Trooper Larry James proposed to Margaret McKenna, and at war's end returned to Northern Ireland to marry her. More than fifty years of marriage and four sons ensued. Lillian Forbes of Belfast accepted the marriage proposal of Pfc. Charles P. Blankenship of South Carolina. Blankenship died on D-Day in the Town Square of Sainte-Mère-Église, the first Norman town liberated by the 82nd. Forbes kept in contact with the Blankenship family, but she unfortunately died at the age of thirty-nine. A friend wrote to Blankenship's mother: "I was told by my mother that Lillian never really recovered from Charles's death. She never married, and, indeed, the loss of Charles may even have contributed to her early death."[30]

The paratroopers' primary overseas mission was to make war, not love. At the end of 1943, Portrush's Urban Council hosted a dinner at the Trocadero Restaurant for 100 officers and enlisted personnel of the 507th. The President of the British Legion spoke, remarking that the British appreciated that the United States had first provided moral support and military matériel in the "dark days" of 1939 to 1941. He added that his nation had been "buoyed up with the hope that one day we would see her young men and young women over here by our side in the struggle." The speaker concluded by celebrating the fact that "that day has come."[31] Shortly thereafter the 507th was formally attached to the 82nd Airborne Division. As Sgt. Hinchliff observed, the men were "very enthusiastic" to join the 82nd because of the division's "prestige." Bob Bearden of Texas seconded Hinchliff, remembering that "it was a great day when we sewed that bright red, white, and blue 82nd Airborne Division patch on the sleeve of our jumpsuit jackets."[32] In early March 1944, the paratrooper infantry regiments stationed in Northern Ireland began to move out. With little fanfare, the regiment boarded a train for Belfast, took a ship to Glasgow, and finally a train to Nottingham, England, arriving at its new base on 13 March 1944. Ed Isbell of the 507th summarized the previous three months by noting that "the good people of Northern Ireland treated us Yanks as their own."[33]

Until the end of May 1944, the paratroopers lived at Tollerton Hall, a country estate near the village of Plumtree, just outside of Nottingham in the Midlands of England. Regimental supply officers preceded the move to England. They secured Tollerton Hall, a castle-like structure, for officers. They ordered German and Italian POWs to build a tent city for enlisted men. Each tent had a floor, cots, mattresses filled with straw, and a stove. Six men resided in a tent. The outside ground was muddy, and through April the English weather stayed cold and damp, warming only in May with advancing daylight.[34] That 507th officers permitted such a disparity in living conditions frustrated General Gavin, albeit he confined his disgust to his diary.[35]

General Gavin and General Ridgway had an immediate issue to resolve with the 82nd in England. In Nottingham and the city of Leicester, to which some parachute infantry regiments deployed, African-American military units had been stationed. Racism reared its hideous head. Paratroopers began to attack black soldiers, when they noticed them in the company of white English women. The paratroopers indulged themselves in ugly racism, imagining that interracial sexual relations were occurring. Knifings took place. Gavin, who disdained racial prejudice, recorded in his diary that "English people, especially the lower classes do not discriminate in any way. In fact, they prefer the company of colored troops. The colored troops have been in this community for almost a year and they are well entrenched."[36] Gavin and Ridgway became especially alarmed when they learned that Lt. Colonel Herbert Batcheller vowed to give the entire 505th regiment a pass. As one historian has noted, Batcheller's "intentions were obvious."[37] The generals put Leicester off limits and ordered military police and armed officers to patrol. Ridgway told his officers that they must respect uniforms and assured the English that he would keep the peace.[38] But the solution was segregation, moving the African-American military units to other places in England.

General Gavin was well pleased when he met his new additions to the 82nd Airborne Division, the 507th and 508th regiments. The constant marching and running in Northern Ireland had kept the men fit. He compared the two regiments favorably with his battle-tested 505th regiment, conceding that the two units lacked the proficiency of the 505th, "but what they lack they more than make up for in their zeal and interest in doing the correct thing. They will do all right."[39] To be sure, General Gavin was General Gavin. He constantly groused about the fighting abilities of his classmate, Colonel Millett, labeling him as "overweight," the worst epithet in the general's vocabulary. Other officers reminded Gavin that Colonel Millett had built the 507th from scratch and that the regiment was battleworthy.[40] Gavin also constantly worried that he was not pushing his two new regiments hard enough in training. By May, Gavin informed his daughter that he was working from 7:30 a.m. to midnight.[41]

Once in England, the paratroopers immediately noticed that the intensity of training had picked up. They reasoned that combat was looming, but they had no reliable information on where or when they would jump. As was the case in Northern Ireland, the troopers had difficulty finding space to carry out regimental- and battalion-sized maneuvers. They focused on small unit tactics, calisthenics, and long marches. Captain Sophian wrote to his family about fifteen-mile marches.[42] The 507th Regiment managed to carry out practice jumps, but with mixed success. Bad English weather kept planes grounded and, when there was good flying weather, the skies over England became too crowded with aircraft. One exercise in April 1944 led to numerous injuries, because the paratroopers jumped when the wind was blowing at over thirty miles an hour. Pfc. James P. James from Wisconsin was spun around by the wind and his arm hit the plane, knocking him out. He landed face down. He was away from his company for three weeks, recovering the use of his arm. Fred Boyle of Headquarters Company asserted that eleven of the seventeen men in his "stick" broke one bone or another on this jump.[43] In the middle of May, the paratroopers had a successful night jump along the Grantham Canal in Midlands farm country. The practice jump was marred, however, by an air accident, when two C-47s collided after they had dropped their paratroopers. The jump, codenamed "Exercise Eagle," proved a dress rehearsal for D-Day.[44]

When free from training, the paratroopers could fish in the region's pleasant streams. More often, the men devoted their time and jump pay to meeting English women. Social life in England was as it was in Northern Ireland, only more so. Colonel Millett had declared the village of Plumtree off limits, but nearby Nottingham was a fair-sized metropolitan area. And, as one paratrooper puckishly observed, "as luck would have it, virtually all the eligible young males were away in the armed forces."[45] Many British women in the rollicking pubs were in uniform, serving in the Auxiliary Territorial Service, the Women's Land Army, and the Women's Auxiliary Air Force. Paratroopers proposed marriage, and postwar Anglo-American alliances took place. Marital engagements were also broken by death. Pvt. David Berardi, who was nineteen, promised to marry the similarly youthful Dorothy Cumberland after the war. The paratrooper was killed in action in the Ardennes Forest on 6 January 1945. Dorothy Cumberland would thereafter visit her deceased fiancé's family in the United States.[46]

One extraordinary relationship involved S/Sgt. Charles W. Penchard (1918–2000) of the 507th Regiment and his bride, 1st Lt. Olga Louise Campbell Penchard (1921–1980). S/Sgt. Penchard would be one of the defenders of Graignes. Penchard had initially enlisted in the cavalry but volunteered for the paratroopers. In 1942, he and Olga Campbell married. She enlisted in the Women's Army Corps (WAC) and rose to officer rank. Like her husband, Lt. Penchard was sent overseas, and she worked in military communications in England. Lt. Penchard and her husband spent time together when they were both stationed in England. If military protocol was honored, S/Sgt. Penchard was duty bound to salute his wife! Penchard rose in rank to first sergeant, after he won the Silver Star for gallantry in Normandy in late June 1944.

Figure 2.2 First Lieutenant Olga Louise Campbell Penchard proudly displays the uniform of the Women's Army Corps. Photograph courtesy of her grandson, Michael Heaney.

On 20 May 1944, the paratroopers realized that military combat was imminent. Colonel Millett assembled the regiment, mounted a platform, and gave one, sharp, succinct command: "Sharpen your jump knives." The Colonel then saluted the men and left. The paratroopers sent their trench knives, bayonets, and switchblades to Nottingham for sharpening.[47] Astute paratroopers might have already sensed an impending development. The source of their protein had changed from daily allotments of lamb to beef, which was in short supply in England. Pfc. James of the 507th Regiment thought that "they are fattening us up."[48] Paratroop officers had learned that the 82nd and 101st Airborne Division would be assaulting German positions in Normandy. As early as 19 April, General Gavin sent his coded reminder to his daughter to renew magazine subscriptions. He repeated his "I am about to jump" warning on 2 June.[49] Junior officers, like Lt. David Marr, received preliminary briefings in late May.[50] On 26 May, the 507th Regiment was put on "full alert" and confined to Tollerton. On 28 May, the regiment marshalled and boarded buses for airfields. The 1st Battalion went to Fulbeck Airfield, and the 2nd and 3rd Battalions bused to Barkston Heath airfield, about thirty miles from Tollerton. At Barkston Heath, seventy-two C-47 airplanes had been assembled to transport the 1,230 paratroopers of the two battalions to Normandy. The men were assigned cots to sleep on in airplane hangars. There, in T/5 Robert Davis's words, "sealed in strict, barbed-wire security, we were briefed on our mission."[51]

The Mission

President Franklin D. Roosevelt and key military advisors wanted to land US troops on Western European soil as soon as possible. Planning for a cross-English Channel invasion began on 27 March 1942.[52] The president wanted to take the fight to the enemy, liberate traditional friends like the French, and relieve pressure on the Soviet Union, which was doing the bulk of the fighting against Nazi Germany. The United States was not, however, fully mobilized for war until 1943–1944. Thus, President Roosevelt had to defer to the wishes of his ally and friend, Prime Minister Winston Churchill. The prime minister was reluctant to sacrifice another generation of young men on Western European soil, as the United Kingdom had done during World War I. The British also had traditional political and economic interests and military ties in the Mediterranean region. The compromise was to attack indirectly, by launching an invasion of North Africa in 1943 and then attacking Sicily and Italy. President Roosevelt began to assert his authority over Churchill once the United States became militarily powerful. At a conference in Tehran, Iran at the end of November 1943 between Roosevelt, Churchill, and Soviet leader Josef Stalin, President Roosevelt made a firm pledge to Stalin to launch an invasion of Western Europe in 1944.

US and British military planners would, of course, decide to liberate Western Europe and invade Germany by first invading Normandy. "Operation Overlord" was the codename for the overall Norman campaign. "Operation Neptune" was the codename for the landing of assault troops via air and sea on French soil on 6 June 1944, D-Day. Landing on a broad front in Normandy provided several advantages. The US, British, and Canadian forces would be able to capture the strategic port at Cherbourg and ports further west in Brittany. The terrain in the southern part of Normandy would facilitate the movement of tanks, trucks, and artillery through France and toward the Rhine River and the heart of Germany. Once in control of Normandy, the Allies could also move toward Paris and liberate the cultural center of Europe. Allied planners rejected landing at what, at first glance, seemed the most logical place – Pas de Calais. The closest distance between England and the continent was between Dover and Pas de Calais. But it was the most heavily fortified area of France, because German military planners anticipated that the Allies would launch a major assault on Pas de Calais. Allied military and intelligence planners developed an elaborate scheme, dubbed "Operation Fortitude," to deceive the Germans. They created an invasion force on paper and appointed a prominent figure, General George S. Patton, Jr., to command it. They further launched a massive "disinformation" campaign to persuade the Germans that General Patton would lead his fictional army into France via Pas de Calais.[53]

The US military had responsibility for the Cotentin Peninsula of Normandy. The US assignment was to take control of the Cotentin Peninsula and, above all, to seize Cherbourg, the port at the northern point of the peninsula. Once the US military had control of Cherbourg, it could rapidly transfer equipment and supplies into Europe. On D-Day, the 4th Infantry Division had the mission of assaulting "Utah Beach," and the 1st Infantry Division supplemented by the 29th Infantry

Division would land at "Omaha Beach." Both landing areas were on the eastern side of the Cotentin Peninsula. They were separated by the strategic town of Carentan, which is inland but is connected to the sea a few miles away via a canal. Military planners foresaw the paratroopers of the 101st and 82nd Airborne Divisions playing a central role in successful beach landings, especially at Utah Beach. The 101st would jump directly behind Utah Beach. The "Screaming Eagles" of the 101st would secure the Barquette Canal, which was about two miles north of Carentan. The canal controlled the flow of the Douve River, a major artery in Normandy, to the sea. The 101st would also capture the four causeways that crossed over the lagoons behind Utah Beach. Without US control of the causeways, the 4th Infantry would be trapped on the beaches and be subjected to deadly artillery fire. Finally, the 101st would take control of Carentan and prevent the Germans from driving a wedge between US troops on Utah and Omaha.[54]

The "All Americans" of the 82nd Airborne Division had similarly crucial assignments to complete. The three regiments of the division would touch down around Sainte-Mère-Église. The 2,004 paratroopers in the 507th Regiment, for example, were supposed to land in Drop Zone T near the village of Amfreville, about four miles west of Sainte-Mère-Église. The small crossroads town of Sainte-Mère-Église was judged militarily significant because it was situated near Route 13 (N-13 today), the major road that connected Cherbourg to Paris. Beyond liberating Sainte-Mère-Église, the 82nd was ordered to take control of bridges that crossed the Merderet River. Control of the bridges would hamper a German counterattack coming from the western part of the Cotentin Peninsula on US infantry emerging from Utah Beach. Finally, the 82nd was asked to be ready to assist gliders landing with supplies, ammunition, jeeps, light howitzers, and troops from the 325th Glider Infantry Regiment. The 325th Regiment, which was part of the 82nd Division, would land during the daylight hours of D-Day.[55]

The proposed deployment of the 82nd and 101st Airborne Divisions sparked heated debate among military planners. Chief of Staff General George C. Marshall once wrote to General Eisenhower recommending that the paratroopers be dropped near Paris. Eisenhower rejected the advice, warning that the paratroopers would be trapped far behind enemy lines, if the beach landings went wrong.[56] Air Chief Marshal Sir Trafford Leigh-Mallory offered a different argument. The British officer opposed the paratroopers jumping into Normandy, predicting that it would lead to catastrophic casualties. Leigh-Mallory oversaw air operations for Operation Neptune and reported directly to General Dwight D. Eisenhower, the commander of the Normandy invasion. Leigh-Mallory protested to Eisenhower the "futile slaughter" of the 82nd and 101st. He calculated that only 50 percent of the paratroopers would be capable of fighting. Unarmed C-47s would be vulnerable to enemy fire, whether it came from German fighter planes or anti-aircraft batteries on the ground in Normandy. The low-flying glider planes would suffer a 70 percent destruction rate, because they would be especially vulnerable to anti-aircraft fire. The paratroopers and glider men who made it to the ground would face enormous difficulties. In a confused and disorganized state and behind enemy lines, the men of the 82nd and 101st Airborne Divisions would have immediate contact with a formidable enemy.[57]

Leigh-Mallory's nightmare scenarios forced General Eisenhower to reconsider the idea of an airborne assault into Normandy. He would later observe that this was the most difficult of his D-Day decisions, even more difficult than his decision to commence the attack on 6 June, a day with problematic weather. As Eisenhower wrote, Leigh-Mallory's strong dissent forced upon him "the unbearable burden of a conscience justly accusing me of the stupid, blind sacrifice of thousands of the flower of our youth." At the end of May, Eisenhower retreated to his tent to ponder his options. He knew that General Omar N. Bradley, the field commander of US ground forces, unequivocally opposed the idea of cancelling the airborne assault. US ground troops needed to get off Utah Beach, cross the causeways, and be in a position to move toward the first big military prize of Operation Overlord – the port of Cherbourg. Without the support of the paratroopers, the invasion of Utah Beach might as well be cancelled. As he reviewed the D-Day plans, Eisenhower reasoned that "the Utah attack was an essential factor in prospects for success. To abandon it really meant to abandon a plan in which I had implicit confidence for more than two years." Eisenhower informed Leigh-Mallory of his decision in a letter, noting that his staff, General Bradley, and General Matthew Ridgway, the commander of the 82nd, supported his decision to maintain the airborne assault.[58] Nonetheless, Eisenhower took Leigh-Mallory's view seriously, and he worried. The general visited with the paratroopers of the 101st in the evening of 5 June 1944. As one scholar has written, it has long been known that the famous picture of Eisenhower with the

Figure 2.3 In this iconic photograph, General Eisenhower speaks with members of the 101st Airborne on the evening of 5 June 1944. The confident paratroopers reassured the anxious general. They promised Eisenhower that they would accomplish their missions. US National Archives photograph.

paratroopers the night before D-Day reflects his concern over having to put aside his advisers' written objections to the American airborne operation because of excessive casualties.[59]

In his response to Leigh-Mallory, Eisenhower ordered "there is nothing for it but for you, the Army Commander and the Troop Carrier Commander to work out to the last detail every single thing that may diminish these hazards."[60] Leigh-Mallory's idea that the C-47s stay at a high altitude over Normandy to avoid flak from anti-aircraft guns was rejected. Dropping from 1,000 feet or above would subject the paratroopers to a long period of being exposed to ground fire. The British officer's argument that glider planes should not try to land at night, however, for the most part won out. Although he was not involved in the final decisions, General Gavin seems to have anticipated Leigh-Mallory's concern about confusion and disorganization on the ground among paratroopers. Paratroopers became paratroopers because they were intelligent, fit, disciplined men capable of showing initiative. Once on the ground, paratroopers would form themselves into fighting units with paratroopers from other companies, battalions, regiments, and even divisions. On D-Day, men from the 101st Airborne Division joined Headquarters Company, 3rd battalion, 507th Regiment of the 82nd Airborne in the defense of Graignes.

Air Chief Marshal Leigh-Mallory probably never believed that Eisenhower made the proper call on the airborne assault. In his diary, he recorded the warning that "the 82nd Division will have a most sticky time of it."[61] Scholarly judgments on Leigh-Mallory's pessimism have been harsh. US fighter planes protected the C-47s on their way to Normandy. Anti-aircraft fire over Normandy was intense, and C-47s suffered damage and some crashed. Of the 82nd's 369 transport planes, 9 C-47s were destroyed or missing, and 115 suffered "heavy damage."[62] The C-47s managed, however, to drop the paratroopers, albeit often far from designated drop zones. Both the 82nd and the 101st accomplished their assigned missions. The liberation of Sainte-Mère-Église on D-Day remains a proud moment in US and French history. Hence the distinguished historian of World War II Gerhard L. Weinberg wondered why Leigh-Mallory held his position and noted that "the issues associated with this rigid, prickly individual remain something of a puzzle."[63] Leigh-Mallory never had a chance to answer critics in a memoir or postwar interviews. He died in November 1944, on the way to a new military assignment, when the plane he was on crashed into the French Alps. In the postwar period, Leigh-Mallory might have pointed out that his vision of unspeakable casualties became tangible. One analyst calculated that the total battle casualties (killed and wounded) of the 82nd Airborne's paratroopers and glider men amounted to 35 percent on D-Day alone. No US military division has ever before or since suffered such casualties in a twenty-four-hour period.[64] General Eisenhower had cause to worry on the night of 5 June.

The paratroopers who waited at Barkston Heath airfield were unaware of the debates among generals and air marshals over their fate. The enlisted men also knew nothing about the timing of the attack or that their drop zone had been changed. Military planners targeted the dates of 5–7 June as the opportune time to launch the invasion of Normandy. These dates offered the best combination of moonlight, favorable tides, and time of sunrise to accommodate the needs of the paratroopers and ground troops arriving via the sea. Since they would be dropping at night, paratroopers needed ample moonlight. They also wanted winds to be moderate, preferably at less than twenty miles per hour. General Eisenhower scratched the 5 June date, because of stormy weather. He issued his famous "OK, we'll go" order for 6 June when a meteorologist he trusted advised him there would be a period of fair weather for that day. To go past 7 June would have meant at least a fourteen-day postponement of the invasion. Eisenhower believed that morale would suffer, if his invaders had to wait an additional two weeks.[65]

In late May, the drop zone for the three regiments of the 82nd Airborne Division had been moved ten miles eastward, closer to Utah Beach. Intelligence analysts had discovered that the German 91st Air Landing Infantry Division led by *Generalleutnant* Wilhem Falley was near the proposed landing zone around Saint-Sauveur-le-Vicomte, which is in the middle of the Cotentin Peninsula. In the region also was the 6th Parachute (*Fallschirmjäger*) Regiment led by Major Friedrich August Freiherr von der Heydte. The US paratroopers would be at a distinct military disadvantage if they landed in the middle of heavily armed German units. Officers of the 82nd Airborne Division had conducted map and sand table studies to learn the terrain and landmarks around Saint-Sauveur-le-Vicomte. As D-Day approached, the officers were forced to renew their studies for the new landing zones near Sainte-Mère-Église.[66]

In the airplane hangars at Barkston Heath, enlisted personnel of the 2nd and 3rd Battalions of the 507th Regiment also studied maps, reconnaissance photographs, and sand tables. The paratroopers had time to kill, for they were essentially confined to the hangars for a week. Latrines were installed within the hangars. The men could leave the hangars only in small groups to guard against German aerial reconnaissance noticing the assembly of paratroopers. German intelligence personnel understood, however, that paratroopers would soon assault occupied France. The paratroopers listened on the radio to the German propaganda outlet hosted by "Axis Sally," also known as the "Berlin Bitch." Axis Sally was Mildred Elizabeth Gillars, an American employed by Nazi Germany. She played popular big band music of the 1940s interspersed with taunts about what German soldiers would do to US troops. She identified the 507th as a "virgin parachute regiment," which had replaced the 504th Regiment in the 82nd Airborne Division. The 504th, which had fought in Italy, had been "chewed up" by the Germans, according to Axis Sally. A "warm welcome" could be expected by the 507th when they entered combat, for "their blood would grease the wheels of German tanks." Sgt. Ed Jeziorski of New York remembered that the "Berlin Bitch" followed those threats by playing "tear-jerking songs."[67]

While listening to the radio, the paratroopers entertained themselves, playing cards and throwing dice. They had some new money to play with, as each man was issued French francs for the upcoming invasion. They also received visits from Generals Ridgway and Gavin, but not General Eisenhower. Both Ridgway and Gavin discouraged a visit from the Supreme Allied Commander, thinking it would distract the men. Officers did read aloud, however, Eisenhower's encouraging letter to the invading forces, in which he told them that they had embarked on a "Great Crusade" and that "the eyes of the world are upon you." Generals Ridgway and Gavin were both frank about what lay ahead. Ridgway said: "Some of you will die, this participation in world history may be just a thought that you can take with you. You are assured by me that you will be on the winning side." Gavin echoed Ridgway's somber thoughts, admitting that "some of us will lose our way." But Gavin also expressed conviction in his men, expecting them to do "a hell of a good job."[68] For his part, the battle-tested Gavin remained confident. As he assured his daughter, "I even amaze myself sometimes with the speed with which I can get under a flat rock."[69]

The paratroopers had plenty of time to think in the pre-invasion week. Neither fear nor hatred characterized their thoughts. They had trained intensively for this assignment for more than a year and wanted to get on with it. They always wanted to prove themselves to their colleagues. As Ed Isbell of the 507th recalled, being killed or wounded was not the biggest concern, but rather "worrying about holding up in combat, being so frightened you would disgrace yourself in the eyes of your buddies and reacting to the killing of another human, were our fears. These thoughts were foremost in our minds."[70] Isbell's thoughts were also shared by the infantry troops who would assault France from landing boats. Forrest C. Pogue, who served as an official historian for the US military, moved among the landing troops. He detected no hatred of the enemy but enthusiasm for action. The men were tired of the endless training. As such, "with no worry about the fact that the first day of battle might be the last of their lives, they hailed the announcement that they were going to Normandy." The men also had the false comfort provided by a recent article in *Stars and Stripes*, the official organ of the military. The article emphasized that the invaders would feel little pain or shock if wounded. Unconsciousness or morphine injected by a medic would soon take over.[71] The soldiers who lay bleeding on Omaha Beach or the paratroopers who struggled to avoid drowning in the flooded *marais* of Normandy might subsequently disagree with the article's rosy assessment of pain.

On 5 June 1944, the paratroopers of the 507th busied themselves checking and cleaning their weapons and equipment. Red Cross nurses served coffee and doughnuts. For the second day in a row, the paratroopers sat down to a sumptuous dinner of steak, fries, and apple pie. Black humor reigned, with paratroopers comparing the all-you-can-eat feast to the condemned person's last meal before execution. Father John Verret of the 3rd Battalion celebrated Mass to the largest group of communicants of his military career – Catholics and non-Catholics alike.[72] Colonel Millett, the regimental commander, conducted the ultimate ceremony. His remarks to the men, some of whom would soon be landing near Graignes, Normandy, sent them into a frenzy. The regimental commander reviewed the unit's history and "all the trouble it had caused him." The paratroopers had brawled their way through Georgia, Nebraska, Denver, and Nottingham. Towns and villages from Columbus, Georgia to Plumtree, England had been placed off limits to them. But the paratroopers could now atone for their "list of sins." They could "make it all up to me tonight." The colonel paused and then declared: "We are going in tonight." As recounted by Lt. Frank Naughton, "at those words I thought the top of the hangar would come off. The morale of the men was just incredible. It was electrifying. I get goose bumps now just recalling those moments." Naughton, the career military officer, then elaborated: "Through 33 years of service I never did see, hear, or feel that way. I never saw troops as fired up as they were on that particular afternoon. About 3 or 4 hours later, we were airborne and on our way."[73]

The paratroopers were on their way to a France that had been occupied by Nazi Germany since June 1940. The shock of sudden defeat left the French population confused and overwhelmed. Many French people initially collaborated with the Germans or at least accommodated themselves to the occupation. But French resistance to Nazi tyranny grew. The French resented their loss of independence and the sickening racial laws that the Nazis imposed on their country. Increased German demands for forced labor and the continued imprisonment of French soldiers inflamed the French. In the seemingly placid Norman village of Graignes, locals seethed about the occupation. But even as French attitudes hardened, Germany dispatched more of its troops into France, anticipating the Allied invasion. This included a new unit, the 17th *Schutzstaffel* (*SS*) *Panzergrenadier* Division. Elements of the 17th *SS Panzergrenadier* Division would attack Graignes on 11–12 June 1944. The paratroopers would need the help of the aroused villagers in order to survive.

3 OCCUPIED FRANCE

As paratroopers of the 82nd and 101st Airborne Divisions left England for Normandy during the late evening hours of 5 June 1944, they hoped for many things. They needed the help of the people of occupied France. Effective French resistance to German occupation would go a long way in facilitating the invasion effort. In particular, French citizens could provide intelligence about German military installations and impede German military movements by sabotaging transportation networks. As exemplified by the heroism of the villagers of Graignes, the French had come to the point in 1944 at which they were prepared to risk everything to aid the Allied invaders. The paratroopers understood that liberation ultimately depended on them and their military colleagues defeating Nazi Germany. They believed that their training had prepared them to take on the formidable German army in France. What they did not anticipate was that Germany had introduced forces into France that operated outside the traditional boundaries of warfare.

France under Occupation

By mid 1940, Germany led by Führer Adolf Hitler of the National Socialist German Workers' Party (Nazi Party) dominated most of Western and Central Europe. German aggression had been relentless. Hitler violated the Treaty of Versailles (1919), rebuilding German armed forces and moving troops into the Rhineland. In 1938–1939, Germany absorbed Austria and most of Czechoslovakia.

On 1 September 1939, World War II officially began in Europe when Germany invaded Poland. By the end of September, Germany, in conjunction with its temporary ally the Soviet Union, had conquered Poland. After a few months of relative inactivity, the German war machine was again on the march. In April, Germany attacked Denmark and Norway. On 10 May 1940, it launched its *Blitzkrieg* ("lightning war") campaign against Belgium, Luxembourg, the Netherlands, and France. The Germans coordinated dive bomber attacks with rapid tank and infantry movements, taking advantage of their superior communications to outflank and shock their enemies, especially the French army. Within six weeks, the German military had subdued the four Western European countries. German troops marched into Paris on 14 June 1940.

The French government, army, and people, who had held firm and ultimately defeated Germany during World War I, were in a state of bewilderment and shock in 1940. Civilian politicians of the Third Republic (1870–1940) resigned and were replaced by Marshal Philippe Pétain (1856–1951), the conservative military leader from World War I. Marshal Pétain was popularly known as the "Lion of Verdun" for his dogged leadership and determination in resisting German advances in the battle at Verdun that lasted over 300 days in 1916. On 22 June, at Pétain's direction, France signed an armistice with Germany. Germany gained military control of about 60 percent of the country's territory – northern and western France, the Atlantic Coast, and Paris. Pétain's government, having abolished the Third Republic, was nominally in charge of the entire country, with French civil servants managing routine affairs. The old *maréchal* and his advisors resided in Vichy, a spa town in central France. Beyond accepting German military occupation, the French were forced to agree to onerous terms in the armistice. France had to pay Germany 400 million francs ($8 million) per day for the occupation, demobilize and disarm its military forces, and prevent all resistance to Germany both at home and in French colonies. Germany subsequently incorporated French territory, Alsace and Moselle, into the Reich and impressed 130,000 men from these regions into the German military. To ensure French compliance with the armistice terms, Germany kept hostages, approximately 1.5 million French soldiers who were held as prisoners of war. Over 900,000 French soldiers would not be repatriated until the end of the war.[1]

Two competing analyses surfaced in 1940 that purported to explain, in historian Robert O. Paxton's words, France's "shattering trauma" of defeat. A compelling explanation is that at a critical time France suffered from weak civilian and especially military leadership. Civilian leaders throughout Europe, like Prime Minister Édouard Daladier of France and Prime Minister Neville Chamberlain of the United Kingdom, failed to grasp the nature of the threat that Hitler's Nazi Germany posed for Western civilization. More important, French generals were still fighting World War I, which had been characterized by static trench warfare. In the 1930s, French military planners had placed France's security in the Maginot Line, a series of fortifications, concrete bunkers, and artillery installations on France's borders with Italy, Luxembourg, Switzerland, and Germany. Unlike German generals, French military men had not adapted to technological change – fast dive bombers, powerful tanks or *Panzers*, and wireless communications. To be sure, some French officers, including Charles de Gaulle, dissented, arguing for mobile armored forces. German forces went over and around the Maginot Line and did so at amazing speed in the *Blitzkrieg*. Ironically, German military planners had studied de Gaulle's treatises on the tactical advantages of mobile armored forces. As Philip Nord, a historian who analyzed France's defeat observed, "it was the army command that lost the Battle of France, not civilian error or a disinclination to fight, let alone faults, real or imagined in French society as a whole."[2]

Marshal Pétain and his authoritarian advisors favored, however, a false narrative to explain France's defeat and surrender. They blamed parliamentary democracy, trade unions, feminism, secularism, cultural diversity, and the eternal scapegoat, Jewish people, for France's military defeat. German occupation provided an opportunity for French right-wing authoritarians to impose their vision of the proper life on the civilian population. Strong-man government, anti-labor policies, work, family, and fatherland would replace the ideals of the French Revolution – *liberté, égalité, fraternité*. Of its own volition, the Vichy government imposed discriminatory laws against Jews and would subsequently accede to German demands that Jews be deported to death camps. It also persecuted defenders of the rights of industrial workers, Socialists and Communists. Collaboration and collusion characterized the relationship between Vichy and Nazi Germany, as symbolized by Marshal Pétain's handshake with Hitler on 24 October 1940 at

Montoire-sur-le-Loir, a small town in central France. As Pétain explained, "a collaboration was planned between the two countries. I accepted the principle of it."[3]

At the outset of Vichy, French citizens largely accepted the concessions that had been made to Nazi Germany. General Charles de Gaulle had fled to England and on 18 June and on 22 June 1940 made appeals, via the British Broadcasting Corporation (BBC) radio, to the French people to resist. The French had lost a battle, but the global war was not over. The general further warned that the French would fall into slavery if they acquiesced in German rule.[4] Few French people at the time agreed with the general's analysis. The potentially powerful United States remained a neutral nation. Germany was allied with Italy and Japan, and the three aggressor nations planned to integrate their military plans. Germany also had a non-aggression pact with the Soviet Union. England seemed doomed. One defeatist French general predicted that within three weeks "England's neck will be wrung like a chicken." Germany would soon rule all of Europe. As such, France's best course would be to accommodate itself to German suzerainty. Prior to 1942, resistance to German occupation and Vichy malevolence was sporadic and limited. Few French military veterans heeded de Gaulle's call to join him in London and become founding members of the Free French movement. Acts of sabotage within France were infrequent. In 1941, only thirty attacks on railroad lines were recorded. Étienne Achavanne, a veteran of World War I, became the first martyr of the Resistance, when on 20 June 1940 he sabotaged telephone lines between an airfield and German field headquarters in Rouen. Achavanne was apprehended, court-martialed, and executed by firing squad on 6 July 1940.[5]

The course of wartime events both abroad and at home transformed French attitudes toward the occupation and the Vichy collaborators. Britain, led by Prime Minister Winston Churchill, proved up to the task of facing down the Germans. The country withstood the massive German bombing of cities like London and Coventry. The Royal Air Force and its famed "Spitfire" fighter planes gained control of the skies over the United Kingdom. An aroused United States joined the war in December 1941 and converted its industrial base into war industries that built staggering numbers of airplanes, tanks, and ships. Through the Lend-Lease Program (1941–1945), the United States transferred $50 billion in military matériel to its wartime allies. After Germany launched in June 1941 "Operation Barbarossa," its invasion of the

Soviet Union, French Communists began to be actively hostile to the German occupiers. The confidence of the Communists to attack Germans grew as the Soviet Union repeatedly turned back during 1942–1943 German assaults on Stalingrad. In November 1942, the Allied invasion of North Africa, "Operation Torch," further inspired the French to resist the occupation and turn against Vichy. In response, the Germans and Italian Fascists on 11 November 1942 invaded previously "unoccupied" Vichy territory.

Internal developments gave further cause for the French to resist the occupation. The Vichy government enacted discriminatory laws, removing Jews from government jobs and expelling foreign-born Jews from France. Right-wing groups defaced and bombed synagogues. But the Nazi occupiers began to demand more. French Jews were required to wear the Yellow Star in public places. In June 1942, Heinrich Himmler, *Reichsführer* of the SS, demanded that France deport 100,000 Jews. Vichy's security forces cooperated in rounding up people. Approximately 75,000 Jews were deported to killing camps like Auschwitz. Only 2,600 people survived this holocaust. Outraged French citizens who valued basic human rights responded with individual efforts to save Jews, both foreign- and native-born. The names of 2,000 French citizens, who defied the Nazis and Vichy and attempted to save Jews, are engraved on walls in the Israeli Garden of the Righteous Among the Nations.[6]

The Germans intensified the resistance by imposing draconian policies on the population. The occupiers executed 4,000–5,000 French citizens. Men were shot by firing squads, and women were shipped to Germany to be beheaded, shot, or hung. In October 1941, three young Communists shot Lt. Colonel Karl Hotz in Nantes. Germany responded to this and other assassinations by executing fifty innocent French citizens for each German killed. The occupiers further repressed the population by imposing in 1943 the *Service du travail obligatoire* (STO, Obligatory Work Service) on the young population. Under the STO, young people were ordered to Germany to work in war factories as slave laborers. Over 200,000 men and women went into hiding. Many would join the *Maquis*, the French underground. Nonetheless, there were perhaps 1.75 million French men and women toiling in German factories. Beyond being subjected to forced labor, the French grew hungry. Agricultural output fell in France, because so many agricultural workers were in German POW camps. As Germany began to experience military defeats and Allied bombing, it responded by depriving the French of food. The occupiers shipped French livestock to Germany. They also rationed salt, fearing the French would salt meat and hide it. Caloric intake for French adults fell to 1,200 calories per day. The Vichy government instructed schools to teach children how to forage for acorns and chestnuts. The one million Germans in France continued, however, to eat well.[7]

In the dark days of June 1940, General de Gaulle had rejected submission and defeatism and promised his country a global war against the aggressor nations. As he avowed, "somewhere must shine and burn the flame of French resistance." By 1942–1943, the French viewed de Gaulle as prophetic. His emblem, the Cross of Lorraine, became a rallying symbol for the French. It was chosen to remind the French of the perseverance of Joan of Arc and as an answer to the Nazi swastika. Each evening, the BBC provided the Free French with a five-minute slot. The broadcast reached a wide audience, for there were five million radios in the cities, towns, and larger villages of France. The broadcast began with the opening chords of Beethoven's Fifth Symphony. Beethoven's memorable opening chords resembled the three short taps on the Morse Code for the letter "V" for "Victory." The opening words of the broadcast were "Ici Londres! Les Français parlent aux Français" ("London here! The French speak to the French").[8]

The metric of attacks on railways demonstrated how the resistance became more active. Instances of railroad sabotage grew from 30 in 1941, to 108 in 1942, to 1,384 in 1943. During the first eight months of 1944, which included the D-Day invasion and its aftermath, the instances of railway sabotage amounted to 4,523. Railway traffic fell by 50 percent in the weeks surrounding 6 June 1944. Saboteurs became adept at unbolting tracks and then placing them at an angle to produce derailments.[9] The German military relied on the railroad for transportation, because, as the war evolved, they faced a chronic shortage of vehicles and fuel. To resolve shortages, the Germans ordered vehicles from French factories, but found that they received defective goods. When the vehicles were put in reverse, the differential gear malfunctioned. The French factory workers had deliberately built parts to fail. The Renault auto factory built three-ton trucks for the German military but delivered them without tires. The Germans were forced to buy tires on the black markets near the Renault factory.[10]

The occupying force troops had difficulty controlling the swelling resistance in 1943–1944, because it was so diffuse. General de Gaulle and the Free French movement worked with resistance organizations in France. Allied forces dropped to them, by parachute, supplies such as rifles, ammunition, and radios. Beginning in January 1944, with "Operation Sussex," two-person French reconnaissance teams parachuted into France. Their special mission was to gather intelligence on the number and location of German *Panzers*.[11] But most French patriots were not members of a centralized "Resistance," operating on orders from London. Instead, they participated in the resistance movement as individuals or in small groups. A historian of the French resistance has calculated that the "army of shadows" consisted of 200,000 by D-Day. When unarmed civilian resisters are added, the total number of those in the movement amounted to 300,000 to 500,000.[12] Historian Ronald C. Rosbottom has noted that young people in their teenaged years or early twenties were especially significant in the resistance movement. These young people with their "moral certainty" proved an inspiration to the general population.[13] What the Allies in London wanted from the movement was intelligence about German military facilities and movements, transport to safety for downed Allied pilots, and the sabotage of transportation networks. The movement also developed a significant underground press that supplemented news of the war from the BBC. The Allies, including General de Gaulle, discouraged attacks on German soldiers, because of the heavy retribution exacted on the French population after assassinations of high-ranking officers.

In the aftermath of liberation and General de Gaulle's triumphant return to Paris, the mythical memory grew of a "glorious page of national history." The French, except for a few Vichy scoundrels, "contributed toward saving the nation," as an edict signed by de Gaulle proclaimed. The Free French awarded 1,038 *Ordre de la Libération* medals to Resistance heroes. These decorations ignored the daily contributions of many to the cause and had the effect of creating another myth that resistance was a masculine affair. Only six women received the *Ordre de la Libération*.[14] In fact, French women, as in the village of Graignes, worked to undermine the German occupiers, who were disparagingly known as the *boches*. The historical truth is that many French people spent the war focused on surviving and stayed apolitical. And a significant percentage of French clung to the Vichy government to the end. In 1943, Vichy established, for example, the

Milice française, a state militia of blue-uniformed thugs who hunted after those who resisted. This repugnant behavior had the ironic effect of further undermining Vichy, for it identified the Pétain regime with the German occupiers.[15]

Although the history of France under German occupation is complicated, it probably can be said that by June 1944, the majority of the French were sick of the occupation, saw victory in sight, were prepared to fight, and were now willing to risk their lives for their liberation.[16] In their memoirs, the paratroopers of the 82nd and 101st Airborne Divisions universally testify that when they were lost and confused on D-Day, Normans provided advice, guidance, and sustenance. Liberation would prove costly for France. General Dwight Eisenhower worried when he received estimates of 80,000 civilian casualties for Operation Overlord.[17] Civilian casualties would be high in cities and towns like Saint Lô, Coutances, and Valognes, and physical destruction would be widespread in Caen, a city of 60,000 people. Allied bombing and shelling killed the mayor of Carentan. Nonetheless, subsequent studies would show that Normans and the rest of France were "overjoyed" when the Allies landed. In Carentan, the aged, infirm vice-mayor, Alfred Joret, emerged from hiding in his cellar after six days of fighting, stretched out his hand and, without irony, said in French, "Welcome to Carentan," to the French-speaking Major John Maginnis of the US Army.[18]

Graignes, Normandy

The patterns of life for citizens who lived in Normandy, the Cotentin Peninsula, and the village of Graignes largely mirrored the experience of citizens in other parts of occupied France between 1940 and 1944. But there were some meaningful differences. In invading at Utah and Omaha Beaches, US military planners chose to attack the Germans in the Cotentin Peninsula, which is part of Lower Normandy. In governmental terms, the area is part of the Department of *la Manche*. A notable physical feature of the region is its soft, damp ground. At one time, the Cotentin Peninsula was almost an island, connected to land only at Lessay, in the northwestern part of the peninsula. Over the centuries, Normans managed to dry the sea beds and splice the peninsula to Normandy by building barriers, locks, dykes, and canals to control the flow of seawater into the low-lying peninsula. But for the barriers, the seawaters of the Bay of Gran Vey on the east coast would reach to the middle of the peninsula at Saint-Sauveur-le-Vicomte. A key engineering feat was the construction in the middle of the nineteenth century of the La Barquette Lock just north of Carentan. The lock regulated the flow of the Douve River into the sea. Eastward rivers and streams, like the Merderet River, all flowed into the Douve. By opening or closing the lock, according to the tides, engineers could regulate the flow of fresh water to the sea or turn the swamplands or *marais* near Carentan into a shallow, salty lake.[19]

The hydraulic engineering that the Normans perfected helped them build a sturdy agricultural economy. The meadows flanking the

Figure 3.1 The globally famous Norman or *Normande* cows graze at Le Port St. Pierre, about three kilometers from Graignes. Author's photograph.

Douve, Merderet, Taute, and other rivers and streams are below the level of the sea at high tide. Once drained, however, the bottomlands are lush and perfect for grazing. Norman farmers bred the famous *Normande* or Norman cows and bulls. The animals are big-bodied. A cow weighs 700–800 kilograms, and a bull can weigh up to 1,100 kilograms. The *Normande* also have distinct dark circles around their eyes, giving them the appearance of wearing eye glasses. The milk that cows produce is remarkably high in fat and protein, making the milk suitable for the production of butter and cheese. The cows are also dual-purpose animals. Their meat has good flavor and is marbled with fat. Norman farmers found good markets for their prized products in Paris. In 1940, there were as many cows and horses in Normandy as there were people.[20]

The other distinctive feature of Norman agriculture was the development of hedgerows. The terrain of Lower Normandy is identified as *bocage*, a mixture of woodland and pasture. Farmers divided their fields with hedgerows, an interlocking combination of trees, native plants, and stone that over time became impenetrable. Each field normally had only one opening. The hedgerow system would prove particularly challenging for the US Army, because one German machine gunner could control the opening and stymie enemy movement. The Allied drive toward Cherbourg in the summer of 1944 would be delayed by weeks because of the hedgerow issue. In any case, within the hedgerows, Norman farmers planted truck gardens and orchards. In particular, they harvested apples and pears, which became cider and Calvados, an apple and sometimes pear brandy that is delightfully intoxicating and commands a good price. In order to earn the title of "Calvados," the fruit must be grown in Normandy. The distilling of the fruit also provided employment for Normans.

At first thought, *la Manche* might be considered a region in occupied France that would be receptive to the Vichy regime of Marshal Pétain. Vichy preached the virtues of work, patriotism, cultural homogeneity, Catholicism, and large families. Vichy functionaries looked askance at urban areas, with their diverse populations, support for the rights of women, and tolerance of cultural experimentation. Vichy would hardly, for example, contemplate granting the right to vote for women, a right that women in numerous European countries, whether it be in the United Kingdom or in Germany during the Weimar Republic, had achieved before the outbreak of World War II. In Vichy's view, women should be at home taking care of their babies. The regime enacted a series of pro-natal policies. The last major election in the Third Republic had taken place in 1936. It had been a polarizing election, with the political right pitted against leftists. The men of *la Manche* overwhelmingly voted for conservative candidates. The Popular Front, a coalition of Socialists and Communists led by Léon Blum, won the election and thereafter enacted pro-labor legislation. Blum – a native of Paris, a Socialist, and a Jew – represented everything that Vichy despised. Vichy arrested Blum and ultimately dispatched him to the concentration camp at Buchenwald. Blum survived, although his brother died in a German camp.[21]

Despite signs indicating that the citizens of *la Manche* would collaborate with Vichy and the Germans, they did not. Whether it be in the liberation of Sainte-Mère-Église, Carentan, or the village of Graignes, Normans openly risked their lives to aid the paratroopers of the 82nd and 101st Airborne Divisions. Rural people may have had apprehensions about strangers, but the ultimate strangers in their midst were the foreign occupiers, the *boches*. The memory of German aggression on French soil between 1914 and 1918 remained ever present. The towns and villages in *la Manche* had war memorials, inscribed with lengthy lists of those who perished in the "Great War." Many of the region's middle-aged adults had protected France against Germany during World War I. Alexandre Renaud, a pharmacist and mayor of Sainte-Mère-Église, was a machine gunner at the Battle of Verdun. Abbé Albert Le Blastier (1881–1944), the parish priest of Graignes since 1931, had been a medic during World War I. Doctor Jean Baptiste Caillard, the mayor of Carentan who died from a bomb blast during the town's liberation, had served as a military doctor during the previous war. Gustave Rigault (1898–1975), a butcher and farmer in the Graignes area, still carried German shrapnel in his knee.[22] Veterans of World War I had relatives – younger brothers, nephews, even sons – who now languished behind barbed wire as German prisoners of World War II. Citizens in *la Manche* tended to marry within the community, reflecting a traditional desire among rural folk to consolidate landholding patterns. Extended Roman Catholic families lived in the same village for generations. These endogamous marriage patterns signified that when the Germans dragooned young people from *la Manche* into the forced labor of the STO they infuriated blood-related, Catholic communities. Finally, the women of the region hardly resembled the submissive, baby-bearing Vichy ideal of womanhood. In order to survive, everyone worked on the family farm, including women and girls. In Graignes, women served as teachers, and Germaine Boursier operated the town's café and grocery store.

As early as the chaotic *Blitzkrieg* days of June 1940, the residents of *la Manche* demonstrated that they would not countenance the loss of French freedom. Father Le Blastier found out about three retreating English soldiers hiding in a ditch and asked his fellow veteran Gustave Rigault for his assistance. Rigault and his wife, Marthe, had three daughters to safeguard. Nonetheless, the family resisted. They outfitted the English soldiers with pants, jackets, and a pitchfork to help them blend into the community. The family never found out whether the ruse worked or whether the soldiers made it back to England. The soldiers left the youngest daughter, who was eight years of age and also named Marthe, with a pocket handkerchief and buttons.[23] Mayor Renaud of Sainte-Mère

Figure 3.2 This is a photograph of Gustave and Marthe Rigault with their son, Jean Claude, who was born in 1942. Photograph courtesy of the Rigault/His family.

-Église recalled that, when German troops arrived on 18 June 1940, boys greeted them with "glou, glou, glou," the sound of air escaping a drowning man's lungs. The taunt was designed to inform them what would happen if they tried to cross the Channel and invade England. The Germans responded by placing notices in public places in French and German that they would execute anyone who opposed the occupation.[24]

After Germany's victory over France, Father Le Blastier advised his congregation not to resist the occupation. Odette Rigault (1925–2018), the middle daughter in the family, remembered that her family did not welcome the advice but followed it to avoid physical injury or deportation. Nonetheless, in Odette's words, "it was catastrophic. But we never submitted. No one was ever able to stand the thought of the occupation." Her teenaged years were circumscribed, with no chance to attend dances or social functions. Odette's future husband, Édouard Lelavechef, had to go into hiding to avoid being deported to Germany for forced labor. He hid in the home of one of Odette's aunts. But life was hard for Édouard, because he did not have a ration card to obtain food.[25] Issuing ration cards was a method the occupiers used to control the French population. As with the rest of France, the occupation in Normandy was not as onerous between 1940 and 1942 as it would become in 1943 and 1944, with brutal German demands for labor and food. Graignes was never occupied by German troops, although there were troops in surrounding villages and large German military installations in Carentan, six miles to the north.[26]

Prior to the German occupation, the village of Graignes, with a population of about 900 people, was a typical Norman village that offered the tranquil, rural life. A splendid, twelfth-century Romanesque Catholic Church, which was situated on a hill of altitude fifty meters, dominated the village scene. Graignes was a Roman Catholic village, and residents were members of one, big, extended family. Names like Foillot, Mauger, and Rigault predominated. Nearby the church were the rectory, the schools for boys and girls, the grocery store, and the café. The surrounding areas, especially to the north and west, were *marais* that flooded during the winter months from rain and the rivers and streams overflowing. Contemporary photos reveal a mixture of housing, with some qualifying to being labeled as "chateaus," whereas others were more modest with clay and thatched roofs. Residents could bicycle to nearby Carentan. Only three or four farmers had cars. Villagers could transport their dairy and fruit products to Carentan via canals by poling flat boats. Unlike in nearby villages such as Cantepie, the people of Graignes did not have to deal with Germans on a daily basis, for there were no German troops stationed there. German troops would come at times to conduct live-fire exercises in the marshes. The Germans also once took over the school, forcing students to miss classes for eight days.[27]

The Rigault family lived in the nearby hamlet of Le Port St. Pierre, at about three or four kilometers walking distance from the church. Parents Gustave and Marthe had been born in Graignes. The house was on the very edge of the *marais*. The large house did not have electricity. Rural electrification had not made much progress in pre-war France. The family worked the land and milked cows. From the perspective of the young Marthe Rigault (1932–), "it seemed like we lived on the edge of the earth."[28] On 5 June 1944, no one in Graignes could have possibly imagined what would happen in a week's time. To the villagers' amazement, 160 paratroopers from the 82nd and 101st Airborne Divisions would land or splash down near them. War criminals from the 17th *SS Panzergrenadier* Division would subsequently destroy their church, and German troops would burn down Graignes. Graignes would suffer the greatest damage of any Norman village.[29]

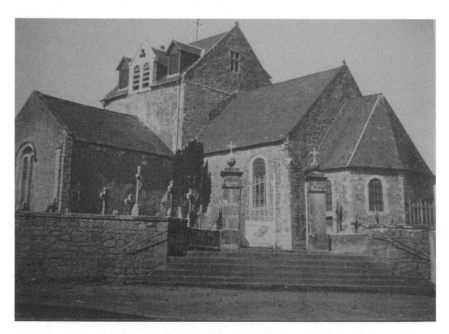

Figure 3.3 The church at Graignes as it appeared before its destruction. Photograph courtesy of the Mayor's Office of Graignes.

Suffering severe military losses on the Eastern Front and calculating that the Allies would invade Western Europe, Nazi Germany demanded more from Normans in 1943–1944. The Germans began building the Atlantic Wall, including a bevy of fortifications and heavy-gun emplacements on the coast of the Cotentin Peninsula. German engineers of the Todt Organization supervised the conscripted workers from Eastern Europe who were euphemistically labeled "International Workers." The Todt Organization also built concentration camps throughout Europe.[30] The Germans disrupted regional life by expropriating coastal lands, razing buildings, and limiting fishing. Normans also faced the threat of deportation and forced labor from the STO.[31] In 1944, the Germans ordered Normans to help with the "defense" of France. In Sainte-Mère-Église, German officers demanded that Mayor Renaud supply labor to dig rings of field defenses around the town. The Germans also stole tools, horses, carts, and automobiles. The German commanding officer showed Mayor Renaud the tree branch upon which the Germans would hang him, if his demands were not met.[32] Throughout Normandy, Germans ordered locals to construct fields of "Rommel Asparagus," six-foot poles placed in fields at intervals to impede the landing of glider planes. Both Mayor Renaud and the new mayor of Graignes, Alphonse Voydie (1904–1980), did their best to temper the German demands. As Mayor Voydie recalled, "I was busy in the administration of my affairs in order to escape as much as possible the annoyances of the Germans."[33] Local officials succeeded in delaying work. The Germans never achieved their goal of stringing the poles with barbed wire and placing mines on them.

The most destructive German action in the Cotentin Peninsula in 1943–1944 was to close the locks at La Barquette to back up the Douve River and its tributaries and flood the regions west and south of Carentan. The objective was to impede Allied military movement and drown the paratroopers of the 82nd and 101st Airborne Divisions. In the area of Graignes, the water in the *marais* was five feet in depth in some places. The water was at full height along river valleys, depriving Norman cows of grazing areas. The bodies of some drowned paratroopers would not be found until the summer of 1945, when the *marais* finally drained. As military historian S. L. A. Marshall later observed, the "enemy had filled the cup" of the low-lying regions.[34]

As a result of German military policies, Normans faced extreme hardship in 1943–1944. The population of Normandy, which was approximately one million in 1940, began to decline, with people fleeing

Figure 3.4 Marthe Rigault and her baby brother Jean Claude are situated on the edge of the family farm. This photograph demonstrates the extent of the flooding in 1943–1944 in areas near Graignes. Photograph courtesy of the Rigault/His family.

forced labor demands. With labor shortages, agricultural production fell. Food became scarce. Prices soared. Ration cards became useless. Germans extorted chickens, milk, and cows from farmers. Every week the Rigault family had to donate one of their cows to the German occupiers. Young Marthe could no longer find the chocolate she so dearly loved at the local store. The Rigault family depended on rabbits and root vegetables they grew for their survival. Finding food was difficult for Normans who did not live on farms.[35] Normans nonetheless persevered, showing some wit and humor amidst the German-produced calamities. In late 1943, an announcement circulated that was ostensibly issued by the Roman Catholic Bishop of Bayeux. Christmas had been cancelled, for "the stable has been requisitioned, the Holy Virgin and the infant Jesus have been evacuated, and St. Joseph is in a concentration camp." The shepherds went "underground" to avoid the labor draft. Their sheep had been "sent away to be consumed by the masters in Berlin." The angels had been "killed by anti-aircraft fire," and the stars had been "impounded by the Chief of State."[36]

A Norman resistance group probably circulated the Christmas cancellation announcement. As in the rest of France, in

Normandy resistance to the occupation grew in 1943–1944. By 1944, perhaps 5,000 Normans belonged to a resistance organization. The vast majority of the rest of the population detested the *boches*. Resisters and their sympathizers tended to be followers of General de Gaulle, who placed his appeals for resistance within the context of French patriotism and not within visions of thoroughgoing socioeconomic change. Members of the *Alliance Confrérie de Notre-Dame*, which was associated with Free French forces, conducted reconnaissance near the Atlantic Wall, producing sketches and maps. One French fisherman stole German flyers warning people to stay away from specific coastal batteries when they practiced firing. The flyers, which inadvertently identified the position of the batteries, made their way to Allied intelligence officers in England.[37] Most reconnaissance was conducted, however, through aerial photography. The photographs did not reveal the extent of flooding, because tall reeds obscured the deep waters. Military photograph interpreters reasoned that, at worst, the ground was soft.

In the first days of June, the people of the Cotentin Peninsula and the German military anticipated an Allied invasion. Mayor Renaud thought that the Germans seemed confused and frantic, constantly changing the positions of their troops, moving from village to village. He also noticed the introduction of troops in German uniforms who were Russian or Ukrainian in ethnic origin.[38] A French farmer, who lived near Sainte-Mère-Église, noticed that Germans did not show up on 5 June to supervise their work planting poles in fields. He surmised that the occupiers sensed the impending invasion.[39] Allied aircraft dropped leaflets with drawings of US and British paratroopers, jeeps, and tanks. Resistance leaders listened carefully for coded messages from the BBC. On 1 June 1944, the coded message alerted Resistance leaders to pay special attention to the next days' messages. The coded message that "the tomatoes must be picked" informed the French to intensify their attacks on railways and to fell trees across roads. The Germans tried to counter this intelligence by ordering the confiscation of radios. On Sunday, 4 June, Albert Mauger (1896–1977) of Graignes, a veteran of World War I and the local Resistance leader, informed his friend Gustave Rigault that the invasion was imminent. On Monday, 5 June, Odette Rigault, who identified herself as a "soldier," rode her bicycle to Carentan. She recalled that people were speaking under their breath that the Allies were coming.[40]

Figure 3.5 Albert Mauger, Resistance leader from Graignes, posed for
a photograph in the immediate postwar period. Mauger collected intelligence
on German installations and ammunition depots in *la Manche* and passed the
information on to contacts in Carentan. His medals reflect his service as
a soldier during World War I and as a member of the French Resistance.
Mauger was decorated with the Legion of Honor, the highest French order of
merit. Photograph courtesy of the Mayor's Office of Graignes.

The German Occupiers

Odette Rigault enlisted as a soldier and Albert Mauger,
a veteran of World War I, reenlisted, because their beloved Normandy
was occupied by the German military. In mid 1944, approximately
one million German troops were stationed in France. Eleven of the fifty-
five German divisions were *Panzer* divisions. Germany had strengthened its forces in France, Belgium, and the Netherlands in anticipation
of an Allied invasion. There were perhaps 200,000 German troops in
Lower Normandy. In the months before the invasion, the German

commanders dispatched an additional 20,000 troops to *la Manche*, even though they continued to expect that the Allies would focus invasion efforts on Pas de Calais.[41] Although the German military had suffered grievous losses at the hands of the Soviet Union in 1942–1943, German officials still had confidence they could hold on to their conquest of Western Europe. In June 1944, the German armed forces numbered 6.5 million, albeit the majority of troops fought on the Eastern Front. There were millions of POWs and forced laborers working in German factories. Allied strategic bombing took its toll, but German war production was 285 percent higher in 1944 than it was in 1940.[42] Adolf Hitler and German military planners also counted on new weapon systems to bolster their military strength. The V-1 flying bomb and the V-2 rocket would be used to terrorize civilian populations in cities like London. Jet fighter planes, notably the *Messerschmitt* Me 262, might restore the *Luftwaffe*'s mastery of the air. German engineers worked on designing powerful *Panzers* to dominate the battlefield. And new U-boats, which were fast and did not have to surface to recharge batteries, could be deployed to counteract the British and US control of the high seas.[43]

The German troops, who in 1944 occupied most of France, performed a variety of missions. Some supervised French civil servants. Others aided Vichy security forces, which included the right-wing, paramilitary organization, the *Milice*, in hunting down members of the increasingly active resistance movement. Historians have estimated that over 100,000 French resisters and Free French soldiers were killed or deported. Much of this repression occurred in 1944. For example, the German secret police, the *Gestapo*, executed eighty French resisters in a prison in the Norman city of Caen on 6 June 1944. Some of the executed included those who had produced maps for the Allies of the Atlantic Wall that the Germans were constructing.[44]

Defending the east coast of the Cotentin Peninsula, where Utah Beach was located, were three *Heer* (Army) Divisions. The 709th Infantry Division had primary responsibility for throwing the invaders back into the sea. Reinforcing the 709th Infantry Division was the 243rd Infantry Division. If US forces succeeded in establishing a bridgehead at Utah, the 91st Air Landing (*Luftlande*) Division was tasked with launching a counterattack. The 6th Parachute Regiment (*Fallschirmjäger-Regiment 6*), which was attached to the 91st Air Landing Division, had responsibility for keeping Carentan under German control.[45] US military planners especially judged the 91st Air Landing Division to be a tough opponent. The division, which was under the command of Lt. General Wilhelm Falley and had 7,500 men, represented a new innovation in German military science, for it had been trained and equipped to be transported by air. The division lacked German *Panzers*, but it had seized light French tanks made by Renault. In May 1944, the D-Day planners had changed the landing zones of the three regiments of the 82nd Airborne to forestall landing on top of General Falley's forces. Nonetheless, the 91st was in position to take on the paratroopers and the Utah Beach invaders. Falley's headquarters was in Picauville, which is only five miles from Sainte-Mère-Église. Two days after landing in Normandy, Colonel George Millett, the commander of the 507th Regiment, and a contingent of paratroopers were surrounded and captured by soldiers from the 91st.[46]

The German troops stationed near the east coast of the Cotentin Peninsula on 5 June 1944 looked more formidable on paper than they were in reality. The German journalist Dieter Eckhertz toured the region in 1944 and was surprised to find that the German defenders of what would be dubbed Utah Beach were unfit or were inexperienced older men. The average age of men in the 709th was in the mid thirties, because the Germans were drafting older men to meet their military needs in 1943–1944. Inside the circular, concrete bunkers known as *"Tobruks"* were veterans who had suffered war injuries on the Eastern Front or in other campaigns. For example, Pfc. Stefan Heinevez, who was a machine gunner in a *Tobruk*, had been wounded in Italy and walked with a limp. Eckhertz also learned from Fortifications Development Officer Gert Hoffman that the Atlantic Wall was months from completion and that the troops had been misled into believing they could throw the invaders into the sea. The actual mission was to slow down invasion forces, until an effective counterattack could be launched. To maintain morale, German officers and military chaplains invoked the memory of Charlemagne, "who stood firm against enemy barbarians," in making clear the duty of the German soldiers to repel the invaders. Cpl. Henrik Naute, who was stationed on Omaha Beach, remembered that he was warned that, if he failed in his mission, the Allies would turn France into a puppet state and use it as a launching pad for an invasion of Germany. German officers probably realized that speeches would not be enough to inspire the defenders of Norman coasts. Medics passed out "soldiers' cocktails" to the old veterans.

These were a combination of morphine and methamphetamine designed to make the soldiers energetic and impervious to pain.[47]

Compounding the military challenges that Germany faced in the Cotentin Peninsula was that about a quarter of the men in the 709th Infantry Division were not Germans. Overall, there were forty-five *Ostbataillone* (Eastern Battalions) in the region. These were units made up of "volunteers" from parts of the Soviet Union, such as Georgia, Russia, and Ukraine. Some were fierce anti-Communists, who detested Stalin and the Communist Party. Most were unfortunates who were captured by the Nazis during their invasion of the Soviet Union and given the dire choice of enlisting or being sent to a forced labor camp. These units had German officers and German sergeants and corporals.[48] General Wilhelm von Schlieben, the commander of the 709th Infantry Division, caught the irony in the situation when he noted that "we are asking a lot if we expect Russians to fight in France for Germany against Americans." The general's fear was borne out, for *Ostbatallione* were no match for the 101st Airborne and the 2nd Armored Division in fighting around Carentan in the weeks after D-Day.[49]

If the men from the 82nd and 101st Airborne Divisions who landed near Graignes had been dropped on their respective targets, they would have encountered the 91st Air Landing Division and the 6th Parachute Regiment. On D-Day, 1st Lt. Malcolm D. Brannen and his men from the 508th Regiment of the 82nd ambushed and killed General Falley near his chateau in Picauville. Falley, who was attending a military conference in Rennes, had rushed back to take charge of the counterattack against the invasion. Men from all three regiments of the 82nd subsequently engaged the 91st for control of the La Fière bridge over the Merderet River. The battle started on D-Day, lasted several days, and resulted in extensive casualties for both sides. By 24 June, the 91st had lost 85 percent of its infantry soldiers and was no longer a functioning military unit. Within a few days after landing in Normandy, the 101st Airborne Division accomplished its mission of liberating Carentan, when it drove the 6th Parachute Regiment from the town and subsequently rebuffed repeated German efforts to retake Carentan.[50]

The defenders of Graignes, men of Headquarters Company, 3rd Battalion of the 507th Regiment and their nineteen colleagues from the 101st Airborne, would face, however, a different and more ominous enemy than the 91st Air Landing Division or the 6th Parachute Regiment. On the afternoon and evening of Sunday, 11 June, the paratroopers and the villagers of Graignes would be attacked by elements of the 17th *SS Panzergrenadier* Division. During World War II, German Army units committed war crimes, especially on the Eastern Front. But in Normandy, the German Army did not routinely execute captured paratroopers and offered medical assistance to wounded paratroopers. Paratroopers gave accounts of German units discovering unarmed US medics administering first aid to wounded US soldiers and deciding to move on and let the medics do their work. On 7 June, during the battle for the bridge over the Merderet River at La Fière, German soldiers proposed, and the 82nd Airborne Division accepted, a thirty-minute ceasefire to allow each side to retrieve wounded soldiers.[51] To be sure, paratroopers who became POWS have provided horrifying accounts of their treatment by their German captors.[52] *Waffen-SS* soldiers, however, made a habit of violating customary laws of war. Germans retreating from Utah Beach on D-Day noticed several dead US paratroopers who were in a kneeling position with their hands tied behind their backs. They appeared to have been methodically shot in the back of the head. The retreating soldiers remarked that "this must be the work of SS boys, who apparently had a taste for such things."[53] At the postwar Nuremberg Trials, the *Waffen-SS* was judged to be a criminal organization because of its ties to the Nazi Party and its consistent commission of war crimes and crimes against humanity.

The 17th *Waffen* ("Armed") *SS* (*Schutzstaffel* or "Protection Squad") *Panzergrenadier* Division "Götz von Berlichingen" was authorized by Adolf Hitler at a Führer Conference on 3 October 1943. *Waffen-SS* military units pledged their loyalty to the Nazi Party and Hitler. Their leader was *Reichsführer* Heinrich Himmler, who reported directly to Hitler. Consistent with Nazi racial policy, only men of Germanic origin were eligible to serve in the *Waffen-SS*, although units consisting of foreign nationals would subsequently be authorized. *Waffen-SS* personnel wore the *Totenkopf* (death skull) insignia, signifying in Himmler's words that they "would not spare their own or foreign lives when it comes to the well-being of the *Reich*."[54] The 17th *SS Panzergrenadier* Division took the name of Götz von Berlichingen (1480–1562) in honor of an untamed, educated medieval knight who was a mercenary, poet, and thief. In the eighteenth century, Johann Wolfgang von Goethe wrote a play about his life depicting the struggles of a free-spirited rebel confronting the norms of civilized society. The special insignia of the 17th *SS Panzergrenadier* Division was the iron fist, for von Berlichingen had lost his right hand in battle and replaced it with a prosthetic hand made of iron.[55] Werner Ostendorff (1903–1945) became the commander or *Oberführer* (Senior Leader) of the division in January 1944. A Nazi Party member who joined the *SS* in 1935, Ostendorff, who was born in Königsberg in East Prussia, had fought in World War I as an infantryman and had participated during World War II in the invasions of France and the Soviet Union.

Between October 1943 and June 1944, the 17th *SS Panzergrenadier* Division built its military strength. The division was authorized to have a force of approximately 16,500 men. The heart of the unit would be two *Panzergrenadier* (armored infantry) regiments, the 37th and 38th Regiments. The infantry regiments would be backed by artillery and anti-aircraft units and the motor pool. The twelve 88 mm anti-aircraft guns could be lowered to fire at targets on the ground. The division did not have tanks but did have twenty-five *Sturmgeschütz* (*StuG*) IV "assault guns," turretless armored vehicles built on tank chassis that were powerfully armed and could destroy tanks. The enlisted personnel consisted of volunteers and conscripts recruited or drafted from Germany and Austria or foreign lands, where people of German culture and language resided. The division had a significant number of men from German-speaking regions of Romania. The enlisted men were young, with more than 50 percent being under the age of twenty. There were boys who were sixteen years of age in the 17th *SS Panzergrenadier* Division. Younger men served in the infantry. Men who were over thirty years of age fired the artillery and anti-aircraft guns or drove the trucks and other mechanized vehicles.[56]

Combat veterans who had served in other *SS* units became the officers and senior enlisted men of the division. Beyond teaching military science to the young volunteers and draftees, the *SS* veterans imparted Nazi ideology to impressionable young men. The 1st Battalion of the 37th Regiment attacked Graignes on 11–12 June 1944. Jacob Fick (1912–2004) led the 37th Regiment. His low service number – 3 247 – signified that he joined the *Waffen-SS* shortly after its inception. He worked his way up the command ranks in the *SS*, serving as a company and then battalion commander, and was awarded a Knight's Cross for his military accomplishments. The initial commander of the 1st Battalion was Ernst Häußler (1914–1979) who joined the SS in 1933 and saw significant combat on the Eastern Front. Häußler's tours of duty included a stint from 1936 to 1939 at the Dachau Concentration Camp near Munich. At the time, Dachau held political prisoners, but the SS was developing techniques that would be subsequently used against European Jews. The company commanders of the 1st Battalion who served under Häußler and then Christian Reinhardt were also all veteran SS officers. Otto Binge (1895–1982) led the artillery company, which bombarded Graignes and destroyed the twelfth-century Romanesque Church. Binge, who served as an artillery man in World War I, joined the Nazi Party in 1922 and served in the party's protection police (*Schutzpolizei*) until 1939.[57] At a briefing on 12 June 1944, shortly after the destruction of Graignes, fellow *Waffen-SS* officers described Binge as a "loveable old man, who wins all the hearts."[58]

The 17th *SS Panzergrenadier* Division assembled and trained in 1943–1944 in areas around Thouars in western France. Thouars is located about 380 kilometers (236 miles) south of Carentan. The Germans chose to base the new unit in France for several reasons. They anticipated an Allied invasion in France and wanted to be prepared to counterattack. On 26 April 1944, *Oberführer* Ostendorff attended a military conclave in Paris, where he was informed that the impending invasion would begin with the drop of a significant number of paratroopers. The division also trained in France because German cities and training grounds were under constant Allied bombardment. For example, US and British bombers raided Stuttgart, the sponsoring city of the 17th *SS Panzergrenadier* Division, fifty-three times during the war. While in France, the officers and enlisted men helped themselves to French food and French-owned cars and trucks. They quartered themselves in French barracks, schools, halls, and chateaus.[59] The Germans deluded themselves that the French welcomed the occupiers, as they spoke of the "nature of the friendly, life-loving population of middle France." Hans Stöber, who was a veteran of the 17th *SS Panzergrenadier* Division, included photographs of alleged friendly interactions between Germans and French citizens in his history of the division.[60]

The officers and men celebrated the 17th *SS Panzergrenadier* Division's commissioning at a grand ceremony near Thouars on 10 April 1944. *Reichsführer* Heinrich Himmler presided at the ceremony, which included music from Ludwig Beethoven and Richard

Wagner, readings from Goethe, and the singing of songs, including the *SS* loyalty song (*Treuelied*). *Oberstleutnant* (Lt. Colonel) Dittrich von Berlichingen, a descendant of the medieval knight, was a guest of honor. The ceremony was dubbed a "cuffing ceremony," as the division earned the right to wear stripes or cuffs on the lower arms of uniforms. In his speech to the troops, Himmler spoke of the need for loyalty to Hitler and the *Reich* and the *SS* commitment to "the most strenuous selection of race and form." He noted that the war was in its fifth year and that Germans continued to fight "against plutocrats and bolshevism, with Slavs, Western Europeans, and Americans." He also praised the "fighting spirit" of Götz von Berlichingen and reminded the men that they should remember the medieval knight's scatological response to a surrender demand: "You can kiss my ass."[61]

As D-Day approached, multiple problems bedeviled the new division. The division exceeded its authorized strength with 17,000 men. But it was short of battle-experienced officers and non-commissioned officers. The appalling casualty rate on the Eastern Front was beginning to take its toll. Officers assigned battle-experienced privates and lance corporals to positions normally held by sergeants and corporals. The division also lacked modes of transportation. French workers were subtly sabotaging trucks that the Germans had ordered from French factories. The Germans depended on French drivers to transport them in "wood-fueled" French-made cars. The drivers began to disappear as expectations of the Allied invasion mounted. The German soldiers had little idea about how to service these unique vehicles. As in the rest of France, resistance groups became more active in May and early June of 1944. The division planned to transport its larger tracked vehicles, like the *StuG* IV, via railroad to whatever battlefront developed. On orders from London, French resisters were focusing on disrupting railway service. The 1st Battalion of the 37th Regiment was ordered to establish roadblocks to counter increased activity from armed resisters, the *Maquis*. The battalion confiscated a cache of British-manufactured Sten submachine guns. The British were increasing their drops of weapons to the Resistance. German officers also noted that French officials became "obstinate and sullen."[62] Mayor Renaud in Sainte-Mère-Église and Acting Mayor Voydie in Graignes were simultaneously displaying the same attitudes toward the occupiers.

The most fearful development for the 17th *SS Panzergrenadier* Division was that US military officials began targeting it from the air. US paratroopers in the 82nd Airborne considered the P-51 Mustang their best friend. The fighter-bombers provided close air support for them, for example, when they assaulted Hill 95 in western Normandy in early July 1944. The P-51 Mustangs terrified the Germans. They labeled them the *Jabos*, short for *Jäger-Bomber* (hunter- or fighter-bomber). In early June, the *Jabos* started harassing the 17th *SS Panzergrenadier* Division's military engineers, as they tried to repair sabotaged rail lines or build bridges over the Loire River near Saumur to facilitate the division's move northward. The attacks forced the engineers to work at night. And once the 17th *SS Panzergrenadier* Division received orders to move out toward Carentan, the *Jabos* became the division's constant traveling companion.[63]

At 4:00 a.m., on 6 June 1944, *Oberführer* Ostendorff summoned his staff to division headquarters in Parthenay, just south of Thouars. He passed the codeword, *Blücher*, for an alert. Ostendorff had been informed that paratroopers had landed in the Cotentin Peninsula, and an armada of ships had been spotted on the horizon. On 7 June, the 1st and 2nd Battalions of the 37th and 38th *Panzergrenadier* Regiments began to jump into trucks for the journey to Carentan. The 3rd Battalion of each regiment and other elements of the division would have to follow on trains or by bicycle, on horseback, or on foot. The Germans requisitioned every French automobile they could find, but the French drivers vanished. The *Jabos* repeatedly attacked. The 17th *SS Panzergrenadier* Division's assigned mission was to keep Carentan a German-occupied town.[64] But before they could approach the strategic town of Carentan, the division would confront the paratroopers of the 82nd and 101st Airborne Divisions who held the village of Graignes, six miles from Carentan.

As the first week of June 1944 arrived, both the people of France and their occupiers from Germany expected that the Allied troops who had assembled in England would invade the continent of Europe. The French had prepared for that moment. The first Allied troops the citizens of Normandy would meet would be paratroopers from the United States and the 6th Airborne Division of the United Kingdom. On D-Day and the days that followed, Normans would demonstrate they were eager to aid the men they praised as "the liberators." The French who lived in the village of Graignes would display extraordinary courage in aiding the US paratroopers who unexpectedly landed near their farms and homes.

4 LIBERATORS AND FRIENDS

The grand campaign to preserve the principles and ideals of Western civilization began in the late evening hours of 5 June 1944. The paratroopers of the 82nd and 101st Airborne Divisions boarded C-47 transport planes for their momentous journey to Normandy to begin the liberation of Western Europe and to save Germany from itself. During their month of combat in Normandy, the paratroopers would accomplish their missions, albeit at a staggering price in casualties. For the members of Headquarters Company of the 3rd Battalion of the 507th Regiment, there would be the shock of landing hopelessly off target and having to wage their own private war. That so many of these paratroopers survived can be explained only by the astonishing heroism of the citizens of Graignes.

The Liberation Riders

Approximately 12,000 US paratroopers left England from various airbases for Normandy on 5 June 1944. Three regiments from the 101st Airborne went first, followed by three regiments from the 82nd. Of the 82nd, the combat-experienced 505th Regiment went first, followed by the "green" regiments, the 508th and then the 507th. General Matthew Ridgway jumped with the 505th, and General James Gavin jumped from the lead plane of the 508th. Preceding the departure of the six regiments were the "pathfinders." Their mission was to jump first and set up beacons and markers so that the hundreds of C-47s that would follow could drop their cargoes of men and war matériel on their designated targets.

The 3rd Battalion of the 507th Regiment began to board their planes at about 10:00 p.m. As they moved toward their planes, the service and security personnel of the Barkston Heath airbase stood at attention in a silent tribute to the paratroopers. They understood the significance of what they were witnessing. Paratroopers at other airbases received similar homages. General Dwight D. Eisenhower briefly boarded some of the C-47s carrying members of the 101st to wish them well. Eisenhower then stood on the tarmac and saluted the airplanes as they took off. He stayed until midnight, until every plane had departed.[1]

Paratroopers needed assistance boarding the transports, because they were carrying so much equipment and ammunition. A paratrooper

Figure 4.1 This photograph is of mortar men S/Sgt. Stephen E. Liberty (middle) and S/Sgt. Rene Rabe (right) in preparation for the jump over the Rhine River on 24 March 1945. Liberty, from the Flathead Reservation in Montana, was one of the two Native Americans at Graignes. The photograph demonstrates how heavily loaded the paratroopers were, when they made combat jumps. Machine gunners and mortar men preferred to carry M1A1 carbines, with folding stocks. Rabe had one. Photograph courtesy of the Poss family.

carried main and reserve parachutes and a life jacket. Fighting tools might include an M1 rifle, a pistol, bullets for the firearms, hand grenades, and four types of knives – a bayonet, an entrenching knife, a jump knife, and a hunting knife. Paratroopers also carried a musette bag filled with personal items and three days of rations. The uniforms of paratroopers were purposely designed to be baggy, containing numerous pockets in their jackets and pants. Paratroopers weighed as much as 300 pounds when fully loaded with equipment. In Headquarters Company, Fred Boyle carried a 9-pound land mine. Pvt. Willie Coates jumped with a Browning Automatic Rifle (BAR), which weighed 21 pounds. Sgt. Edward Barnes had a telephone switchboard, which weighed 60 pounds, tethered to his leg when he jumped.[2] The machine gunners and mortar men did not carry their heavy weapons when they jumped. The machine guns and mortars fell into the *marais* or hit land in parapacks attached to color-coded parachutes dropped from the C-47s. For example, the C-47 that carried mortar men Coates, Stephen Liberty, Homer Poss, and Rene Rabe dropped six parapacks attached to blue parachutes. The parapacks, which weighed between 203 and 288 pounds, contained the company's two 81 mm mortars and mortar rounds.[3] The amount and weight of the equipment signified that the paratroopers were being dropped behind enemy lines and would need to be self-sufficient.

During the time before takeoff and during the flight over the English Channel, the US paratroopers displayed various emotions. All implicitly understood that the jump into Normandy would be the defining episode of their lives. The majority of the men were quiet, deep in thoughts of parents, siblings, wives, and girlfriends. Bob Bearden of Texas recalled that 1st Lt. Thomas P. Woodward showed him a letter from his wife describing the birth of their first child accompanied by a photo of their baby girl. Woodward and his wife would ultimately have five children and thirteen grandchildren.[4] Some paratroopers silently prayed. Captain John Verret, the Roman Catholic chaplain, led his stick in an improvized version of the Lord's Prayer, confessing that "we haven't always played square with you, but Father, forgive us" and "deliver us from evil."[5] Others relieved tension with humor. Some merrily chatted about the "French gals" they hoped to meet. General Ridgway remembered that his plane was filled with comedians, who "jeered and offered gratuitous advice" on the efforts of nervous, cold paratroopers who had to relieve themselves. It was difficult for men strapped in and loaded with gear "to find anatomy."[6]

Fatalism took hold of some paratroopers. The paratroopers had been told by General Gavin to "remember you are going to kill, or you will be killed." John Hinchliff reminisced that S/Sgt. Kenneth Gunning, a leader of the machine gunners, told him: "Johnny, take as many of them bastards with you before you go." S/Sgt. Gunning died in Graignes. The glider pilots who landed near Graignes, Lt. Irwin Morales and Lt. Thomas Ahmad, made a pact to visit their respective parents, if either died. Lt. Ahmad was killed at Graignes by a German sniper.[7] On the other hand, Lt. Colonel Arthur A. Maloney, the commander of the 3rd Battalion of the 507th Regiment, chose to be optimistic. He had all of his traveling companions on the C-47 autograph a 100 franc note. Lt. Colonel Maloney earned the Distinguished Service Cross for his leadership and bravery in Normandy. He was, however, severely wounded on 7 July 1944 and had to retire from the Army. Maloney's son retains the autographed French currency.[8]

The C-47s that carried Headquarters Company to Graignes began to fire up their engines beginning at 11:00 p.m. on 5 June 1944. Sgt. Hinchliff checked his watch and saw it was 11:59 p.m., when his plane lifted off. Sgt. Major Robert A. Salewski recorded in his diary that he hit ground near Graignes at 2:38 a.m.[9] The 159-minute air journey involved several steps. The seventy-two C-47s that took off from Barkston Heath first circled, as they assembled into a "V" of "Vs," where three planes flew as a "V" and three "Vs" made a flight of nine planes. The C-47s traveled in serials of thirty-six aircraft made up of four nine-plane "Vs of Vs." The aircraft flew south over England, hitting the first checkpoint, "Flatbush," at the Isle of Portland at the edge of the English Channel. Once over the Channel, the C-47 pilots turned leftward, after receiving a submarine signal, at "Checkpoint Hoboken." The planes turned between the Channel Islands of Alderney and Guernsey and Jersey. The Germans occupied the Channel Islands. The C-47s proceeded to cross over the western section of the Cotentin Peninsula. The planes were scheduled to be over occupied France for twelve minutes before reaching the eastern coast of the Cotentin Peninsula and the English Channel. General Gavin calculated that he should be dropped eight minutes and thirty seconds after crossing the western coast of the Cotentin Peninsula. Troopers would first receive a red warning light from the cockpit to stand up and ready themselves, followed by a green light to jump immediately. The pilots were instructed to adhere to their flight plans to insure precise drops on the designated landing zones. The pilots' orders also included the injunction to drop all paratroopers.[10]

Those paratroopers who sat near the open doors of the C-47s gained confidence, as they viewed what was near them and below them. Captain Robert M. Piper, of the 505th Regiment, took advantage of his officer status and sat in the open door with his feet in the breeze.[11] The skies were clear over the English Channel, with reflections of moonlight on the sea. In Bob Bearden's words, "there was not a ripple in the sky, and the moon glistened on the channel water about a thousand feet below, reflecting like stars of the sea." T/5 Eddie Page wrote about "seeing a sight that will probably never be seen again," with "hundreds of C-47s traveling like a sheet of steel across the sky with P-38 and P-51 fighter planes as escorts." Battalion surgeon Dave Thomas of the 82nd recalled that "in the bright moonlight, as far as I could see behind were echelon of C-47s, each filled with troopers. Boy I thought this is going to be a piece of cake. We are really organized."[12] The parade below of more than 5,000 naval vessels surging toward Normandy overwhelmed the men. One trooper from the 82nd exclaimed: "ships so many ships it looked as if you could walk from England to France without getting your feet wet." Ed Isbell of the 507th agreed, noting that "it looked as if you could step from one ship to another." Isbell added that "it was hard to believe the armada we saw below. It made us feel a lot better knowing they would be hitting the beaches in a few hours to back us up."[13]

As the C-47s, the "sheet of steel," approached the western shores of the Cotentin Peninsula, the battle plan seemed perfect. The weakened German *Luftwaffe* had not challenged the air armada. German batteries on the Channel Islands had fired at the C-47s. But the anti-aircraft guns were ineffective, because the transport planes were too far away and too high at 1,500 feet altitude. General Ridgway saw glints of anti-aircraft fire. The general did not worry, however, for he and his men were "like flying ducks watching a hunter and knowing they were too high and far away to be concerned."[14] Aided by the work of the pathfinders, the pilots would hone in on the landing zones. The paratroopers would hurl themselves out of the planes at the altitude of about 800 feet.

The last few minutes of the journey to Normandy proved chaotic and deadly for the paratroopers. The C-47s hit dense cloud cover, just as they crossed over the Cotentin Peninsula. The wing tips of the aircraft had been a mere 100 feet apart in the respective "Vs." Over the English Channel, the paratroopers could readily see the blue lights on the wing tips of the C-47s. Now they could not see the wing tips of their own airplane. Fearful of mid-air collisions, the pilots began to break formation, often going lower in search of visibility. The dense clouds also created turbulence. The C-47s bounced and weaved and rocked and swayed "like nothing I had seen before," according to Bill Bearden. Air sickness buckets were passed along. Rene Rabe ruefully recalled that someone in his stick stumbled and kicked over the vomit bucket. He sighed: "We did not jump out over Normandy, we slid out."[15]

Intense German anti-aircraft fire started striking the C-47s. The intensity of the fire increased, as the Germans became fully aware of the air invasion. The 507th Regiment, which jumped last, encountered the full fury. The proverbial "all hell broke loose" became the common expression of those who survived. John Hinchliff remarked that the flak was so intense that he thought he could walk on it. The planes seemed engulfed in red and green tracers and the "sky was full of golden, orange, and red blossoms of fire." The spectacle reminded General Ridgway of a Fourth of July celebration on the Mall in Washington, for "the sky was covered with stuff, rockets and tracers were streaking through the air and big explosions were going off everywhere."[16] The perspective from the ground was similarly awesome and alarming. Mayor Alexandre Renaud of Sainte-Mère-Église noted that "the sky was continuously crisscrossed with the fugitive lights of tracer bullets, and sometimes these lights would seem to disappear into the huge fuselages."[17]

Mayor Renaud correctly surmised that the C-47s were being hit. Pfc. James P. James of the 507th Regiment witnessed Major Joseph Fagan, who was standing in the doorway, take a non-fatal head wound. The next paratrooper in line pushed Fagan out and seven troopers followed. But the damaged C-47 went into a nosedive and crashed, killing the crew and seven paratroopers who did not have time to jump. The right motor of Ed Isbell's plane was hit by flak and the plane was losing altitude. When the green light went on, "out the door we went – do or die." Other paratroopers told of improvised exits from their aircraft. Private Bill Bowell's plane had a "bad hit" and the plane began to lurch and vibrate. The standing paratroopers fell to their knees. But "somehow we managed to get out of the door; some of us crawled out." Others dove, rather than jumped, out of the C-47, because pilots struggled to keep their planes level to the ground.[18]

Pilots reacted to attack by increasing their air speed and varying their altitudes. Paratroopers wanted an air speed of about 95 miles per hour to minimize the shock when their chutes opened. Veterans of the 82nd and 101st Airborne Divisions swore that their planes were speeding at 125 to 150 miles an hour. "The opening shock was terrific" recalled a paratrooper who injured his back. The opening shock ripped off equipment attached to the paratroopers, and items in their pockets burst through bottom seams. General Gavin felt a watch being ripped from his wrist.[19] Within seconds after the chute deployed, paratroopers were on the ground or in the water. Veterans of the 82nd estimated that they jumped from altitudes as low as 400 to 250 feet. During his practice jumps, Rene Rabe's first act, after the opening shock, was to push up his helmet from over his eyes. In Normandy, he pushed his helmet up and immediately hit hard. Homer Poss, who jumped behind Rabe, also hit hard, suffering a hair-line fracture of his left ankle.[20] From the ground, Mayor Renaud saw "a wave of transport planes, with all lights on, [that] came over at treetop height." And then "something like enormous confetti came out of their bellies and dropped rapidly to earth." Sixteen-year-old Jeannette Pentecôte, who lived in the mayor's town, could see a paratrooper standing in the doorway of his C-47 that was skimming the roof of her home. The paratrooper "seemed surprised by the meager height from which he had to jump." In later years, she saw in her mind's eye "this paratrooper's face as he prepared to jump and was stunned to find himself so low."[21]

Without time to maneuver their parachutes to find a good landing place, the men of the 507th Regiment landed everywhere but in Drop Zone T near Amfreville. T/5 Bob Davis summed up the adventure: we landed "in trees, on roofs, in villages, on paved roads, in cemeteries, on top of German units and more often in water." Davis elaborated: "many were drowned, severely injured, wounded, shot to death or captured."[22] One historian has characterized the landing experience of the 2,004 paratroopers in the 507th Regiment as "nothing less than a disaster," with only a handful of the C-47 crews successfully dropping the men on target. The pathfinders of the 507th had landed near Amfreville but had difficulty in setting up beacons, because they were immediately attacked by German troops.[23]

The other two regiments also fared poorly. In the lead plane of the 508th, General Gavin landed three miles off target. The green jump light had gone on thirty seconds later than Gavin expected. The veteran 505th Regiment was relatively successful, landing near Sainte-Mère-Église. The unit's pathfinders had accomplished their mission. Experience also helped. Lt. Colonel Benjamin Vandervoort, and his 2nd Battalion had the most accurate jump of all. Vandervoort stood in the doorway studying terrain. He ordered the nervous pilot to turn off the green light, because they were not yet near the drop zone. Nonetheless, men in the 505th experienced disasters. One trooper died when he landed in the middle of a burning building in the town. Pvt. John Steele's parachute famously caught up on the steeple of the splendid church in the center of Sainte-Mère-Église. Henry Langreher of Iowa landed in a greenhouse near the church. Langreher had luck, however, for the dangling satchel tethered to his leg, filled with blast caps and explosives, broke the glass of the greenhouse ahead of his descending body.[24]

It may not have been surprising that perhaps 80 percent of the 82nd Airborne Division's men landed off target. As Bob Bearden observed, "it was nothing new." In practice jumps, his 507th Regiment never landed in proximity for easy assembly.[25] But the scattered drop had some unintended, positive consequences. German military leaders had difficulty discerning the paratroopers' objectives. The landings also terrified the German troops. The commander of the German paratroopers near Carentan, *Oberstleutnant* Friedrich-August Freiherr von der Heydte, admitted that "the Allied airborne landing was a terrible shock – even to my paratroopers. For at least one or two hours we were not far from panic."[26] The US paratroopers did not panic. General Gavin had planned for this day. Paratroopers had been trained to be self-reliant, to not depend on officers, and to excel in small-unit combat. Men from the three regiments formed up into combat teams, often joined by lost men from the 101st, and took the fight to the enemy.[27] Despite the chaos and dreadful casualties, the 82nd liberated Sainte-Mère-Église and took control of two vital bridges over the Merderet River on D-Day. The paratroopers would subsequently repel repeated German efforts to reverse those gains. As Cornelius Ryan, author of the influential *The Longest Day* (1959), concluded, the paratroopers of the 82nd achieved General Eisenhower's objectives. They confused the enemy, disrupted communications, and blocked the movement of enemy reinforcements toward Utah Beach. They did so within five hours of landing in Normandy.[28]

Paratroopers Come to Graignes

Of the 378 aircraft in their "V of Vs" that carried the 82nd Airborne Division's paratroopers toward Normandy, one group logically had to earn the dubious distinction of being the most off target. This was a nine-plane formation that carried the majority of the Headquarters Company of the 3rd Battalion of the 507th Regiment. On these nine planes were 143 paratroopers. The distance between the villages of Amfreville and Graignes is 31.2 kilometers or about 19 miles via the N 13 highway. Some men were initially farther away than that, as they were dropped south of Graignes near the villages of Le Mesnil-Angot and Tribehou. Why the planes flew so far off course cannot be precisely explained. The commonplace account is that the planes were trying to avoid flak. Sgt. Frank Costa, who stood in the doorway of his C-47 to combat motion sickness, saw that the lead plane, which carried Major Charles D. Johnston, "turned tight." The other eight planes followed. Perhaps the lead pilot confused the Taute River with the Merderet River, as suggested by one chronicler. But, writing fifty-five years after D-Day, Captain Dave Brummitt asserted "to this day, I have not received a credible explanation" for why the C-47s veered off course.[29]

Captain Brummitt was confused in his last minutes in the C-47. He had studied for "long hours" maps, aerial photographs, and sand-table mock-ups and could not recognize any familiar landmarks. He also constantly checked his watch and realized that the planned jump time had been exceeded. The red light had not been followed by a green light. But looking out the doorway he noticed that men in C-47s in front and near his plane were jumping. As such, Brummitt "gave the 'GO' command and exited the aircraft followed by his 'stick' of paratroopers." Lt. Naughton, who was in the lead plane, had similar memories. The aerial formation received "intense flak" when it crossed into Normandy, then little flak, and then increased fire just before jumping. Like Captain Brummitt, Naughton thought the red light stayed on for an interminable length of time. He spotted troopers jumping from planes to his left. Finally, the green "jump" light came on. T/4 Eddie Page's plane was on the right flank of the formation. Flak hit the C-47, and "it began to shudder, shake, and vibrate." After jumping, "the worst feeling came over me," for Page feared no one else had jumped. But he looked around in the dark, and "I could see 'pop, pop' other parachutes opening up, coming all around me."[30]

The chaotic jump pattern predictably led to a scattered landing. Some troopers found ground, but most landed in the *marais* that encompassed much of Graignes in an arc of at least 230 degrees. Rabe and Poss landed hard. Pvt. Arthur "Rip" Granlund landed in an apple

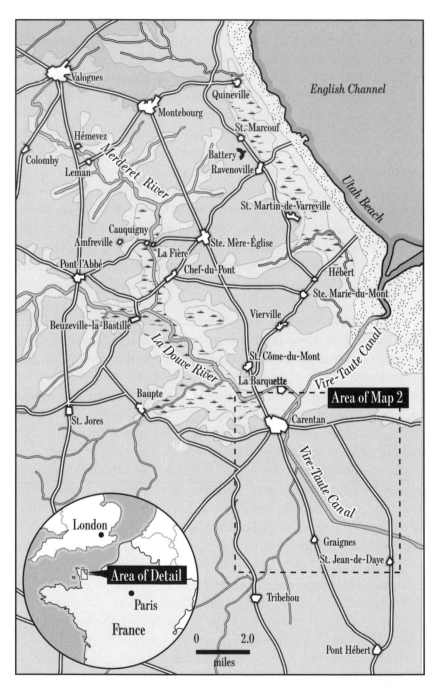

Map 4.1 This map demonstrates how far off target the nine sticks of paratroopers from the Headquarters Company were on 6 June 1944. Their assigned mission was to land near Amfreville, just west of Sainte-Mère-Église, and prevent German forces from reaching the Allied invading forces at Utah Beach. The village of Graignes is about ten kilometers south of the strategically vital port town Carentan. Map by Joe LeMonnier, https://mapartist.com/.

tree and briars after jumping from "a very low, fast airplane." Eddie Barnes and his telephone switchboard had the good fortune for his parachute to be caught up in the branch of a tree, which bent and slowly lowered him to a cow pasture near Graignes. An inquisitive cow then approached him. Fred Boyle estimated that he jumped from an altitude of 250 feet and landed in the swamp. Thereafter, in Boyle's words, "it was just chaos." Lt. Naughton agreed that the altitude at jump was less than 500 feet. When he landed south of Graignes, his head went under water. But he was able to stand and release the parachute, because the depth of the water was about three to four feet. Sgt. Frank Costa landed in a flooded field up to his shoulders. He cut the risers of his parachute with a trench knife. But in the scramble to free himself, he lost his carbine in the *marais*. Eddie Page similarly dropped his weapon upon landing but was able "to reach down and pull my rifle out of the muck."[31]

Machine gunner John Hinchliff landed thigh-deep in water. Hinchliff added, however, that "a lot of guys weren't so lucky and they drowned." Within the *marais*, there were drainage ditches five to seven-feet in depth to help with the seasonal flooding. Madame S. Pezerin, who welcomed paratroopers into her home, noticed several men had severe

Figure 4.2 An unspecified number of paratroopers of the 82nd Airborne Division died from drowning in Normandy on D-Day. US Army photograph.

cuts on their hands from using their knives to cut their parachute lines and free themselves before drowning.[32] Some troopers in Headquarters Company may have had the misfortune to land in a drainage ditch and become entangled in their parachute gear. Five men – Pvt. Allison T. Bliss, Private Robert W. Britton, Pvt. Harold J. Premo, Pfc. Stanley Pytel, and Pfc. George E. Tillett – from the company are listed as having been killed in action on 6 June 1944. Eddie Page recalled that upon landing, he administered a morphine syringe to a "badly wounded" paratrooper. Perhaps this paratrooper was hit by enemy anti-aircraft fire and was Pvt. Bliss, who was in Page's stick. Page and others have concurred with Hinchliff that several men drowned. In the opinion of one veteran of the 82nd Airborne Division, drowning was the "worst" way to die for a landing paratrooper. In later life, Rene Rabe could not approach a body of water without having the flashback of seeing a drowned paratrooper. Pvt. Premo jumped one man behind Rabe.[33]

The Headquarters Company paratroopers, who now numbered 138, had two immediate goals after 2:38 a.m. on D-Day. They wanted to assemble with their buddies, and they needed to find dry land. For a couple of hours, Sgt. Barnes was alone, and "a feeling of loneliness" enveloped him, as he imagined "the entire German Army was trying to locate and exterminate me." At 5:00 a.m., as the skies began to lighten, another trooper, who was behind a hedgerow, challenged Barnes with the password of "Flash." Barnes answered with the countersign of "Thunder." Unlike men of the 101st Airborne Division, members of the 82nd Airborne did not carry the toy metal clickers that made a "cricket" sound as a form of identification. General Gavin had discouraged their use, reasoning they were needless weight to carry. Barnes and his buddy thereafter located four other lost troopers. The six men discerned on the horizon the outline of a church steeple and headed for that.[34] Eddie Page similarly found a group of men, and "we went from swamp to some high ground, saw the steeple of a church and headed for that." Sgt./Major Salewski met six mortar men and some machine gunners and moved toward high ground and the church. Pvt. Marion L. Hatton, a member of the mortar platoon, landed in a plowed field and quickly spotted other paratroopers. He noted that "rifle fire and the sounds of grenades and mortars exploding were in the distance." Hatton had to swim across a canal in order to reach Graignes.[35]

The Romanesque Catholic Church of Graignes became the North Star of Headquarters Company. The maps the men carried were useless, for they surveyed the region near Amfreville. Captain Brummitt carried, however, a "silk map of Normandy" as part of his "escape kit," and, after speaking to a French farmer after daybreak, determined that he was near Graignes. He became one of the first to enter the village and began to assemble paratroopers into a defensive perimeter. Lt. Naughton did not enter Graignes until the afternoon of 6 June. After landing in water, he cut himself out of his chute with a knife. He freed himself of about forty pounds of equipment, throwing away a wet walkie-talkie, wet batteries, and a reel of wire that had been attached to his thigh. He heard some firing in the distance but not near him. He moved slowly and carefully through the *marais*, which was three feet deep, taking care to avoid the deep drainage ditches. Using the password and countersign, he encountered Major Johnston from his stick and three other troopers from another C-47. The two officers eventually saw a paratrooper waving an orange recognition flag and moved into Graignes. As recounted by Sgt. Barnes, Major Johnston, the commanding officer, "was as lost as the rest of us."[36]

The paratroopers of Headquarters Company would be joined in Graignes by men from other military units. At about 4:00 a.m., a glider plane attached to the 101st Airborne Division piloted by Lt. Irwin Morales and Lt. Thomas Ahmad plopped into the *marais*, northwest of Graignes. The tow plane and glider missed the designated target at Hiesville, which was twenty-two kilometers from Graignes, because, in Morales's words, "Jesus! The flak and tracers became so thick that I don't know how the hell we walked through it." The glider carried a jeep and two enlisted men – Norwood Lester and George A. Brown. The four men survived and walked to Graignes. The jeep was no longer operable.[37] A stick of infantrymen from Company B of the 1st Battalion of the 501st Regiment of the 101st Airborne Division also landed south of Graignes. The company's mission had been to help secure causeways that led from Utah Beach. Pfc. Frank Juliano from Staten Island, New York City recalled that the enemy used searchlights and flares to target the drop zones north of Carentan, noting that "we felt like sitting ducks." His C-47 was hit several times by flak and the ranking officer, Captain Loyal K. Bogart, was hit by flak. Bogart further injured himself on the ground. Juliano believed that one trooper died in the jump, drowning in a river. Juliano calculated that sixteen paratroopers from B Company, including Captain Bogart and two troopers who had

military medical specialties, made it to Graignes on 6 June. Mark
Bando, a historian of the 101st Airborne Division, has raised Juliano's
number to nineteen paratroopers from the 101st.[38]

The confusion and surprise that paratroopers of the 82nd and
101st experienced when they discovered they were so far off target was
exceeded by the astonishment that gripped the people of the region
around Graignes when they saw parachutes floating down toward
them. It seemed like divine intervention, or, as one parish priest later
testified, the coming of the soldiers they called the *paras* was emblematic
of "your glory and that of all your holy Church." From the perspective
of the ground, the very early hours of D-Day were marked by bombs,
anti-aircraft fire, the roar of airplanes, and "flames rising in the night
sky."[39] Mayor Alphonse Voydie remembered a large number of airplanes flying over Graignes. Getting up early in the morning, the mayor
went out and saw paratroopers in a field behind his house. Voydie
hurried to make contact with them and those paratroopers that he
heard had already reached the village. Germaine Boursier, the propri-
etor of the local café, witnessed the drop of several *paras* into the swamp
near her home. She ministered to the cold, drenched men by providing
food from her café and the latest intelligence on the whereabouts of the
German occupiers. Other villagers welcomed paratroopers into their
homes, where they could dry themselves by fires and have a shot of
Calvados. As the local history of D-Day recounted, "soon the swamps
were swarming with" the *paras*. "They rallied at the church. They were
greeted warmly. Some of the drenched and wet shivered and rattled their
teeth. Very quickly a flow of sympathy and confidence established
itself."[40]

Normans were coming to the assistance of the paratroopers
from the 82nd and 101st Airborne Divisions throughout the region.
At 9:30 am on D-Day, two paratroopers arrived at a farm, where
seventeen-year-old Roger Lepourry worked. The *paras*, who did not
speak French, carried sketches of a horse and cart. Lepourry hitched
a neighbor's horse to a cart and headed toward Tribehou. Upon the
advice of friends that he met on the road, he took a circuitous route to
avoid German patrols. Arriving at the "wood of Touraille," Lepourry
was greeted by fourteen other paratroopers. The *paras* loaded on the
cart fourteen cases of ammunition, which had landed with them in the
parapacks. Each case weighed forty kilograms. Lepourry, "always very
suspicious" of German activity, drove the cart to Graignes and delivered

the cases to the boys' school, which had become the command post of the Headquarters Company. So overjoyed was Lepourry that he stopped at a café in Bas-Vernay to drink three bottles of wine with friends "to celebrate the liberation." Among the celebrants was Raymond Rigault, a relative of the Rigaults of Le Port St. Pierre.[41] The physically fit, athletic paratroopers were inspiring confidence throughout Normandy. Madame S. Pezerin of Graignes remembered the paratroopers as "solid, well-built, and agile fellows." As a school teacher who lived near Sainte-Mère-Église testified, "everything about them evokes the outlaws of the Wild West; their massive size and big round helmets, the large knife stuck inside the shaft of their beautiful tall, yellow leather boots, their bearing and gait." The teacher, Marcelle Hamel-Hateu, added that the confidence of the *paras* was so contagious that "we consider Liberation to be already accomplished."[42]

A large contingent of the liberators initially congregated at the home of Gustave Rigault, which was on the edge of the *marais* and about a three-kilometer walk via a pathway to Graignes. The Rigault family – the parents, sisters Odette and Marthe, and toddler Jean Claude – had been up since the beginning of D-Day. Little Jean Claude busied himself running around the house. Older sister Marie-Jean worked in a hospital in St Lô. At 1:00 a.m., the family heard planes and the bombing of the coast. "It was a hellish sound," Marthe remembered. Shortly after 2:38 a.m., a disabled neighbor, Lucie Maduit, brought a paratrooper to their house. The family closed the curtains and put on a fire and lit candles to see the paratrooper. The paratrooper reassured the family that thousands would be coming "to rescue us." He spread his map out on the table and learned that where he landed was not on his map. Before leaving after an hour's stay and vowing to find other paratroopers, the paratrooper left some chocolate. Marthe, a life-long *aficionada* of chocolate, judged the gift "very, very good chocolate."[43]

Between 5:00 and 6:00 a.m., Sgt. Benton Broussard of Cajun Louisiana knocked on the door of the Rigault household and surprised the family by addressing them in perfect French. Broussard first ordered his companions to search the house for Germans. A large group of *paras* gathered in the courtyard, drying themselves and cleaning their wet weapons. To Marthe, it seemed like there were 100 Americans in the courtyard. Gustave instructed Odette to milk the cows, "because when dawn comes there is going to be trouble." While milking the cows, Odette began to receive fire, noting splashes in the *marais*, like "someone throwing stones in water." One "splash" hit within a meter of Odette. In Odette's words, the "marshlands were like the open sea." Germans on the other side of the *marais* toward Tribehou had noticed the US paratroopers and opened machine-gun fire. Upon the advice of the paratroopers, the family spent the night of 6–7 June at their grandfather's house, although Marthe tried to return to the house in the evening when the family realized that it had forgotten Jean Claude's bottle. Gunfire discouraged Marthe from accomplishing her mission. Nonetheless, the twelve-year-old was comforted by the sweets and chewing gum that *paras* had left with her. Unaware of chewing-gum protocol, Marthe swallowed her first piece of Wrigley's Chewing Gum.[44]

The Rigault family enlisted in the liberation cause. The nine C-47s that dropped the men from Headquarters Company also dropped, with mainly blue parachutes, fifty-five parapacks. Inside the containers were rations, medical supplies, mines, communication equipment, demolition kits, ammunition, and five light machine guns and two 81 mm mortars. Sgt. Hinchliff and his assistant gunner, Pvt. Patrick Sullivan, a native of Ireland, quickly found their machine gun and ammunition in the *marais*.[45] But most of the containers were scattered and inaccessible in the *marais*. Beginning on D-Day, Gustave Rigault and his daughters took flat-bottomed boats out into the swamps and stored containers they found in their sizeable barn that they called "*Les Curies*." Odette and Marthe also discovered white silk in the discarded reserve parachutes and hid the "silk from the sky" in the barn. The sisters envisioned sewing lovely dresses. Other villagers poled their flat-bottomed boats into the swamps. Fifteen-year-old Ginette Decaumont recalled: "My father, my uncle, my brother . . . [went] out on the marsh many times to look for equipment which they [the paratroopers] had lost."[46] The citizens of Graignes accomplished their missions. Lt. Earcle Reed noted that "we never did recover the full complement of heavy weapons." But Reed, who was known as "Pip," pronounced that the company had "more ammunition than we thought we could ever use." Lt. Naughton, who was in charge of demolition, concurred that "we had lots of Composition C," an explosive material.[47]

The Great Debate

Having concluded by the middle of D-Day that they were way off target, the ranking officers of Headquarters Company had to decide the next move. An acrimonious debate broke out between Major Charles D. Johnston and Captain David Brummitt. The other officers listened, with some sense of amazement at the tenor of the argument. The able and energetic Brummitt was the S-3 officer of the 3rd Battalion, making him responsible for operations, plans, and training. Brummitt had held that position since October 1942 and had participated in all training and pre-combat planning for the Normandy operation. The captain's central argument was that fulfilling the "Battalion MISSION" had the highest priority. This was Headquarters Company. The assigned task was to support the three infantry companies in the battalion. The Headquarters Company consisted of a communications platoon, a light-machine-gun platoon, an 81 mm mortar platoon, a demolition squad, and a medical detachment, all of which had trained to support the three rifle companies. The three infantry companies and the battalion as a whole could not operate effectively without the paratroopers of Headquarters Company. Brummitt reasoned that the company had to find its way to Amfreville and rejoin the 3rd Battalion. Brummitt formulated a night-march plan to ford the flooded swamp area or alternatively go around the surrounding coastline to Carentan. The idea was to link up with US forces who could facilitate the company's return to where the 82nd was fighting. The captain had already carried out a reconnaissance and observed "what appeared to be a portion of the 101st Division attacking German forces in Carentan."[48]

Captain Brummitt also worried that the personnel in Graignes did not have any combat experience and "they were not, and I emphasize not, trained or equipped to fight as rifle squads or even as individual riflemen." In later life, Brummitt conceded that Headquarters Company fought with discipline, skill, and vigor in the defense of Graignes. The paratroopers proved to be "elite troops of the highest order" and were "worthy of commendation." The defenders of Graignes would indeed receive numerous medals and battlefield promotions for their heroism. The captain admitted his plan to abandon Graignes had weaknesses. The company would have to destroy heavy equipment before moving out. For example, the 81 mm mortars would have to be spiked and the mortar rounds destroyed. In addition, paratroopers might panic and drown when they stepped into one of the deep drainage ditches.[49] The specter of paratroopers drowning was already in the memories of the men of Headquarters Company.

Major Johnston "curtly" dismissed Captain Brummitt's withdrawal plans, "turning aside my forceful reference to our stated MISSION." He ordered that the troops in Graignes, including the men from the 101st Airborne Division, would stay in Graignes. The men would organize a perimeter defense around the village and wait for the invading forces at Utah and Omaha Beaches to reach them.[50] Utah and Omaha were respectively 28 and 44.5 kilometers from Graignes. Beginning on 6 June, the paratroopers began to dig deep foxholes around Graignes. The specialist personnel of Headquarters Company reorganized themselves into infantry fire teams. The men of B Company of the 101st, who had been trained as infantry riflemen, deployed to the flanks. The mortar and machine-gun platoons pre-planned their fires. An observation team, led by Lt. Elmer F. Farnham, a native of Pennsylvania and the leader of the mortar platoon, ensconced themselves in the church belfry. Cable wires of communication were set out. The wounded Captain Bogart volunteered to operate the telephone switchboard from the boys' school.

In retrospect, strengths and weaknesses can be found in Captain Brummitt's plans and Major Johnston's decision. During the period 12–15 June, about 120 US military personnel escaped either by foot or flat boat from Graignes through the *marais*. They reached the 101st Airborne Division and the 2nd Armored Division near Carentan. Brummitt's withdrawal plan came to fruition. Captain Brummitt garnered the Silver Star, an extraordinary commendation, for leading about ninety of the men to Carentan. But the military situation was very different in the immediate days after D-Day. The 101st Airborne Division did not liberate Carentan until 11–12 June and had to fight furiously on 13 June to hold the town. Only the arrival of the tanks of the 2nd Armored Division preserved the liberation of Carentan on 13 June. The men who fought to defend Graignes slowed the movement of German troops toward Carentan, thereby aiding the liberators of that strategic town.[51] If the defenders of Graignes had begun a withdrawal on the night of 6 June, they would have likely encountered concentrations of German troops and no allies.

Major Johnston could not have known that his decision to defend Graignes would aid in the liberation of Carentan. But his plan for a static defense had a strong dose of "hope" within it. The major had to hope that the Allied invaders would reach Graignes before a superior German force discovered his men in Graignes. The defenders of

Graignes lacked air, artillery, and tank support. They had no motorized transportation. A patrol went out to look at the jeep in the glider, and Gustave Rigault and his daughter Marthe floated a flat boat out into the *marais* to examine it. The engine of the jeep had been ruined by the swamp water.[52] The company's major weapons were the two mortars and five machine guns. They did not have their usual complement of anti-tank rocket launchers, which were dropped by another C-47 elsewhere. Johnston's officers and enlisted men thought they had sufficient ammunition and explosives. Sgt. Hinchliff judged that his stacked boxes of machine-gun rounds "would last a week."[53] The paratroopers were overly optimistic. There was little chance of resupply. The paratroopers had dropped with carrier pigeons. On D-Day, Major Johnston dispatched a pigeon, hoping that it would reach the headquarters of the 82nd Airborne Division. The message attached to the pigeon gave the coordinates at 415:800, noted the company had recovered blue parachutes of equipment, and informed that it was impossible to reach regimental headquarters. On 8 June, US military personnel found the dead pigeon, and the message was brought to division headquarters. The division subsequently sent out an urgent message, requesting any units in the area to assist, and asked for air resupply.[54] Given the chaos and hard fighting in Normandy that characterized the immediate days after D-Day, the message unsurprisingly went unheeded.

Major Johnston's men had to fend for themselves. Veterans of Graignes have variously estimated the uniformed personnel there numbered from 160 to 182 men. Sgt. Major Salewski wrote that there were 14 officers and 168 enlisted men at Graignes. Chroniclers of Graignes have settled on the figure of 182 men. But that figure may overstate the strength of US forces.[55] There were 138 men from Headquarters Company on the nine planes in the "V" formation who had survived the first hours of D-Day. They were joined by nineteen 101st paratroopers and four glider personnel attached to the 101st Airborne Division. On 7 June, Flight Sgt. Stanley K. Black, an Australian crewman, entered Graignes. Black had been shot down in a Lancaster bomber that crashed near St. Jean de Daye. A Norman farmer hid Flight Sgt. Black in his home and escorted him to Graignes.[56] On Friday, 9 June, two soldiers from the 29th Infantry Division wandered into Graignes. The lost soldiers had landed at Omaha Beach. One carried a Browning Automatic Rifle. Veterans of Graignes remembered the two soldiers but could not recall their names or their fates. It would seem that 164 military men were in Graignes. Two Spanish citizens from the Basque region, who possibly had been subjected to slave labor by the Germans, also entered Graignes with French gendarmes. They may have helped build defenses and fortifications, but they were not trained soldiers. Because they spoke Spanish and French, they may have helped with translation by communicating with those Latino paratroopers in Headquarters Company who were bilingual.

The Spaniards were not the only non-combatants in Graignes. The battalion surgeon, Captain Abraham Sophian, was accompanied by five other troopers who had medical training and were tasked with the mission of operating 3rd Battalion's medical aid station. One – Pvt. Robert W. Britton – died on D-Day. Two paratroopers from B Company – Cpl. James M. Naff and Pvt. James A. Nebeling – had medical specialties. Medical personnel normally did not receive weapons training and did not carry weapons into combat. As explained by T/5 John "Jack" Dunn of Milwaukee, Wisconsin who served as a medic and surgical assistant with the 82nd Airborne Division, being a medic was inherently dangerous. When a medic crawled toward a wounded paratrooper on the battlefield, he hoped not to be targeted. Not carrying a weapon and wearing a Red Cross insignia on his helmet and shoulders would ostensibly keep the medic safe from hostile fire.[57] It cannot be determined whether any of the medical personnel took up arms in Graignes. Medics presumably accompanied the numerous patrols that the paratroopers carried out from Graignes. On D-Day, Captain Sophian accompanied Sgt. Hinchliff and Pvt. Sullivan, when they spotted a German machine-gun squad in the *marais* and unsuccessfully attempted to cut the enemy off.[58] But the presence of seven medical personnel probably reduced Major Johnston's combat forces, leaving about 155 armed military personnel to defend Graignes.

Major Johnston's order to keep the paratroopers in the village was not made in isolation. The overwhelming enthusiasm that citizens of Graignes displayed for their unexpected guests facilitated Johnston's decision. On D-Day, Mayor Voydie met with Major Johnston and pledged cooperation. Voydie arranged for food to be provided to the paratroopers.[59] Farmers and villagers had guided bewildered paratroopers to Graignes and warned them where they believed German soldiers were deployed. Villagers had welcomed soaked paratroopers into their homes and helped dry them. As Denise Boursier-Lereculey, daughter of Madame Germaine Boursier, explained, "we made them a good fire, because the poor men were chilled to the bone and shivering; most of them had fallen into the water in their parachutes."[60] Other citizens were hauling into Graignes the crates of equipment dropped by the blue parachutes. On 7 June, Acting Mayor Voydie and Father Albert Le Blastier assembled the village's heads of households in the church. Gustave Rigault attended. The assembly unanimously voted to accept Voydie's resolution to ally with the paratroopers.[61] The men of Graignes would not have the last word. Shortly after the church assembly, Madame Boursier organized the women in the village in a round-the-clock operation to provide the paratroopers with two meals a day. The Headquarters Company of the 3rd Battalion had left most of its "Mess Section" behind in England. The cooks would land later in Normandy via ship.[62] Madame Boursier would assume the honored title of "Mess Sergeant."

Figure 4.3 On D-Day, Alphonse Voydie was the "Acting Mayor," because Mayor Albert Defortescu was too old and ill to continue in office. Voydie assumed office in April 1944 and served as the village's mayor from 1944 to 1977. Photograph courtesy of the Mayor's Office of Graignes.

In the words of one historian, US soldiers and the people of Graignes had "turned their town into an outpost of liberty in the heart of enemy territory."[63] But in pledging to aid the paratroopers, the citizens of Graignes would be putting their personal lives, the lives of family and neighbors, and their property at extreme risk. On 10 June 1944, for example, a *Waffen-SS* unit massacred 642 inhabitants in the village of Oradour-sur-Glane in central France for alleged anti-German actions. The Nazis also obliterated the village. Mayor Voydie understood that summary execution awaited those who aided US troops. He declared, however, that "since France was being liberated by the Americans, the liberated would take their chances with the liberators, and that freedom was worth the price."[64] Odette and Marthe Rigault remembered that "Papa said we should never forget" that freedom had a price. That price seemed especially dear when the family was informed shortly after D-Day that older sister Marie-Jean had died when Allied bombs hit the hospital in Saint-Lô where she was working. The news did not deter the family from hiding in their barn for three days desperate, fleeing paratroopers. As the sisters asserted in 2004, "we wanted liberty." Fortunately, the family would later learn that their beloved Marie-Jean was still alive.[65]

Having decided to await relief from invading ground forces, the paratroopers of the 82nd and 101st Airborne Divisions proceeded to do all they could to protect themselves and their new-found allies. They worked to fortify their defense of the village. They also constantly patrolled to gain intelligence on enemy troop movements and to block potential avenues of attack. Village men accompanied the patrols, providing tactical guidance and knowledge of local landmarks. And, as happened in Northern Ireland, the young paratroopers began to bond with the children of Graignes. All were largely unaware, however, that a German *Waffen-SS* Division of 17,000 men was heading toward Carentan. The paratroopers and citizens of Graignes were in their way.

5 DAYS OF FRIENDSHIP, HOPE, AND WAITING

Between 7 June and 10 June 1944, US paratroopers and French citizens worked together to create and preserve a liberated village in the midst of occupied Normandy. The US paratroopers built a sophisticated defense system around the village of Graignes. They also launched numerous patrol missions to keep themselves apprised of enemy activity in the surrounding areas. The citizens of Graignes joined with the paratroopers in the fight for liberation and liberty. They found the weapons and supplies of the paratroopers that had landed in the *marais*. They conducted their own missions to gather intelligence. They spread rumors to confuse the Germans. They also fed the paratroopers. And they came to consider the paratroopers as their friends. The citizens of Graignes had chosen to place their liberty over their personal safety. They understood that they faced reprisals and death, if the Germans seized their village. Both the US paratroopers and the villagers hoped that Allied forces who had landed at Omaha and Utah Beaches would reach them before the Germans attacked them. But unknown to soldiers and citizens was that as each day passed, their peril was mounting. A German military division, stationed in the south-central part of France, was heading directly toward Graignes.

Digging In

Major Charles D. Johnston (1918–1944) commanded the paratroopers of the 82nd and 101st Airborne Divisions in Graignes. Johnston was the executive officer of the 3rd Battalion of the 507th

Regiment. Like many of the officers and enlisted men he led, Johnston had a challenging early life. Johnston was born in Knoxville, Tennessee, the home of the University of Tennessee. His father, who was a native of Tennessee, died when Johnston was an infant. For a time, he lived with his grand uncle, W. C. Dum. His widowed mother, Katherine, eventually moved with her son into the home of her brother. She worked as department store decorator. She would have the sad task of arranging her only child's final burial in Lynnhurst Cemetery in Knoxville. At the University of Tennessee, Johnston enrolled in the Reserve Officer Training Corps (ROTC) and was subsequently commissioned in the US Army and volunteered for jump school. The jump into Normandy was Major Johnston's first combat experience.[1] At Graignes, Johnston focused his energies on coordinating with local officials, especially Mayor Alphonse Voydie and Abbé Albert Le Blastier, the long-time parish priest. He often communicated with the officials through Sgt. Benton Broussard of Louisiana. Johnston received full cooperation from the French. He established his command post in the boys' school. Father Le Blastier offered the facilities of his church to the paratroopers. Officers met for coffee in Madame Germaine Boursier's café.

Captain Dave Brummitt became the tactical commander of the uniformed personnel in Graignes. He devised the defense of the village, and, once under attack on 11 June, he adjusted the deployment of the paratroopers to repel German forces. Despite his opposition to Major Johnston's decision to stay in Graignes, Brummitt turned to his new assignment with alacrity and skill. The captain had some tactical advantages on his side. The paratroopers commanded the high ground. The surrounding area was at or below sea level. The Roman Catholic Church and its adjoining cemetery were in the center of Graignes at the top of a hill measuring approximately fifty meters in altitude. From the belfry of the church, Lt. Elmer F. Farnham, the leader of the mortar platoon, could, with binoculars, see vast distances. Brummitt could foresee that any attack would originate from the south generally, which included the southwest and southeast. The *marais* ironically provided some protection. Lt. Earcle Reed and Lt. Frank Naughton estimated that the flooded areas were in an arc of 230 to 240 degrees, generally north of Graignes, in the direction of Carentan. Brummitt also calculated that the paratroopers might have some time to plan their defense. Paratroopers had heard the sounds of warfare in the early hours of D-Day, but direct contact with the enemy was minimal on 6 and

Figure 5.1 Captain Leroy David Brummitt directed the defense of Graignes. He won the Silver Star for his leadership and bravery at Graignes. Captain Brummitt subsequently fought with the paratroopers of the 507th Regiment in Normandy, at the Battle of the Bulge, and in the jump over the Rhine River in March 1945. Photograph courtesy of the Brummitt family.

7 June.[2] Perhaps most notably, Brummitt found that the paratroopers embraced their new roles. The captain had worried that a headquarters company lacked the training and equipment to be transformed into a rifle company engaged in a static defense. He found, however, that the paratroopers were "eager to accomplish the missions assigned." The officers and enlisted men would prove "beyond a doubt that they were elite troops of the highest order."[3]

In clipped, military-style language, Captain Brummitt explained his defense plan. The paratroopers "went on both reconnaissance and combat patrols, mined the key Graignes bridge, manned outpost and perimeter defense positions set up with final protective fires, targeted gaps with pre-planned mortar fires and established wire and radio communications."[4] In the vernacular, this meant that Lt. Farnham, usually accompanied by an aide, mounted the belfry of the church to direct mortar fire. The two 81 mm mortars were placed just south of the cemetery in "dug-in" positions. Their initial aiming was calculated to drop mortar rounds on likely avenues of attack, such as roads. Communication wires were run from the mortars to the church and the command post. Communication wires also connected most other positions. The injured Captain Loyal Bogart operated the switchboard. Radio equipment was camouflaged in a vegetable garden near the school. Lt. Reed directed the machine gunners, who were placed down the hill, about 250 meters south of the church. The paratroopers had five .30 caliber light machine guns. Technician Fifth Grade (T/5) Eddie Page recalled that one machine-gun emplacement was on the roof of a building. The machine guns were aimed so that there would be an interlocking crossfire. Invaders would meet the proverbial "wall of steel" once the machine gunners started firing. In military terms, the machine gunners would provide the "main line of resistance" to an enemy attack. To protect the flanks of the village, Brummitt dispatched riflemen, especially members of the 101st Airborne Division from B Company, who had training as infantrymen. Men were assigned sectors of fire to ensure that all potential avenues of attack were covered with fire. Anti-tank mines were positioned on approaches to the church and village. As an added precaution, Brummitt dispatched observation teams to areas where attacks seemed unlikely. T/5 Page and Sgt. Frank Costa were in a foxhole facing the *marais*.[5]

Everyone in uniform took up arms to defend Graignes. This included those who were not paratroopers. Lt. Naughton estimated that there were about 100 riflemen on the defense perimeter. Lt. Irwin Morales, the glider pilot, took up position in an outpost on the right flank, defending the hill top. Morales's co-pilot, Lt. Thomas Ahmad, was below the cemetery and in charge of a group of men. Sgt. Edward Barnes was in a foxhole in the cemetery. Captain Brummitt especially relied on Lt. Naughton to provide him with intelligence on battlefield conditions. Naughton was below the hill, constantly checking on the US lines of defense. Naughton was nominally in charge of communications for the 3rd Battalion. But Brummitt found that Lt. Naughton "proved to be a dedicated leader capable of performing many duties far beyond his communication function."[6]

Captain Brummitt also prepared for the inevitable aftermath of a battle for Graignes. Captain Abraham Sophian, the battalion surgeon, and his medical team oversaw the medical aid station, which was located in the "small school." On 11–12 June, Father Le Blastier permitted Dr. Sophian and the medics to tend to the wounded in the church sacristy. But prior to the attack on Graignes, the medical team had plenty to do. Several men, such as Cpl. Edward W. Stranko of Pennsylvania, had badly cut their hands and wrists with their knives, while freeing themselves of their parachutes. This had happened throughout Normandy as paratroopers, often underwater, slashed at the risers of their parachutes. Other paratroopers had deep bruises and sprains that needed medical attention. The paratroopers of Headquarters Company had jumped at too low an altitude from planes that were flying at too rapid a speed. The battered paratroopers received shots of novocaine to relieve their pain. The medical team tended to Captain Bogart, who had been hit by flak. Captain Sophian also made "house calls." Gustave Rigault suffered a minor coronary incident. Sophian walked to Le Port St. Pierre to examine Rigault in his home. Such care prompted Madame S. Pezerin of Graignes to say that Captain Sophian "wins all hearts: with his sweetness and gentleness."[7]

Captain Brummitt supplemented the defensive posture at Graignes with day and night patrols to gather intelligence on enemy movements, or, as T/5 Page put it, "every day and night we'd patrol and see if we could find out what the hell was going on."[8] As early as the afternoon of D-Day, Brummitt had led a thirty-man patrol to forage for equipment that had been dropped in color-coded parachutes. Between 8 and 10 June, the patrolling paratroopers made contact with German forces. Prior to D-Day, there had been concentrations of German troops in areas near Graignes. Homer Poss recalled that there was a German garrison about three miles from Graignes. On patrol, Pvt. Marion Hatton spotted a German tank convoy about four miles from Graignes. Hatton guessed that the convoy, which had bivouacked for the night, was heading for the invasion beaches.[9] Once the bulk of the 101st Airborne Division landed north of Carentan and began to move toward the town, some German troops began to flee southward toward Graignes. As recorded by Sgt. Major Salewski in his diary, on 8 June, a patrol led by Lt. Lowell Maxwell of Smith County, Texas encountered a retreating German unit, with horses pulling field artillery. A skirmish broke out, with Staff Sgt. Nelson F. Hornbaker of the medical unit being "clipped" on the wrist. The intelligence that Lt. Maxwell delivered was that "the manner in which the outfit was acting [suggested that] they were a bit battle weary."[10]

Lt. Maxwell's patrol encountered the German unit near a steel and concrete bridge that crossed the Vire-Taute Canal and led to

Carentan. This was the bridge at Le Port des Planqués. Major Johnston ordered the bridge destroyed to prevent Germans from Carentan moving toward Graignes. On Friday, 9 June, Lt. Naughton led a small patrol of the demolition squad with supporting troops to the bridge. The paratroopers carried their "demolition kits," with them. Sgt. Harry W. Murray of North Carolina informed Naughton that it would take twenty minutes for the demolition team to set the explosives. Naughton dispatched Sgt. Costa and Pvt. David Purcell to the far side of the bridge to watch for enemy activity. They carried a Browning Automatic Rifle. Just as the twenty-minute deadline approached, Costa and Purcell spotted a German unit. They scurried back across the bridge to warn the lieutenant. Sgt. Murray's team had taken exactly twenty minutes to prepare the explosives. Lt. Naughton ordered the pressing of the plunger, just as the Germans approached the bridge. Concrete and steel filled the air. A firefight broke out, with the Germans scattering into the *marais*. Sgt. Costa told his son, at a fiftieth anniversary ceremony of D-Day, that he killed a German soldier trying to wade through the canals. Costa regretted the German soldier's death.[11]

Figure 5.2 Colonel Frank Naughton (Ret.) stands on the bridge that his team destroyed on 9 June 1944. The new bridge was named in honor of the 507th Regiment. To the left is Frank Costa, who guarded the approach to the bridge. To the right are the Rigault sisters, Marthe and Odette. In the background is the Vire-Taute Canal. Photograph courtesy of the Rigault/His family.

An ominous confrontation with German troops erupted on Saturday, 10 June. A contingent of the paratroopers from the 101st Airborne Division in Graignes, led by Lt. George Murn and including Pvt. Frank Juliano, spotted three motorcycles with side cars approaching them from the south. They were traveling up Route D 29, which was west of Graignes and led to Carentan. According to Juliano, the paratroopers opened fire, killing four Germans. One motorcycle and side car escaped, and its crew presumably reported the contact to their superiors.[12] The paratroopers searched the pockets of the dead Germans and discovered documents. The papers, as Captain Brummitt noted, identified them as members "of the reconnaissance battalion of an Armored Division."[13] These were men from the 17th *SS Panzergrenadier* Division. Major Johnston and Captain Brummitt and all under their command were now on full alert. Throughout Saturday and into the evening, the paratroopers on patrol were increasingly spotting German troop movements. As Mayor Voydie remembered, "on Sunday [11 June] it is very quiet in the morning, we find that the paratroopers are very nervous, and are up very early, their individual holes already dug."[14]

Major Johnston's decision to stay in Graignes and wait for relief from the US invading forces now seemed problematic. The paratroopers had not been without hope in the previous days. The villagers had proved to be dependable, competent allies. The arrival in Graignes, on Friday, 9 June, of two men from the 29th Infantry Division from Omaha Beach suggested that invading forces were getting close. Since June 6, the paratroopers had taken only one human casualty – the wound to Sgt. Hornbaker's wrist. The paratroopers had, however, "sacrificed" the remaining carrier pigeon on Saturday, 10 June, because it was making too much noise.[15] Through extensive contacts with friends and relatives in Carentan, villagers could report to Major Johnston that the 101st was in position to liberate Carentan. Paratroopers and villagers also spotted numerous Allied planes flying low over Graignes. According to Madame S. Pezerin, "large, pink phosphorescent signs were extended on the lawns in front of the school buildings" to dissuade the Allies from bombing Graignes.[16] Perhaps the pilots of the aircraft would notice the defenses that the paratroopers had built and inform their commanders.

Although danger was looming, Major Johnston cannot be faulted for his decision to stay in place and defend Graignes. During the first days after D-Day, the paratroopers of the 82nd and 101st Airborne Divisions who landed near Graignes were safer than their colleagues who landed closer to their drop zones. Paratroopers of the 82nd Airborne Division landed close to German positions and had to surrender to overwhelming forces. The prisoners of war included the regimental commander of the 507th, Colonel George V. Millett, Jr. Enlisted men – Bob Bearden, Ed Isbell, and James James – of the 507th Regiment emerged from captivity in 1945 weighing less than 100 pounds. Isbell recalled that when, on 8 May 1945, a US officer first saw Isbell and his fellow prisoners at a prison camp in Germany, he was shocked by the appearance of men "in dirty clothes, in rags, wooden shoes, unkept hair, not shaved in months." During the first week of the Normandy campaign, the three paratrooper infantry regiments and the 325th Glider Regiment of the 82nd Airborne Division were also taking catastrophic casualties, as they fought to keep control of the bridges over the Merderet River at La Fière and Chef-du-Pont. As Colonel Mark J. Alexander, a battalion commander in the 82nd, described the fight over the bridge and causeway at La Fière, "man did they have casualties."[17] When the 82nd Airborne Division's mission in Normandy concluded after the first week of July 1944, the division's casualty toll in terms of killed, wounded, missing, and prisoners amounted to 46 percent. The 507th Regiment's casualty toll was 61 percent. As dawn broke on Sunday, 11 June 1944, members of the Headquarters Company of the 3rd Battalion were about to become part of the 507th Regiment's grim statistics.

French Allies and Friends

If paratroopers of the 82nd and 101st Airborne Division harbored doubts about their mission in Graignes, their concerns would have been alleviated by the dedication of the villagers to the cause of liberation and victory over Nazi Germany. Between 7 and 10 June, the people of Graignes gathered intelligence and weapons for the paratroopers. They served as guides for paratroopers on patrol. They counseled US military officers about the nature of the German occupying forces and monitored the movements of potential French collaborators. The leaders of Graignes further tried to confuse the enemy by disseminating disinformation. The women of Graignes not only fed the paratroopers but risked their lives traveling through the countryside in search of food. The young people of Graignes especially bonded with the paratroopers, many of whom were similarly young. T/5 Page, in his plain, direct manner of speaking, summarized: "The people of the village were so good to us."[18] After the battles of 11–12 June, the villagers played critical roles in aiding the escape of their liberators, including Page. For all of this, the people of Graignes were subjected to cruelty and war crimes from German troops. They endured their punishment with pride in their mission.

Acting Mayor Alphonse Voydie was the leader of his village during the first two weeks of June not only in name but also in purpose and in commitment. Every paratrooper who survived Graignes and wrote or spoke about his experience testified to Voydie's character. In Lt. Frank Naughton's words, the mayor was "a man of remarkable vigor and personal charm." He was "a good leader – a great man" and he "laid down the law on this matter of giving us assistance." Captain Brummitt added that "Mayor Voydie was especially influential in obtaining support of all sorts from citizenry."[19] By force of personality, Voydie obtained unanimous consent from the male adults to support the paratroopers. He then assigned tasks to citizens. They took their flat boats out into the marshes to retrieve equipment. Villagers also retrieved color-coded parachutes that got hung up on trees and roofs. Young, able men accompanied the paratroopers on patrol. Other men found matériel for fortifications. Madame Germaine Boursier began to organize her field kitchen. Mayor Voydie also took actions to forestall trouble. Word spread quickly throughout the region of the arrival of the paratroopers to Graignes. Rural people streamed into Graignes to take a look at the seeming miracle. After 7 June, the mayor forbade outside visitors. He also understood, probably from past experience, that not everyone could be counted on to not pass information to the German occupiers. Vigilance was established over suspects.[20] No evidence has surfaced, however, that any citizen of Graignes collaborated with the Germans, during the period from 6 to 16 June 1944.

Beyond organizing his constituents, Voydie, along with Father Le Blastier, Albert Mauger, and Gustave Rigault, gathered intelligence and provided insight into the German occupiers. The mayor used his contacts to pass information that would deceive the Germans. He tried to create the impression that a US battalion, which would normally consist of about 650 military personnel, had arrived in Graignes. Albert Mauger, the leader of the local resistance, traveled throughout the region. Mauger made contacts with his allies in the Liberation-North Resistance network, and passed intelligence about German troop movements to Major Johnston. Gustave Rigault conducted similar missions.[21] Father Le Blastier had mediated between the German occupiers and outraged parishioners during the period from 1940 and 1944. His experience gave him insight "concerning the enemy's propaganda ploys and the tactics and techniques used to force French citizens to defect." Lt. Naughton and Lt. Reed testified that Le Blastier shared his knowledge about the enemy "freely and thoughtfully" with US officers. Father Le Blastier, a veteran of World War I, also had his own contacts with patriotic French citizens. He encouraged them to help with the supply of the paratroopers.[22]

Two young men, Joseph Folliot and Charles Gosselin, served as scouts and navigators for US paratroopers on patrol. Reflecting the nature of the extensive kinship ties in Graignes, Folliot, a farmer, was the nephew of Gustave Rigault. Both Folliot and Gosselin were fierce, had chafed under German occupation, and were eager to drive the Germans out of their country. The paratroopers had to discourage Folliot and Gosselin from firing on German troops. Capture might mean becoming a prisoner of war for the paratroopers. But the Germans would have summarily executed the two Frenchmen for aiding the enemy. During the Battle of Graignes, both men served as ammunition bearers and messengers. Both aided paratroopers in escaping the village. Folliot was especially instrumental in helping paratroopers make it to Carentan on flat boats via the canal system. Gosselin successfully went underground after the German forces captured Graignes.[23] Folliot has been reported as having been eventually captured by the Germans and executed. His father was also a victim of the Germans. Shortly after the last paratroopers made it to Carentan on the night of 14 June, Isidore Folliot went out in the *marais*, when he spotted a parapack with US rations. He was killed by German machine-gun fire.[24]

Isidore Folliot's death signified that villagers had to be circumspect when they floated out into the *marais*. German troops were spying on them. Transferring the containers with ammunition and supplies to Graignes also involved risk. On 7 June, two paratroopers came to the Rigault home and asked for help in transporting the containers the family had salvaged from the *marais* on D-Day. Madame Rigault agreed, and Odette volunteered for the assignment. She hitched a cart

Figure 5.3 Members of the Rigault family pose with "Pom-Pom." In the background is the Rigault family home at Le Port St. Pierre. Photograph courtesy of the Rigault/His family.

to "Pom-Pom," the family's horse. Troopers loaded the cart. Odette used sacks of feed and fertilizer and mounds of hay to cover the cargo and set off for Graignes, three to four kilometers away. Odette Rigault took the route nearest the marshes to minimize contact with Germans.[25] Five decades after the event, Lt. Naughton was still astonished at what he had seen, stating that "I remember this young lady bringing in weapons concealed under a load of hay. She left right under the Germans' eyes, and she drove that into our perimeter."[26] Odette did not, however make it to the village center. Her father, who was returning from the church meeting, stopped her, because he had just been informed that there were enemy troops in the vicinity. Gustave Rigault and his daughter left the horse and cart in the care of the two paratroopers, who brought in the cargo. The family subsequently retrieved the noble "Pom-Pom."

The expression "an army marches on its stomach" has been attributed to Napoleon Bonaparte of France or Frederick the Great of Germany. The paratroopers of the 82nd and 101st Airborne Divisions in Graignes never forgot the efforts of villagers to feed them. Major

Johnston told Mayor Voydie that supplying food for the paratroopers was what he especially needed from the civilian population. On 7 June, Sgt. Major Robert Salewski recorded in his diary that he had only one meal that day.[27] Villagers butchered pigs and calves, which locally were in short supply, for the paratroopers. Madame Rigault cooked the pig her husband butchered, and the meat was shared at church.[28] However important such individual efforts were, what was needed was a methodical feeding program. Mayor Voydie assigned the energetic Germaine Boursier, the owner of the local café and grocery store, the mission of feeding the young, hungry paratroopers.

Madame Boursier organized the women of Graignes, which included her adult daughters, into a village cooking campaign. The women vowed to supply the paratroopers with two meals a day. The

Figure 5.4 This is a photograph of Madame Germaine Boursier, the "mess sergeant" of Headquarters Company in Graignes. In 1986, at the age of ninety, Madame Boursier, accompanied by her daughters, would be recognized for her heroism and be awarded a commendation and medal from the US Secretary of the Army. Courtesy of the Mayor's Office of Graignes.

kitchen operated twenty-four hours a day. Major Johnston assigned two soldiers to assist the women. Children brought cooked meals to the paratroopers in their foxholes. Such efforts required not only hard work but also bravery. There were approximately 165 uniformed personnel in Graignes. And other men, like the French-speaking Spaniards, had entered Graignes. Existing food supplies were scarce. The German occupiers had seized surplus food. They also forced Normans to purchase food with ration cards. Boursier and her sidekick, Renée Meunier, outwitted the Germans. Mademoiselle Meunier was a patriotic member of the community who frequently inveighed against the detested German occupiers in her friend's café. Boursier and Meunier went out in their horse-pulled wagons, often at night, to forage for food in the region. They traveled on roads that had been mined. They went into German-occupied villages such as Saint-Jean-de-Daye. Boursier clandestinely contacted her suppliers in the food industry and persuaded them to misrepresent the amounts of basic foodstuffs that she was authorized to sell in the village. The women hid food supplies under hay in their wagons. When stopped by German patrols, they protested they were simply gathering food for their neighbors. Other villagers engaged in the deception, journeying to mills in larger towns to obtain flour, for Graignes did not have a flour mill. These heroic efforts meant that the paratroopers had veal, vegetables, and bread to eat.[29]

These interactions created a strong bond between the paratroopers and the people of Graignes. However brief, the experience in Graignes replicated the experiences of the paratroopers in Portrush, Northern Ireland and Tollerton, England. The situation was similar. The men were young, lonely, missed their parents, their siblings, and their wives and girlfriends, and had been away from home for a long time. The difference was that they were in harm's way in Graignes, Normandy. The paratroopers did the expected by passing out chocolate and chewing gum to the children of the village. One trooper promised Marthe Rigault that he would send to her and her sister Odette dresses when he returned home. The trooper had sisters in the United States who were the same ages as the Rigault sisters. Children gathered around the paratroopers when they took time out to clean their weapons. They taught each other songs in French and English. Marthe sang for the paratroopers her favorite song, *Ma Normandie* (*My Normandy*) with the opening lyrics – *J'aime à revoir ma Normandie! C'est le pays qui m'a donné le jour* ("I love to see my Normandy! The land that gave to me the light of day"). In turn, the paratroopers taught children *It's a Long Way to Tipperary* (1912), the universally popular song of soldiers that expresses a longing for home. In later life, Rigault His characterized the experience of singing with the paratroopers as "all that is unforgettable."[30]

The adults of Graignes also reacted warmly to the paratroopers. Like others in Normandy, the villagers were first struck by the overwhelming physical authority and confidence of the paratroopers. As Denise Boursier-Lereculey, daughter of Madame Boursier, recalled, the paratroopers announced their presence with the cry: "*Bonjour*, we are your friends, we have come to save you." But beneath the bravado, she found that "all of them were charming and impeccably correct in their dealings with the population." Madame S. Pezerin, a school teacher, spoke about what happened when paratroopers were invited into village homes. She noted that the paratroopers were younger than they looked. They showed photographs of their families, and "a very young father, who is wearing a rosary around his neck, kept forcing us to admire the portrait of his wife and little girl." Others reminisced about the girlfriends they had left behind in America.[31] Inevitably, flirtatious conduct began to mark the exchanges between the paratroopers and young, unmarried women of the village. Sgt. Benton Broussard, the French-speaking Cajun from Louisiana, especially attracted attention. In an interview in 2019, Danielle His Peros, the niece of Odette Rigault, suggested that her aunt had fallen hard for Sgt. Broussard. Seventy years after Broussard's death in Graignes, Odette Lelavechef, approaching ninety years of age, recorded a message for Broussard's family, wishing that she could meet them and that she "was happy with him" during the last week of Sgt. Broussard's life.[32]

Throughout Normandy, citizens cheered the arrival of paratroopers on D-Day and thereafter risked everything to aid them – providing battlefield intelligence about concentrations of German troops and hiding paratroopers in their barns and cellars. Liberation exacted a heavy toll on Normans. During the first two days of the invasion, 3,000 Normans died. The death count would subsequently rise due to bombing and street fighting in urban areas like Caen, Saint-Lô, and Valognes. An estimated 19,890 civilians lost their lives during the Allied campaign to liberate Normandy.[33] US military planners worried that the heavy civilian casualties would cause the Norman spirit to flag. Supreme Headquarters Allied Expeditionary Force (SHAEF) ordered a study team organized by the Psychological War Department to interview 1,000 residents of the Cotentin Peninsula south of Cherbourg. Ten young French men and women conducted their interviews. The researchers found that the vast majority of Normans were "overjoyed" and given new hope by the Allied landings. Only 2 percent of the respondents complained about damaged homes. To be sure, 20 percent had complaints about excessive behavior by Allied troops, including 3 percent mentioning improper attitudes toward Norman women and 1 percent citing rape. But the report concluded that the stories by Normans "of their contacts with the troops are replete with agreeable and friendly relations for the most part."[34]

Antoine Anne of Saint-Georges-d'Elle, a village northeast of Saint-Lô, typified the attitudes of Normans toward the suffering they endured. He echoed the views of Mayor Voydie, Gustave Rigault, *Curé* Le Blastier, Joseph Folliot, Madame Boursier, Mademoiselle Meunier, and the Rigault sisters when he proclaimed "there are costs to resurrecting freedom." His village's "aim was to rediscover our freedom and dignity so that the servitude we had endured would no longer be anything but a memory." Antoine Anne lamented, however, that "our village after Liberation had the sad privilege of being called the 'capitol of ruins.'"[35] The village of Graignes would be in a similar state of devastation fewer than ten days after D-Day. Nazi troops from the 17th *SS Panzergrenadier* Division would murder over thirty civilians, and other German troops would set fire to the village. The villagers were punished because they had dared to aid those who came in the name of liberation.

The March toward Graignes and Carentan

The clock would run out for the paratroopers and the people of Graignes when, beginning on the afternoon of Sunday, 11 June 1944, the 1st Battalion of the 37th Regiment from the 17th *Waffen-SS Panzergrenadier* Division, known as the "Götz von Berlichingen" Division, launched attacks on the village. It had taken the *SS* men of the 1st Battalion four days to make the journey of 241 miles (388 kms) from the Thouars region to Graignes. The 1st Battalion launched its first probing attack on Graignes even as the 101st Airborne Division was beginning its assault on German troops in Carentan. The paratroopers of the 101st would liberate Carentan the next day. By the morning of

12 June, the SS men would be in control of Graignes. If either the 1st Battalion had been delayed for another day in reaching Graignes, or the 101st could have liberated Carentan a day or two earlier, the paratroopers in Graignes might have been able to make it to Carentan safely. And the villagers might have been spared the vicious fury of the Nazis.

At 4:00 a.m. on D-Day, the commander of the 17th *SS Panzergrenadier* Division, *Oberführer* Werner Ostendorff, woke his staff, informing them that he had received the alert signal that the Allies had launched their long-expected attack against Western Europe. By 4:15 a.m., the alarm was transmitted to the Reconnaissance Section and shortly thereafter to all units in the division. By 6:15 a.m., Ostendorff received a briefing from the First Orderly Officer of the Chief of Staff with a preliminary analysis of the attack. US paratroopers, in 600 to 800 planes, had landed in the area of Normandy from Cherbourg to Caen, and the airborne assault continued to strengthen. Land troops would be in battle, for enemy warships were landing an invading force near the historic town of Bayeux. By 9:00 a.m., *Oberführer* Ostendorff had received orders from Lt. General Fritz Kraemer to ready the 17th *SS Panzergrenadier* Division to march.[36] The news excited the *Oberführer*'s staff. The division, which had been training since October 1943, was eager for war. A staff officer remembered "everyone was in a good mood and eager to see action again – happy that the pre-invasion spell of uncertainty and waiting had snapped at last."[37]

Oberführer Ostendorff soon learned that his division was assigned to the defense of Carentan. By the early evening of 7 June, the 17th *SS Panzergrenadier* Division began to move out of the Thouars region. Reconnaissance units traveling in *Volkswagens* led the way. But Ostendorff moved faster than the men, reaching Saint-Lô and the headquarters of LXXXIV *Armee-Korps* and an evening conference on 8 June with General Erich Marcks. The LXXXIV *Armee-Korps* bore responsibility for the German defense of the Cotentin Peninsula. General Marcks presented Ostendorf with some unsettling news. Generals in Berlin and Führer Adolf Hitler did not believe that the Allies had launched their major offensive in Normandy. They still held to the conviction that the Allies would focus their forces with an assault at Pas de Calais. Berlin refused to authorize the deployment of *Panzers* to smash the Allied landings on the beaches of Normandy. General Marcks, believing his own eyes and the reports of his officers at the beaches and in the fields in Normandy, rejected Berlin's analysis. He ordered Ostendorff to deploy his troops near Carentan and establish his headquarters at Périers, about twenty kilometers southwest of Carentan. The 17th *SS Panzergrenadier* Division should link up with the 6th Parachute Regiment. General Marcks further advised Ostendorff that the German troops in the Carentan region were poorly trained, older men. In particular, he disparaged the *Ostbataillon* (Eastern troops). The recruits from places such as Ukraine in the Soviet Union wanted to fight Stalin and Communists, not Anglo-American troops. Marcks counseled Ostendorff to move his men at night, to avoid main roads, and not to stop in villages. He warned that the Allies owned the skies.[38] General Marcks was prescient. On 12 June, he died from an Allied air attack north of Saint-Lô.

Oberführer Ostendorff presented a similarly dismal military appraisal to General Marcks. His troops were having trouble advancing toward their objective. A fundamental problem was a lack of transportation and shortage of fuel. The division lacked sufficient heavy trucks that could transport men, war matériel, and ammunition to the front lines. Allied bombing in Germany and France had stymied efforts to bring heavy trucks to the 17th *SS Panzergrenadier* Division. French workers in auto factories had sabotaged vehicles that the Germans ordered. Transporting heavy equipment like tracked vehicles via railcars had become problematic. Allied warplanes ruled the skies. The increasingly bold French Resistance sabotaged railroad tracks. The German commanders thought they could rely on the French to drive their wood-fueled trucks and cars and transport men and ammunition. Once D-Day arrived, French drivers disappeared into the general population. The commanding officers of the 17th *SS Panzergrenadier* Division had counted on having ninety tons of ammunition at staging areas for the attack on Carentan. By the time, on 13 June, the 1st Battalion of the 37th Regiment launched its attack on Carentan, only fifteen tons of ammunition had arrived.[39]

The 17th *SS Panzergrenadier* Division, which had reached its authorized strength of 17,000 men, also had firepower and experience concerns. As a *Panzergrenadier* unit, the division was designed at inception to have *Panzers*. It never obtained tanks. It had twenty-five *StuG* IVs, which looked somewhat like tanks, but were essentially anti-tank weapons. The *StuG* IV had a 75 mm gun, but, without a turret, the gun could be turned laterally only 10 degrees. The 17th *SS Panzergrenadier*

Division had an artillery unit, with light and heavy howitzers, and a veteran commander, *SS Obersturmbannführer* (Lt. Colonel) Otto Binge. The division also had twelve 8.8 cm flak guns, which could be used to fire at airplanes or targets on the ground, with an effective ground firing range of over 14,000 meters. The men who would operate these weapons or serve as infantrymen remained very young and inexperienced. For example, 42 percent of the 945 men assigned to the 3rd Battalion of the 37th Regiment were between the ages of sixteen and twenty. The battalion had only ten officers, and its non-commissioned officers had little combat experience.[40]

The 17th *SS Panzergrenadier* Division headed north from Thouars in columns or *Marschgruppen*. The 37th and 38th *Panzergrenadier* Regiments, the heart of the division, took different paths toward the Norman battlefields. The 37th *Panzergrenadier* Regiment veered to the west and then headed directly north. The 38th *Panzergrenadier* Regiment moved north and to the east of the 37th. Because of the lack of motorized vehicles, both regiments left their 3rd Battalion behind. The men of the two 3rd Battalions would have to move north via bicycles. Nonetheless, the *SS* men were in high spirits. They probably expected to be on the road for two days and nights, reaching their staging areas near Carentan by the evening of June 9. The Germans told themselves that their American adversaries were inexperienced and lacked the "British fighting spirit."[41] As recounted to his US captors by a staff officer who became a prisoner of war, "our motorized columns were coiling along the roads toward the invasion beaches. Amidst this rumbling of motors and grinding of vehicle tracks the *Panzer Grenadier* was in his element again." The officer added "then something happened that 'left us in a daze.'"[42]

The "something" that happened was that US P-51 Mustang fighter-bombers had chosen to accompany the 17th *SS Panzergrenadier* Division on its journey. The *SS* men had already had a taste of Allied airpower. On 4–5 June, warplanes attacked bridges that crossed the Loire River near Saumur. Attacks on bridges near Thouars continued on D-Day. The P-51s, the *Jabos*, buzzed the columns of German troops. In the words again of the captive German staff officer, after the aerial attacks, vehicles were "left in flames." The once cocky *SS* troops were "pale and shaky." After a second attack, "the length of the road was strewn with splintered AT guns (the pride of our Division), flaming motors and charred implements of war." The *Jabos* had hit *StuG* IV anti-tank vehicles. It now dawned on the Germans of the 17th *SS Panzergrenadier* Division that "the new enemy that had come to Normandy was different." The men wondered what would happen when they clashed with US troops. They asked: "if things like this happened here, what would it be like up there at the front."[43]

Oberführer Ostendorff followed General Marcks's advice and ordered his advancing columns "to become completely invisible." They were to camouflage their trucks, clear the roads quickly, and use their anti-aircraft weapons when attacked by the *Jabos*.[44] The officer staff of the 17th *SS Panzergrenadier* Division and the 37th and 38th Regiments left the highways and traveled on secondary roads "rimmed with hedges and bushes."[45] Progress inevitably slowed. Delays also came when the columns had to wait for fuel resupplies. On 9 June, an anxious Ostendorff pressed the 38th Regiment, wondering when they would reach their objective. He also asked the regiment to report on its losses of personnel and vehicles and how much fuel the regiment had.[46] Finally, on the morning of 11 June, after five days on the road, the officers of the division staff reached their command post at Saint-Sébastien-de-Raids, a hamlet just east of the small town of Périers. A good road, running northeast and twenty kilometers in length, connected Périers to Carentan. Reaching the command post did not, however, spare the staff the fury of the *Jabos*. Indeed, the "*Jabo* plague became even more serious." The staff looked for cover in trees and sunken roads. While hiding, the Germans heard "the nerve-frazzling thunder of the strafing fighters" and witnessed smoke billowing from vehicles and fuel and ammunition dumps. Common soldiers began to ask their officers about the absence of the *Luftwaffe*. The officers could only give evasive answers.[47]

By 11 June, the 37th and 38th Regiments approached their assigned sectors, north of Saint-Lô. The 38th Regiment was centered near Montmartin-en-Graignes, a village eight kilometers to the north and east of Graignes. This position gave the 38th Regiment the ability to confront invading US forces. German commanders worried that the US troops that landed at Omaha Beach were advancing rapidly, having reached, on 9 June, Isigny-sur-Mer, which lay about twenty kilometers from the coast. The 37th Regiment was positioned west of the 38th and was approaching Carentan. The 37th's new march plan was to skirt the *marais* by proceeding westward through Tribehou to the village of Méautis, which would leave the regiment just south and west of

Carentan.[48] As recorded in the diary of Dr. Delitz, the battalion surgeon, the regiment was two days behind schedule.[49] Neither the 37th Regiment nor the 38th Regiment could count on immediate resupply or reinforcements from their respective 3rd Battalion. Allied fighter planes continued their attacks on rail lines in the Thouars region.[50] The men of the 3rd Battalions stayed on their bicycles.

On Sunday, 11 June, at 9:30 a.m, *Oberführer* Ostendorff issued a new order to the 1st Battalion of the 37th Regiment led by *Obersturmbannführer* Jacob Fick. Before moving to Méautis for the assault on Carentan, the 1st Battalion, which was centered in the village of Saint-André-de-Bohon, was ordered to move slightly east and deploy to the nearby Graignes area. The actual distance between the two villages was minuscule, but the road trip was eight kilometers in length because of the *marais*. One company of the 1st Battalion was already positioned just east of Graignes at a bridge just above Saint-Jean-de-Daye. The 2nd Battalion was ordered to continue its march toward Méautis.[51] What prompted Ostendorff to issue this order cannot be documented, but his reasoning would seem obvious. An advance party on motorcycles and in sidecars of the 17th *SS Panzergrenadier* Division had clashed with the 101st Airborne defenders of Graignes led by Lt. Murn on 10 June. At least one of the Germans escaped and presumably reported the ambush. By 11 June, German troops stationed in the region may have relayed information to Ostendorff's staff that there was a US unit in Graignes. Ostendorff may have also been informed that another German unit, an *Ostbataillon*, was preparing to assault Graignes that Sunday morning. His *SS* men would thereby have the assignment of backing up the *Ostbataillon*. Ostendorff may have further reasoned that it would be an unwise tactical decision to leave an active US unit to his rear, when his forces attacked Carentan. Ostendorff's intelligence about Graignes was less than perfect. He ordered the 1st Battalion to seize and hold the bridge at Le Port des Planqués.[52] But Lt. Frank Naughton, Sgt. Harry Murray, and the demolition team had blown the bridge up on 9 June.

The *SS* commander's 9:30 a.m. order to deploy troops to Graignes proved an ominous development for the US paratroopers entrenched in the village and for the villagers themselves. But it also turned out to be a positive turn of events for the main contingent of the 101st Airborne Division that had landed behind Utah Beach and north of Carentan. The paratroopers at Graignes managed to tie down the overwhelming forces of the 1st Battalion of the 37th Regiment for a day. This meant that the 17th *SS Panzergrenadier* Division was three days behind schedule when, on 13 June, the division launched its attack on Carentan. On the morning of 13 June, the 101st Airborne controlled Carentan, after two days of hard fighting. Moreover, by 13 June, other US forces, including the Sherman tanks of the 2nd Armored Division, had had time to move off the beaches and join the fight for Carentan. The paratroopers at Graignes and the P-51 pilots had contributed to the liberation of Carentan.

The three regiments of paratroopers in the 101st Airborne Division – the 501st, 502nd, and 506th – had the same challenges as the 82nd Airborne Division from D-Day onward. Like the 82nd, they had jumped from C-47s that were going too fast and were flying too low. Paratroopers estimated that they had jumped from 400 feet and had only 5 to 8 seconds after their chutes deployed before they hit the ground or flooded areas. Troopers suffered broken ankles and deep bone bruises. Of the 100 men who landed near the hamlet of Addeville, 25 percent had sprains or broken bones. Many also struggled to survive, as their parachutes pulled them underwater. The men of the 101st also landed everywhere but on their designated drop zones. Of the 6,600 paratroopers who jumped, only 1,100 managed to assemble into fighting forces by 6:30 a.m. on D-Day. By evening that number grew to only 2,500. Several planes dropped paratroopers of the 501st Regiment south of Carentan. Most of these troopers were killed or captured by Germans.[53] The stick from B Company of the 501st Regiment that included Captain Bogart, Lt. Murn, and Pfc. Juliano and landed near Graignes was an exception.

Despite the flawed jump, the 101st Airborne reacted the way the paratroopers of the 82nd Airborne had. They improvised, and they persisted. They secured the causeways that led from Utah Beach, facilitating the movement of men and matériel from the 4th Infantry Division into the Cotentin Peninsula. They gained control of the Douve River locks at La Barquette. By 12 June, the locks had been opened, and the draining of the areas that the Germans had flooded commenced. The 101st also gained control of the Douve valley and captured the key village of Saint-Côme-du-Mont, giving US forces a direct path to Carentan from the north. The battles behind Utah Beach cost the 101st dearly. One section of the road, the RN 13 highway, that connected Sainte-Mère-Église to Carentan would be dubbed "Purple Heart

Lane." The 3rd Battalion of the 502nd Regiment experienced a 67 percent casualty rate as it moved toward Carentan.[54]

On 7 June, General Dwight D. Eisenhower inspected the battlefield at Omaha Beach and reiterated the plan to link Omaha with Utah Beach. Eisenhower's ground commander, Lt. General Omar Bradley, relayed and emphasized those orders, remarking to General Lawton Collins that "if it becomes necessary to save time, put 500 even 1,000 tons of air [bombs] on Carentan and take the city apart. Then rush in and you'll get it." The 101st Airborne Division was tasked with the mission of taking Carentan. Generals Eisenhower and Bradley were not the only well-known military figures to decide on the strategic significance of Carentan. Germany's most famous general, Field Marshal Erwin Rommel, ordered that German forces hold the town "until the last man."[55] Occupying Carentan were two battalions of the 6th *Fallschirmjäger* Regiment (6th Parachute Regiment) led by Lt. Colonel Friedrich August Freiherr von der Heydte. The German paratroopers were reinforced by two *Ostbataillone* and a handful of German troops from other units. In the early hours of 11 June, paratroopers of the 101st Airborne launched their attack on Carentan. All three regiments of paratroopers of the 101st Airborne participated in the liberation of Carentan. Also involved in the battle were men of the 327th Glider Regiment, most of whom had landed via the sea at Utah Beach. By the early evening of 11 June, Colonel von der Heydte began to withdraw his troops from Carentan, moving to positions just southwest of the town. By 12 June, Allied forces controlled Carentan. The French citizens of the town would be able to emerge from their cellars. Carentan suffered civilian casualties, including the death of the mayor, and significant damage, with 250 homes and shops being destroyed.[56]

The fate of paratroopers in Graignes and the security of the village's citizens became linked to the liberation of Carentan. Carentan would be the safe haven that the paratroopers sought, after the battles with the 17th *SS Panzergrenadier* Division on 11–12 June 1944. But conversely the new-found freedom of Carentan depended on the bravery of the paratroopers and villagers in Graignes. Even as the paratroopers were fending off the German assaults on the village, the 17th *SS Panzergrenadier* Division contemplated the recapture of Carentan. In the evening of 11 June, *Oberführer* Ostendorff journeyed to the location where the battered 6th Parachute Regiment had withdrawn. Accompanied by staff officers, Ostendorff met with the weary Lt.

Figure 5.5 The 11 June 1944 meeting of *Oberführer* Ostendorff of the 17th *SS Panzergrenadier* Division (on the left) with the commander of the 6th *Fallschirmjäger* Regiment, *Oberstleutnant* von der Heydte (center). The officer to the right is one of Ostendorff's aides. *Bundesarchiv* photograph.

Colonel von der Heydte. The German paratrooper gave Ostendorff a sober report. The 6th *Fallschirmjäger* Regiment had been in constant combat since D-Day, had taken heavy casualties, and was now low on ammunition. US fighter-bombers and the big guns of the US Navy had incessantly pounded the German paratroopers. Von der Heydte added: "Our adversaries are excellent soldiers, especially the paratroopers." Moving over flooded fields and crossing canals, the paratroopers had been exposed to German fire. Nonetheless, the Americans had mounted "a furious attack" against Carentan. Lt. Colonel von der Heydte judged that his paratroopers still had the will to fight, but he found that the "eastern volunteers," the two *Ostbataillone*, had proved unreliable, with many fleeing the battlefield.[57]

Oberführer* Ostendorff had orders to unleash his 17th *SS Panzergrenadier* Division on Carentan and the town's 101st Airborne liberators. He assumed command of what remained of the 6th Parachute Regiment and the one company of Eastern troops still willing to fight the Americans.[58] But Ostendorff would disappoint his masters in the LXXXIV *Armee-Korps* and in Berlin. He would have to delay the attack on Carentan until 13 June. The troops he would subsequently deploy to lead the attack, the 1st Battalion of the 37th Regiment, were drained from their battles at Graignes. The initial reports that Ostendorff received had assured him that his men had met "a weak enemy" at Graignes.[59] The US paratroopers in Graignes proved, however, to be tough and resilient. They fought for the French citizens who had supported them since D-Day. And, at a time of extreme peril, the villagers of Graignes would remain loyal to their friends and liberators, the *paras*.

6 THE LONGEST DAY IN GRAIGNES

The citizens of Graignes, Normandy experienced five days of joy and liberation from 6 to 10 June 1944. Recalling those days, Madame Odile Delacotte noted that when the paratroopers realized that they had landed near a village where there were no Germans, "they became reassured and friendly." She added that for several days, "we became American, and everyone in the village brought them butter, meat, fruit, and we were all happy." But "alas, it did not last."[1] On Sunday morning, 11 June, German forces launched a frontal assault on the village and the paratroopers of the 82nd and 101st Airborne Division. The paratroopers readily repelled the morning attack and fought back a second afternoon attack. US forces exhausted, however, their ammunition and could not withstand a third German attack that began in the evening and stretched into the early, dark hours of 12 June. At 5:30 a.m., the German Nazis reported that they had occupied Graignes. Death, destruction, and war crimes transpired in the village. D-Day has been popularly dubbed "the longest day" for Allied forces.[2] For the people of Graignes and their liberators, 11–12 June 1944 proved another very long and tragic day.

The First Battles

Sunday, 11 June 1944 started as a promising day. In the words of Madame S. Pezerin, "Sunday, the eleventh of June, dawns a radiant, glorious day." It was the feast of the Blessed Sacrament, "and the church bells are ringing out, muffling the distant noise of the cannon."[3] The beloved *paras* of Graignes were also a bit more relaxed. Saturday had been tense, because of clashes with German patrols. On Saturday night, officers had constantly inspected the perimeter defenses, checking to ensure that men stayed alert. But according to Sgt. Major Robert Salewski, Saturday night and early Sunday morning had been very quiet with "no enemy activity."[4] Major Charles Johnston, the commanding officer, gave permission to the Roman Catholics to attend Sunday mass. About forty paratroopers attended, including Lt. Frank Naughton, Sgt. Benton Broussard, Sgt. John Hinchliff, T/5 Eddie Page, and Pvt. Patrick Sullivan.

Abbé Albert Le Blastier celebrated the sacrament of the mass. He was aided by his acolyte, Charles Le Barbanchon, a member of a religious order. Father Le Barbanchon had been a student of Abbé Le Blastier and had returned to Graignes to recuperate from a bout of tuberculosis. As related by Michel Folliot, who played trombone in a group with five other musicians and accompanied the choir, the religious service was unusually well attended by villagers. Folliot was surprised to see his brother-in-law in attendance. He was uncertain whether the large attendance was a result of curiosity about the paratroopers or devotion inspired by the danger that surrounded the parishioners. In any case, "the Mass was progressing as usual." Folliot noted that many of the US paratroopers took Holy Communion at the service.[5]

Odette and Marthe Rigault also attended the service. Sgt. Broussard had invited the sisters and had dispatched a soldier to accompany them to the church from Le Port St. Pierre. Gustave and Marthe Rigault stayed at home, with Gustave still recovering from his coronary incident. Sometime between 10:00 and 10:30 a.m., a woman, whom Odette described as a "fat, middle-aged woman" with "bosoms out to here," burst into the church. She apparently had been shopping in another village. She shouted: "Hurry! Hurry! The *Boches* are coming! The Germans! Save yourselves, the *Boches* are coming, the Germans are coming!"[6] The Catholic *paras* immediately deployed from the church. Sgt. Hinchliff and his sidekick, Pvt. Sullivan, sprinted to their machine-gun position some 200 meters down the hill. The ever-alert Captain David Brummitt was already in position. He had heard noise and sensed movement from the south, indicating that a substantial German force was moving toward Graignes. Brummitt readied US forces.[7]

In military terms, the uniformed defenders of Graignes essentially made up a company, with 15 officers and 149 enlisted personnel. But nine of the men were not combatants. Captain Loyal Bogart had been injured on D-Day, and Lt. Lowell Maxwell had become seriously ill. Battalion surgeon, Captain Abraham Sophian, and the five medics presumably did not carry weapons. All uniformed personnel were without combat experience, and only a handful of the troopers had been trained as infantrymen. Their "heavy" weapons consisted of two 81 mm mortars and five .30 caliber light machine guns. There were also Browning Automatic Rifles present. The paratroopers commanded the high ground, and, under Captain Brummitt's instruction, had pre-aimed their weapons at likely avenues of attack. The US forces also had support personnel. The two Spaniards, who may have once been slave laborers for the Germans, helped build fortifications. Young men of Graignes, like Joseph Folliot and Charles Gosselin, served as messengers and ammunition bearers. Gosselin may have carried a weapon. Women in the village, like Renée Meunier, continued to cook, braved fire, and delivered food and water to the troops. And "Madame Boursier redoubled her energies using all the foodstuffs that the village had to feed the troops."[8] Such interactions, in Naughton's words "had a calming effect" on the paratroopers.[9] Acting Mayor Alphonse Voydie directed his citizens and stayed in close communication with Major Johnston. According to Denise Boursier-Lereculey, there were other foreigners in Graignes – Russians, Mongolians, and "a Yugoslav translator from Cherbourg." Lt. Naughton confirmed that some German prisoners of war were in Graignes and helped dig foxholes. Naughton commented: "How they got there, I'll never know."[10] Whether they were, in fact, prisoners, or Eastern European troops who deserted from the Germans, or slave laborers who escaped Nazi control cannot be determined. Their fate is also unknown.

The identity of those enemy troops who launched the first attack on Sunday morning has not been definitively determined. The paratroopers who survived Graignes and began in the 1980s to provide accounts of their ordeal largely assumed that the 17th *Waffen-SS Panzergrenadier* Division "Götz von Berlichingen," carried out all three assaults. Numerous historical versions of the battle for Graignes followed that reasoning. But the recorded transmissions of the 17th *SS Panzergrenadier* Division demonstrate that it did not participate in the first attack. The 1st Battalion of the 37th Regiment of the 17th *SS*

Panzergrenadier Division carried out the second and third attacks. In the third attack, the artillery regiment of the 17th *SS Panzergrenadier* Division backed up the 1st Battalion. Astute analysts of the battle now think that the 439th *Ostbataillon*, which was made up of Ukrainian Cossacks, carried out the first attack. The *Ostbataillon* had been based in the village of Les Veys, which is about ten kilometers north of Graignes.[11] This unit may have also been involved in the skirmish with Lt. Naughton's demolition unit at the bridge at Le Port des Planqués on 9 June.

Whatever the identity of the enemy forces who attacked Graignes on Sunday morning, they did not perform well, employing dubious tactics. The paratroopers fired first, surprising the attackers. The battle lasted less than thirty minutes, with the attackers withdrawing. To the surprise and delight of the paratroopers, the enemy moved openly on the roads and lanes that approached Graignes. These were the very areas on which the machine gunners and mortar men had pre-positioned their aiming points. As Lt. Naughton remembered, "the enemy attack was certainly no surprise, and it was badly organized, resulting in what had to be a piecemeal effort that lacked coordination." The attackers "hadn't been very smart," for they "exposed themselves unnecessarily by failing to use covered approaches." Sgt. Hinchliff described the attacking infantry as using "human wave" tactics. Hinchliff added: "it was just wholesale slaughter." Pvt. Marion Hatton recalled that the mortar platoon was "knocking the hell" out of the enemy, with Lt. Elmer Farnham precisely guiding the direction and distance of the mortar rounds from his observation post in the belfry.[12] In their first combat experience, the paratroopers of the 82nd and 101st Airborne Divisions had seemingly replicated the overwhelming victory of the British at the Battle of Agincourt (1415) and immortalized in William Shakespeare's play *Henry V* (1599) and in Henry's St. Crispin's Day speech on "we few, we happy few, we band of brothers." The machine guns, mortars, rifles, and carbines had proven as effective as the medieval longbows. The British suffered only a handful of casualties at Agincourt, whereas the French allegedly suffered thousands of dead and wounded. In their first battle, the paratroopers seemed to have sustained no casualties and inflicted heavy casualties on the enemy.

As the Sunday morning battle erupted, the parishioners took shelter in the nave of the church. Once the first battle ended, Major

Johnston advised Father Le Blastier and the parishioners to continue to seek safety in the church. Most would stay until the early evening. Father Le Blastier preached about the prophesies of Our Lady of Fátima, the Catholic belief that the Virgin Mary had appeared to three shepherd children in the village of Fátima, Portugal in 1917. According to the Portuguese children, the Virgin Mary predicted a future war more terrible than World War I, if people did not stop offending God. Parishioners also said the rosary together.[13] A few people left the church but were immediately dragooned by the enemy into loading the dead and wounded soldiers into carts. Sgt. Major Salewski took advantage of the lull to go out at 11:00 a.m. and "investigate [the] body of [a] dead German cyclist." The dead man had no identification on him.[14] Captain Brummitt, at Major Johnston's direction, surveyed US forces, and tightened and strengthened the defense perimeter.

The second attack commenced at about 2:00 p.m. But, starting at 12:30 p.m. and thereafter, the paratroopers took note of increasing enemy activity. One US outpost (OP3) toward the east attacked a German amphibious jeep (*Volkswagen Schwimmwagen*) and killed one man and wounded two others. A German reconnaissance car had followed the *Schwimmwagen*. The paratroopers spotted enemy mortars. From the church belfry, the paratroopers sighted twelve trucks carrying infantry moving toward Graignes from the south. The trucks disappeared but were subsequently sighted empty. In Sgt. Major Salewski's judgment, the trucks had "detrucked" the infantry. The second attack began in a more traditional fashion, with the Germans using "preparatory fire" before initiating a ground attack. They fired mortar rounds at the US positions. The US mortar men immediately responded and knocked out a German mortar position. Mortar men – Durward Biggerstaff, Stephen E. Liberty, and Rene E. Rabe – likely took out the German mortar position. The three received battlefield promotions to non-commissioned officer ranks immediately after they reached safety and the 82nd Airborne Division headquarters on 16 June 1944.[15]

German troops from the 1st Battalion of the 37th Regiment of the 17th *SS Panzergrenadier* Division participated in the afternoon attack. They had been ordered to move to Graignes at 9:30 a.m. by the division commander, Werner Ostendorff. Two of the battalion's three companies engaged the paratroopers on Sunday afternoon. Such a force would have constituted about 500 to 600 *Panzergrenadiers*. The Germans initially reported to division headquarters that they had encountered a "weak" enemy that numbered sixty "American para-trooper fighters." These initial reports gave confidence to the German commanders that the battle for Graignes would be short-lived and that they could rapidly redeploy the 1st Battalion for an attack on Carentan on 12 June. Later transmissions to division headquarters were more pessimistic. Officers in the 1st Battalion conceded that US paratroopers had "repulsed" the afternoon attack. They further reported that the enemy numbers were at company-level strength. German *Panzergrenadier* companies had 200 to 300 soldiers. They also believed that the paratroopers had one or two mortars and ten to twelve machine guns.[16]

The tenacious resistance displayed by the paratroopers to this second attack on Sunday afternoon probably caused the Germans to exaggerate US strength in Graignes. John Hinchliff characterized his experience as "a machine gunner's dream." A machine gunner normally fired his weapon in short bursts to keep the barrel from overheating. But, given the situation of the frontal assault, "you simply had no choice but to squeeze the trigger and keep up a continuous burst."[17] German bodies piled up near Hinchliff and Pvt. Sullivan's position. The infantry tactics of the *Panzergrenadiers* of the 1st battalion were as suspect as those of the troops who attacked in the morning. Norman Costa, son of Sgt. Frank Costa, told of his conversations with veterans of Graignes. They informed him that "the Germans had to be green troops. They were inexperienced. They stood up and marched right at us, and we slaughtered them with our mortars and machine guns."[18] Like the paratroopers, the enlisted men who made up the bulk of the *Panzergrenadiers* had no combat experience. But, unlike the paratroopers, they had only a few months of military training, and a large proportion of them were teenagers, as young as sixteen and seventeen years of age. The *SS* men, who had about a four-to-one numerical advantage during the second attack, came close to breaching the US defense perimeter. But the US lines held, with Captain Brummitt reorganizing defense positions. Two US outposts were pulled back 200 yards closer to the village. Sgt. Major Salewski recorded in his diary that "enemy activity ceased about 1900" (7:00 p.m.).[19]

Although they had successfully defended the citizens of Graignes for a second time, the paratroopers had two pressing problems by the evening of 11 June. They had begun to take casualties, and they were running low on ammunition. Odette Rigault was "shocked" when she peered through a keyhole in the church door and saw a fighting paratrooper fall dead.[20] Father Le Blastier permitted the paratroopers to set up an aid station in the church sacristy. Medics brought the wounded into the church. Father Le Blastier and Father Le Barbanchon assisted Captain Sophian and his medical team. Also present in the sacristy were Eugénie Dujardin and Madeleine Pezeril, two women who served Father Le Blastier and tended to the church rectory. The Nazis would subsequently murder the two religious men and the two housekeepers for aiding those who were hurt.

Major Johnston had decisions to make after the second battle. He ordered the redistribution of ammunition among his paratroopers. He advised parishioners who had sheltered in the church to take advantage of the lull in the fighting and escape to their homes. In Marthe Rigault's words, "at 7:00 p.m. Major Johnston told us that we should go home because they did not have enough ammunition for the night

Figure 6.1 Sergeant John Hinchliff of northern Minnesota led the machine-gun unit in Headquarters Company of the 3rd Battalion of the 507th Regiment. In retirement, he spoke openly and passionately about his many experiences as a paratrooper in World War II. Hinchliff passed in 2020 at the age of ninety-nine, the last survivor of the paratroopers who defended Graignes. US Army photograph.

and the night was coming." He further advised them, if they encountered Germans on the way home, not to inform them about the US position in Graignes. The three- to four-kilometer walk home became perilous for the two sisters. Paratroopers gave them advice on how to skirt mines that they had laid on the pathway back to Le Port St. Pierre. Marthe remembered that she had to jump or step between each "casserole." As they approached their home, they also met Isidore Folliot, who was guiding a contingent of German troops. They were fleeing Carentan and the 101st Airborne. The Germans did not ask the sisters any questions. Folliot guided them away from Graignes. Odette and Marthe Rigault made it safely to their home and their parents at about 8:00 p.m.[21]

The paratroopers understood that they were in grave danger on Sunday evening. Sgt. Broussard assured the Rigault sisters that he would come back to see them. Broussard also said good-bye to Madame Boursier and her two daughters. He remarked that "the *Boches* are more numerous than ants." Major Johnston had instructed the Boursier family to close up their kitchen because of the danger. Broussard thought about finding civilian clothes, leaving Graignes, using his French-language skills, and finding US reinforcements, perhaps in Carentan. But, as Denise Boursier observed, "he was already too late." The Boursier women decided to leave their home and sleep at a place 100 meters away. On the way there, they saw a soldier hit by a bullet. Throughout the night, they heard the sounds of war – hissing bullets and the crash of artillery shells. The women huddled together in a corner of their shelter.[22]

In retrospect, Lt. Frank Naughton ventured that, after the second attack, "this may have been the time to leave." During the lull between the second and third attack, the officers took coffee in the café and reviewed their defense plan and the status of their ammunition. Captain Brummitt had a "good grasp" of the situation and probably thought they should initiate a withdrawal from Graignes. But he apparently did not argue the point, as he had on 6 June. The young woman who served the officers coffee was singing as she moved from table to table. Major Johnston turned to his officers and said: "I wish I could feel as good about all of this as she does." He ruled that they would stay and fight, despite the shortages of ammunition.[23] Johnston apparently did not dwell on the potential consequences of this fateful decision. But the major undoubtedly felt a deep responsibility to Mayor Voydie and his citizens. Paratroopers abjured the idea of retreat, especially when it meant abandoning civilians who had already risked everything to save American lives.

The Final Battle

What took place between about 8:00 p.m. on Sunday, 11 June and the early morning hours of Monday, 12 June cannot be definitely established. The general outlines are clear, but there are contradictory accounts. Writing fifty-five years after the dramatic events at Graignes, Captain Brummitt made the unassailable argument that "I recognize that others may differ in some of the details, but I hasten to note that the accounts of many battle situations vary, depending on the vantage point and perspective of the individual concerned."[24] Brummitt's perception echoed the points made by analysts from a variety of professions. Military historians and war novelists often refer to the "fog of war." Prussian military analyst Carl von Clausewitz first coined the term in his tome *Vom Kriege (On War)* (1832, first English translation 1873). Combat soldiers, under extreme stress, operate in the twilight, in a realm of uncertainty. Modern life has been shaped by physicist Albert Einstein's theory of general relativity (1915) and the commonsense application that one's measurement of reality is based on one's position in time and space. In the artistic world, the Japanese film director Akira Kurosawa, in his classic *Rashōmon* (1950), depicted eye-witness characters providing subjective and self-serving versions of the same incidents – a murder and a rape. Some "I was there" accounts of events in Graignes differed, and those differences may have reflected the needs of the participants to explain dramatic, even traumatic, incidents to themselves.

The events of Sunday evening and early Sunday morning largely took place in the darkness. The lull in the fighting lasted only one hour. In his diary, Robert Salewski recorded that enemy activity "started up again with renewed vigor about 2000" (8:00 p.m.). Since the summer solstice approached in Normandy, there would have been another ninety minutes or so of limited visibility before night set in. "Renewed vigor" meant mortar attacks from the south and east. The paratroopers responded by drawing their outposts and their defense perimeter or "main line of resistance" closer to Graignes. The sergeant major's last notation about the actual battle reported "they seem to be throwing at us everything but the kitchen sink" and that a trooper from the 101st and one from the 82nd Airborne Division had been hit.[25]

The 17th *SS Panzergrenadier* Division had finally decided to take the paratroopers seriously. Commanders deployed the entire 1st Battalion, more than 900 men, for the assault against what had been initially characterized as a "weak enemy." This gave the German unit about a six-to-one manpower advantage. "Everything but the kitchen sink" meant that the Nazis were deploying big guns, by reinforcing the 1st Battalion of the 37th Regiment with the artillery regiment commanded by *SS-Sturmbannführer* Otto Binge, a veteran of a World War I artillery unit. The defenders of Graignes could hear rumblings of military equipment in the distance. The paratroopers in the church belfry could also observe the movement of heavy equipment. The big guns were placed on a hill at a farm in the hamlet of Thieuville, a few kilometers south of Graignes and beyond the range of Headquarters Company's two 81 mm mortars. Lt. Earcle Reed, peering through binoculars, believed that the Germans were setting up two 88 mm guns.[26] But it also may have been that the Germans had placed 105 mm howitzers, which were part of the artillery regiment's arsenal.[27] In any case, the defenders of Graignes had no response to or defense against a long-range artillery bombardment.

An obvious target for the *SS* gunners was the church belfry, from where Lt. Elmer Farnham, the leader of the mortar platoon, had guided the precise mortar attacks of the first two battles. Alarmed by what he had seen through his binoculars, Lt. Reed went up to the belfry "to coax Farnham and another observer to abandon their position because of imminent enemy artillery fire." Lt. Farnham, characterized by mortar man Marion Hatton as "the bravest man I ever knew," rejected Reed's advice. Lt. Reed looked up and saw a shell obliterate the belfry, killing Farnham and the aide. The aide may have been Pvt. Arnold Martinez of the mortar platoon, who had catastrophic wounds.[28] Lt. Frank Naughton remembered that "I was on the phone with him [Farnham] and the phone went dead when the shell hit." As late as 2004, Naughton was still expressing a sense of deep loss about Lt. Farnham's death.[29] Later in the night, artillery shells demolished the boys' school, which was the command post for the paratroopers. The ill Lt. Maxwell was killed, and Major Johnston and the injured Captain Bogart were buried in the rubble. Some paratroopers apparently believed that their commander had been killed.[30] The artillery bombardment and the "infernal and unforgettable sounds" terrified the civilians. Madame Pezerin testified that "while four of us were hiding

Figure 6.2 This photograph demonstrates the extensive damage that German artillery bombardment inflicted on the twelfth-century Romanesque Catholic Church in Graignes. Photograph courtesy of the Mayor's Office of Graignes.

under the table in the kitchen on the first floor, the school is hit in several places."[31]

The high explosives from the artillery shells were also killing individual soldiers. The two paratroopers from Louisiana, Benton Broussard and Sgt. George S. Baragona, died from the blasts. Broussard was very near the church when hit.[32] Thomas Travers of New York City and two others near him died from an artillery explosion. The parents of Pvt. Travers were informed of the circumstances of their son's death in a letter to them from Pfc. Charles Hammer of Headquarters Company. Hammer gave information that had been told to him by another paratrooper. Hammer was severely wounded at the Battle of the Bulge and spent three months in a military hospital. He composed the letter, which was dated 25 February 1945, while on board ship heading home and mailed it from the United States. Military censors would not have permitted Hammer to speak about casualties.[33] John Hinchliff noticed, while withdrawing from Graignes, that one of the 81 mm mortars was destroyed.[34] Along with Lt. Farnham and Pvt. Martinez, Cpl. Marvin H. Allen, Pfc. Lacy H. Reaves, and Pvt. Jesse J. Rushing were three other mortar men who died at Graignes. Villagers apparently escaped death from the artillery barrage, although Denise Boursier remembered that shrapnel wounded some civilians.[35]

Despite the barrage, the paratroopers of the 82nd and 101st Divisions held off the numerically superior *Panzergrenadiers* for several hours on Sunday evening. Lt. Naughton recalled the German attackers armed with machine-pistols or *Schmeissers* shooting indiscriminately in the night as they began to breach the ever-tightening US perimeter.[36] Paratroopers hid behind cemetery stones and fired back, or they crouched deep in their foxholes, let a wave of *SS* men pass, and then fired at them from behind. Lt. Reed witnessed one of his machine-gun teams catch a platoon of the enemy in the open and cut them down.[37] On the other hand, Sgt. Eddie Barnes, who was in a foxhole in the cemetery, saw Lt. Thomas Ahmad, a glider pilot, take a bullet to his head from a sniper.[38] The lack of ammunition ultimately made resistance futile. T/5 Eddie Page recounted the story of a machine gunner on a roof who expended his ammunition and "started to pull slate off the roof and throw it at them."[39] Sgt. John Hinchliff noted that he started Sunday morning with stacks of machine-gun ammunition, commenting that "you'd have thought we had enough ammunition to last for a week." By the end of Sunday evening, Hinchliff and Patrick Sullivan had a box and a half, about 250 rounds, left. Hinchliff added: "This would last you about five minutes in heavy combat."[40] The mortar men were no longer as effective without Lt. Farnham's guidance. As the enemy approached the cemetery, they raised their tubes to an angle nearing 90 degrees and fired away. At about 11:00 p.m., the Rigault family in Le Port St. Pierre saw red flares bursting in the sky over the village. Gustave Rigault, a veteran of World War I, knew that red flares signified distress and impending defeat.[41] The outnumbered paratroopers, without ammunition, had been overwhelmed by the 1st Battalion of the 37th Regiment of the 17th *SS Panzergrenadier* Division. As Mayor Voydie summarized, "our paratroopers defend themselves heroically,

[but] it's an unequal fight. They put out of action many opponents but must give in lieu of the number."[42]

"Out of ammunition for all practical purposes," in Lt. Naughton's words, the paratroopers withdrew from Graignes at the end of Sunday and the first hours of Monday. Some acted of their own volition. With the Germans "swarming in," Naughton led the men he was commanding, about twenty-three soldiers, northward, while simultaneously trying to circumvent the swamps.[43] Hinchliff and Sullivan, who did not see the red flares, decided "we better get the hell out of here." In his haste, Pvt. Sullivan forgot to take the remaining boxes of ammunition, forcing Hinchliff to run back up the hill to retrieve them.[44] Many of the mortar men apparently made individual and small group decisions to abandon Graignes. According to Captain Brummitt, Sgt. Major Salewski informed him that "Major Johnston gave the order to abandon the position and attempt to return individually to friendly lines." Brummitt recalled that Salewski told him that Johnston "and others in the command post have gone." Brummitt checked the command post and found that report to be accurate, although he later found out that Major Johnston "had been killed during the move." Here, the dilemmas of the "fog of war" seem especially evident, for Brummitt's account varies from other reports that Major Johnston was buried alive in the rubble of the boys' school. In any case, Brummitt issued the order to Salewski and Lt. Harry E. Wagner "to round up all the people you can find and follow me." The captain decided to follow the march-plan to withdraw from Graignes that he had devised on D-Day and which had been rejected by Major Johnston.[45] Brummitt's order reached some of the paratroopers. Pvt. Harvey Richig remembered that "we were told by our officers to disassemble our crew-served weapons, pair off, and try to make it to Carentan or Sainte Mère Église as best we could."[46] Salewski recorded in his diary that they walked until just past midnight and "ended up in a section of hedgerows bordering the swamps." When daylight broke on Monday, 12 June, Brummitt's group encountered groups led by Lt. Naughton and Lt. Reed. Naughton's group included Captain Richard H. Chapman. By mutual agreement, Brummitt assumed command of the combined groups, which he calculated to include eighty-seven paratroopers and the two friendly Spanish citizens.[47]

In the process of withdrawal, the paratroopers faced several harrowing combat clashes. Captain Brummitt witnessed two machine

Figure 6.3 Sgt. Fredric Boyle (right) is pictured here with S/Sgt. Rene E. Rabe in the Rhineland area in the closing days of World War II. Beyond the campaign in Normandy, Boyle participated in the Battle of the Bulge, the jump over the Rhine River, and the occupation of Berlin. In civilian life, Dr. Boyle worked as a chiropractor and served as mayor of Keosauqua, Iowa. Rene Rabe photograph.

gunners and two other troopers being killed by small-arms fire. Brummitt discarded his carbine, scooped up the machine gun (minus the damaged tripod), leapt over a wall, and silenced the enemy with bursts from the machine gun.[48] Sgt. Hinchliff, who had left his machine gun and carbine with Pfc. Sullivan, had to make a mad, zig-zag dash down the hill when a German, armed with a *Schmeisser*, spotted him retrieving the machine-gun ammunition. Hinchliff remembered that "bullets were flying all around me" and that he expected to be hit. To Hinchliff's dismay and anger, Sullivan had not stayed in his position, but had left Hinchliff's carbine there. As he tried to follow Sullivan's path, Hinchliff encountered two Germans about to bayonet S/Sgt. Charles W. Penchard, who had run out of ammunition. Hinchliff shot the Germans. He subsequently found Sullivan and "chewed him out" for leaving his post.[49] Mortar man Fred Boyle also had to skirt Germans. Boyle related to his son, Jonathan J. Boyle, that for a time he played dead and that a German soldier walked over his hand. He told historian William B. Breuer that "there were Krauts swarming all over the place, but in the darkness and confusion, my comrade and I slipped out of Graignes and promptly bumbled into a column of parked trucks, and heard the Germans standing beside them talking." Boyle and his buddy moved away and scrambled over a hedgerow, but then encountered a dark figure with a "coal-bucket helmet," who yelled "Halt!" Boyle concluded: "My comrade pumped his last three bullets into the German's belly."[50]

War Crimes

By the time Sunday turned into Monday, 12 June, the majority of the paratroopers who had survived the three battles had withdrawn from Graignes. They had not been able to preserve the liberation of Graignes. They had, however, inflicted a terrible toll on the morning's attackers, presumably the 439th *Ostbataillon*, and then the *Panzergrenadiers* of the 1st Battalion of the 37th Regiment of the 17th *SS Panzergrenadier* Division. Estimates of casualties of men in German uniforms vary widely, from 50 to 1,200. Lt. Frank Naughton noted that the "great" machine gunners, who were well protected behind earth berms and had excellent fields of fire, poured virtually every round into the advancing enemy. Because of the darkness, Naughton could not count casualties, but he thought the paratroopers had inflicted 500–600 casualties. Later, in 1998, he added that "we found that their losses had been far greater."[51] Dominique François, the astute Norman historian of the 507th Regiment and the author of *La bataille de Graignes*, settled on a figure of about 500 enemy casualties.[52] The German occupiers certainly kept villagers busy in the aftermath of the three battles, forcing civilians to retrieve their dead. In determining the casualty numbers, no help will be found in the works of the chroniclers of the 17th *SS Panzergrenadier*

Division – Massimiliano Afiero, Antonio J. Munoz, or Hans Stöber. All three produced useful, detailed books. But they declined to mention, much less analyze, the battles of the 1st Battalion of the 37th Regiment on 11 June 1944. To do so would undermine their central premise that the 17th *SS Panzergrenadier* Division did not engage in war crimes and that its soldiers had no knowledge that other *SS* units engaged in crimes against humanity. Instead, these authors argue that the *SS* men fought bravely, suffered greatly, and ultimately were defeated in battle to the point of annihilation.[53]

More confidence can be attached to an analysis of the deaths of the defenders of Graignes. Over the past eight decades, the villagers, US veterans, and the French and US governments have memorialized what happened in the village in the first two weeks of June 1944. Over time, the memorials have been updated, refined, and corrected. In 2021, the Memorial Wall, which stands next to the preserved bell arch of the Romanesque church, lists the names of fifty men who perished trying to liberate Graignes. The list includes thirty-five members of the 82nd Airborne, twelve members of the 101st Airborne, Lt. Thomas Ahmad and Pfc. George Brown from the glider plane, and the Australian, Flight Sgt. Stanley K. Black. What happened to the two unidentified soldiers from the 29th Infantry Division has never been determined. Of the fifty deceased uniformed personnel, five members of the 82nd Airborne perished on D-Day, presumably from drowning or anti-aircraft fire. This included one medic. Regarding the other forty-five dead, three key findings can be established. Twelve of the nineteen members of the 101st Airborne Division died in or near Graignes. In addition, eight of the nine medical personnel – Battalion Surgeon Abraham Sophian and the medics – died in or near Graignes. Finally, Graves Registration, the military unit responsible for finding and identifying dead soldiers, found forty-nine bodies in and around Graignes in 1944–1945. S/Sgt. Nelson F. Hornbaker, a medic and a married man, is listed on Line 22, Tablet 20, in the Garden of the Missing at the American Cemetery in Colleville-sur-Mer, Normandy.

On the morning of 11 June, 164 uniformed men defended Graignes. Villagers have testified in various forums that the *SS* executed US paratroopers, who were either wounded or captured. Most accounts settle on the figure of nineteen Americans being murdered. By the conclusion of the three battles, German forces had killed in combat only twenty-six paratroopers and soldiers or perhaps twenty-eight men, if the two 29th Infantry Division men also were killed. If the defenders of Graignes inflicted 500 casualties on those in German uniforms they had exacted a toll of Battle of Agincourt-like proportions. The artillery bombardment notwithstanding, paratroopers have affirmed that they remained confident and would not have withdrawn, if their ammunition had not run out. The vast disparity in casualties seems to support that claim.

The high number of US medical personnel who died at Graignes points to how the *SS* committed war crimes. There are French eyewitnesses and evidence from US and German sources. Wounded US soldiers were brought to the sacristy of the church. Captain Sophian was in charge and was presumably assisted by some of the medics. Also present were the two French clerics and their two housekeepers. The transmissions in the German military *Tagebuch* inform that the 1st Battalion reported that combat had ceased by 23:30 hours on Sunday evening. This corelates with the US evidence that the paratroopers were firing their red flares and withdrawing as midnight approached. Thereafter, until 5:30 a.m., the Germans were involved in what they called "cleaning up," and subsequently reported that the 1st Battalion would not be ready to leave Graignes until 7:30 a.m. This gave the Nazis of the 1st Battalion several hours to engage in wholesale murder.[54]

Captain Sophian and most of the medics did not withdraw from Graignes. Whether they decided to stay with the wounded or whether they never received a withdrawal order can probably never be established. Captain Brummitt has written that he only discovered on Monday, 12 June, that Sophian, the medics, and the wounded had not departed Graignes. He noted that "had I been aware of this situation, I would have made a specific move to bring them along." Brummitt ventured that Sophian and his team may have decided to stay with the wounded, expecting to be treated as prisoners of war.[55] It may have been that Sophian and his medics were unaware of the withdrawal order. As Brummitt pointed out, the aid station in the church was some distance from the command post in the boys' school. In truth, not everyone received the withdrawal order. Both Lt. Naughton and his group of twenty-three and Sgt. Hinchliff and Pfc. Sullivan decided to withdraw of their own volition, because they were out of ammunition. And Charles Buscek, Frank Costa, and Eddie Page, who were in their large foxhole down the hill from the village and facing northward toward the *marais*, were not informed that their comrades were

withdrawing. When dawn broke on Monday, 12 June, the three paratroopers were unaware that they were in imminent danger.

Captain Sophian's relatives wrote that in April 1945 US military
personnel came to the Sophian home in Kansas City, Missouri to inform
the family about the circumstances of the captain's death. They told the
Sophian family that Captain Sophian walked from the crumbling
church structure to the front entrance and waved a white flag.[56] If so,
the signal given by Sophian to the Germans was consistent with the steps
taken by other paratroopers with medical assignments in Normandy.
George Koskimaki, a paratrooper who jumped with the 101st Airborne
on D-Day, interviewed numerous non-combatant paratroopers – chaplains, doctors, and medics – about their experiences in Normandy.
Captains Felix Adams and Stanley Morgan, both doctors assigned to
the 101st Airborne, became prisoners of war. Both doctors worked with
German doctors and medics, aiding both wounded German troops and
US paratroopers. In another case, US medical personnel established an
aid station near St. Martin-de-Varreville. They put up a white flag and
cached the weapons of the wounded. These actions persuaded a German
patrol to pass by and not disturb the medics or the wounded. Germans
also asked US doctors and medics to tend to their wounded.[57] To be
sure, these accounts reflect the actions of the regular German army, the
Heer, and not the *Waffen-SS*.

The villagers were the only reliable witnesses to what happened
in Graignes, after the bulk of the US paratroopers withdrew on 11–
12 June. If the Sophian family accurately recalled what was told to them
in April 1945, then they were hearing what villagers had told the US
Army in the late summer of 1944 and thereafter. The villagers subsequently took notes and provided oral histories of the horrors they
witnessed. They also provided evidence in June 1947 to a US military
team that investigated the massacre. Once they entered the village, the
SS men of the 1st Battalion acted like a marauding horde, engaging in
gratuitous violence – pillaging, looting, and burning. Madame Pezerin
accused the Germans of ransacking houses and grocery stores and piling
the goods into a military truck. Pezerin added: "They make fun of us,
come over to break the necks of bottles in front of us while crying out
with joy, greedily swallowing the cake they find, and loading blankets,
dishes, even children's dolls and toys onto their vehicles."[58] They also
broke into stores of alcohol and became horribly drunk. Denise Boursier
recorded in her notes that "we were afraid that they would shoot us,

because they had consumed so much alcohol." Boursier was repelled by the sight of the SS, noting they had "really crazy and rough heads." An SS officer, who spoke good French, warned her about what was to happen. He asserted: "We killed the Americans. Besides, they are very bad boys. They have killed of us a thousand men." That is why, the officer swore, "we are going to take revenge."[59]

The SS had about nineteen US soldiers in their custody. Three of the men were badly wounded and probably could not stand. The SS executed them in the sacristy of the church. Boursier testified that the "bandits" shot one of the men in the leg "to make him scream," before finishing him off.[60] Five men were wounded but apparently could get on their feet. The SS also tortured them, plunging bayonets into the paratroopers, before murdering them. Pezerin saw one wounded paratrooper, whose arm was bleeding, forced to keep his hands behind his neck, while the drunk Germans taunted and yelled loudly, "Invasion! . . . Invasion!"[61] The Germans dumped the bodies of the five men in a small pond near Germaine Boursier's property. Some of the men may have still been alive. Odette and Marthe Rigault told of the common knowledge in the village that the dying paratroopers were "just clutching themselves in the bog."[62] Boursier's daughter, Denise, recorded that the Germans then "covered them with ammunition for the sole purpose of making them disappear, to hide their crimes." The Germans then "went back to load the dead in their trucks."[63]

Mayor Voydie told military investigators in 1947 that he went to the village on the morning of the 12 June and retrieved the bodies of the three men in the church and the five men in the pond and put them in a field. In Odette Rigault's words, the men in the pond "were found huddled together with knives in their backs." Voydie found two other bodies in a field. In an obvious attempt to intimidate the people of Graignes, the Germans ordered that the US dead should not be buried but be left to decompose above ground. Mayor Voydie and his constituents were finally given permission, about two weeks after the battle, to collect the battlefield casualties and the executed and bury them together.[64] Pauline Russ Baragona Cook (1923–2012), widow of Sgt. Baragona, stated that her husband's body was discovered in a common grave that contained twenty-four bodies.[65]

Not all of the paratroopers in German custody were wounded. Madame Pezerin referred to "able-bodied" captives.[66] These may have been some of the medics and men of the 101st Airborne. The paratroopers of the 101st were deployed to the flanks of the perimeter defense and may have been surrounded by the *Waffen-SS*. A different, but equally hideous fate, awaited nine men. Even in their drunken rage, it may have occurred to the *SS* men that they should not continue to murder people in front of French witnesses. The *SS* moved nine men to the village of Le Mesnil-Angot, about three kilometers south of Graignes. Mayor Jean Poullain told US investigators that he saw the Germans forcing the men into his village.[67] There, in a field west of the village church, the Germans ordered the nine prisoners to kneel and then shot them in the back of the head. The murderers stripped the paratroopers of their jump boots and then loosely covered them with dirt. Within days, a farmer, who was a teenager, spotted the stockinged feet of the men sticking up from the ground. Historian Mark Bando has identified Pfc. Richard J. Hoffman and Pfc. William H. Love, members of the 101st, as two of the victims. In 2004, the farmer who saw the bodies escorted Phil Hoffman, who was a child during World War II, to the spot where his brother was executed.[68] US Army personnel collected the bodies at Le Mesnil-Angot in July 1944 and moved the deceased men of the 82nd Airborne Division to a temporary cemetery at Blosville, which is near Sainte-Mère-Église. The 603rd Burial and Registration Command had developed the Blosville cemetery. Three medics – Jesus Casas, Edward J. Pillis, and Joseph Stachowiak – were buried near one another in the T section of the cemetery. It is possible that they died together at Le Mesnil-Angot.

Captain Sophian and Captain Loyal Bogart of the 101st Airborne Division died in a different place. Most accounts maintain that the two officers were separated from the enlisted men, moved to a German encampment at Tribehou, interrogated, and then executed. Their bodies were found in February 1945, off the side of the road (D-57) that connected Tribehou and Graignes.[69] Sophian's body was temporarily interred at the US cemetery in Marigny, which was south of Graignes and east of the city of Saint-Lô. Sophian's parents arranged to have their son's remains buried at Ft. Leavenworth, Kansas.[70] Captain Bogart's body lies at permanent rest in the Brittany American Cemetery. The part of the cemetery at Marigny that had US bodies was closed in the postwar period, and the remains of US personnel were transferred to the new Brittany American Cemetery. The Marigny cemetery still holds the remains of 11,000 German military personnel, including the remains of men who served in the 17th *SS Panzergrenadier* Division.

Figure 6.4 Pictured here is Pfc. Richard J. Hoffman (1921–1944) of B Company, 1st Battalion of the 501st Regiment of the 101st Airborne. Hoffman, who was from Indiana, was murdered by *Waffen-SS* troops. Photograph courtesy of the Mayor's Office of Graignes.

Determining how the commanding officer, Major Johnston, died is more problematic. Martin Morgan, the long-time analyst of the battles, initially thought Johnston died in the bombardment of the boys' school. Ten years later, he ventured that Johnston had been pulled alive from the rubble of the school by the enemy and had been executed with Bogart and Sophian.[71] Morgan discovered a document that complicated analyses. On 22 January 1946, Technical/Sgt. George E. Colli gave a statement to military investigators inquiring about the circumstances of Major Johnston's death. Colli claimed that he and another enlisted man accompanied Johnston, Lt. Lowell Maxwell, and one other officer and left Graignes in search of friendly forces. They headed westward looking for a bridge to cross what was presumably the Taute River, and encountered German guards at the bridge. Everyone sought cover in the surrounding *marais*. The guards shot both the unidentified officer and

Lt. Maxwell. Maxwell was hit in the stomach. According to Colli, the guards ordered Johnston and the enlisted man out of the water. Colli escaped by swimming underwater away from the Germans.[72] Colli's account may be plausible, but there are problems with it. Lt. Maxwell was buried in Blosville in the S section of the cemetery. His remains were buried near paratroopers, such as Pvt. Arnold Martinez and Pvt. Thomas Travers, who have been identified as dying from indirect fire and whose bodies were discovered in Graignes.[73] This tends to support accounts that the ill Maxwell died in the boys' school from the German artillery bombardment. In any case, Major Johnston's body, which was found on the road to Tribehou, was not located until after the war. He was temporarily buried in a new section of Blosville. His family brought his remains back to his native Tennessee.

The SS members of the 1st Battalion did not just commit war crimes against the paratroopers. The boast that "we are going to take revenge" was also directed at the people of Graignes. The Memorial Wall lists the names of thirty-two villagers who died in the defense of Graignes.[74] During the first hours of 12 June, the SS set up machine guns in Graignes. Villagers feared that mass executions would soon follow. The drunken SS men burst into various homes, ostensibly looking for hiding paratroopers. They trashed and looted homes and poked revolvers in the backs of citizens. The indomitable Madame Germaine Boursier challenged the brutes, asking "Why are you looting my house? I'm just a shopkeeper who makes a living."[75] During the tense early hours of 12 June, villagers witnessed awful scenes. Their beloved village had been smashed. In Madame Pezerin's words, the school presented "a sad sight with its broken windows, its hanging drainpipes, its holes in the roofs, and its windows enlarged due to missiles, their shutters torn away." Pezerin also saw on the steps to the cemetery "traces of blood, with an American helmet resting nearby."[76]

The men of the 1st Battalion perpetrated unspeakable evil in Graignes. Soldiers invaded the rectory. They riddled Father Le Blastier's body with bullets and shot Father Le Barbachon in the back of the head. As told by Madame Pezerin, the first villager to see the dead clerics found their bodies "covered with sticks, riddled with bullets, the skulls shattered." Le Blastier's face bore "the marks of great suffering." The murderers also stole the money and watches of their victims.[77] The SS men compounded their war crimes by murdering the rectory's terrified housekeepers – Eugénie Dujardin and Madeleine Pezeril – who sought

Figure 6.5 Abbé Albert Le Blastier (1881–1944) served as the parish priest of Graignes from 1931 until his murder by Nazi henchmen on 12 June 1944. Le Blastier had been a medic in the French Army during World War I. His remains are interred near the Memorial Wall in Graignes. Photograph courtesy of the Mayor's Office of Graignes.

safety in their bed. The SS men also rounded up forty-four villagers and tried to intimidate them into confessing to collaboration by threatening them with execution. No one broke. The Germans demanded to know the whereabouts of the mayor. The villagers responded with the casuistry that the mayor was dead. Acting Mayor Voydie had, however, gone into hiding. The SS did not shoot the villagers, but forced them into the day-long toil of collecting the dead bodies of their comrades.[78]

The village of Graignes would soon endure another criminal act. The 1st Battalion left the village on 12 June. Since the afternoon of 11 June, the battalion had been receiving orders from the commanders of the 17th *SS Panzergrenadier* Division to move to the village of Méautis, the staging area for an assault on Carentan. The march time was moved from 5:30 a.m. to 7:30 a.m. on 12 June. Division command thought it would take four hours to move from Graignes to Méautis, which is south and slightly west of Carentan. The complete 37th

Regiment did not, however, make it to Méautis until 4:00 p.m.[79] Perhaps the men of the 1st Battalion needed time to sleep off their drunken, murderous spree. In any case, the SS men did not initiate the torching of the village. Other German troops, perhaps part of the original occupation force in the region, moved into Graignes. Madame Odile Delacotte recalled that "German soldiers stayed in the village and inhabited the houses." She identified them as members of the *Wehrmacht*, with six soldiers staying in her residence.[80] These occupying troops decided to burn the bodies of the two dead priests. The fire raged out of control. Of the 200 structures in Graignes, only two escaped unscathed from either artillery bombardment or fire. Sixty-six homes, the church, the boys' school, and the café were destroyed.[81]

The murder of prisoners of war and non-combatants in Graignes by the SS men in the 1st Battalion met the legal definition of war crimes. The SS had violated the Geneva Convention Relative to the Treatment of Prisoners of War (1929) and various agreements on the treatment of non-combatants going back to the original Geneva Convention (1864). Germany was a signatory to such agreements. When interviewed in the 1990s, T/5 Eddie Page put the issue of legal and moral culpability starkly in explaining what the Nazis did to captive paratroopers and civilians at Graignes. "Just murdered them. Not war. Murder."[82]

Both general and specific causes can be offered in assessing why the officers and enlisted personnel of the 1st Battalion of the 37th Regiment of the 17th *SS Panzergrenadier* Division turned out to be not soldiers but murderers. Historian Steven P. Remy, who has dissected the Malmedy massacre of 17 December 1944, when eighty-four US prisoners of war were machine-gunned to death by members of the 1st *SS Panzer Division Leibstandarte SS Adolf Hitler*, has offered compelling insights. The massacre took place during the Battle of the Bulge in a snowy field near Malmedy, Belgium. *SS Obersturmbannführer* Joachim Peiper and seventy-three of his principal subordinates were subsequently found guilty of war crimes at trials held at Dachau in 1946. Forty-three of the defendants, including Peiper, received death sentences, although no executions were carried out. The massacre at Malmedy was only one of numerous atrocities during the Battle of the Bulge. The battle group led by Peiper (*Kampfgruppe Peiper*) murdered hundreds of US soldiers in December 1944. In Remy's assessment, these war crimes in the Ardennes Forest were consistent with other war crimes committed by *Waffen-SS* units in France before and after D-Day. On 1 April 1944, the 12th *SS Panzer* Division executed 86 French men near Lille and, between 7 and 12 June 1944, the same unit executed 155 Canadian soldiers in Normandy. On 9 June 1944, elements of the 2nd *SS Panzer* Division murdered 124 civilians in the village of Tulle, and, on the next day, soldiers of the same division slaughtered 642 people in Oradour-sur-Glane for alleged resistance activity.[83]

In Remy's judgment, the *Waffen-SS* perceived itself as "an instrument of terror war, a mode of warfare in which the boundaries between lawful combatants, prisoners of war, and civilians were erased and fear deployed as a weapon." The *Waffen-SS* was not just a normal military unit, as apologists would have it, that was separate and distinct from the *SS* units that butchered Jewish people in concentration camps. In Remy's words, "the *Waffen-SS* was an integral part of the *SS* and a principal weapon of its campaigns of conquest and terror." Führer Adolf Hitler ordered the *Waffen-SS* to be merciless and to spread fear and panic among enemy soldiers and civilians in Western Europe. As one German colonel explained, the *Waffen-SS* would bring their "Russian education" to the Western front.[84] These *SS* terror tactics were well understood by German soldiers who were members of the regular army, the *Heer*. German soldiers have testified that when they passed by the bodies of US paratroopers, who appeared to have been executed with shots to the back of the head, they immediately assumed that this was the work of the "*SS* boys" who had a "taste for such things."[85]

The 17th *SS Panzergrenadier* Division's history of committing war crimes was not limited to Graignes. Erwin Wilhelm Konrad Schienkiewitz, a senior non-commissioned officer in the Headquarters Company of the 38th *Panzergrenadiers*, was convicted on 4 April 1947 at a war crimes trial held at Dachau for overseeing the execution of two US soldiers. The execution took place on or about 17 June 1944 in Montmartin-en-Graignes, which is less than ten kilometers east of Graignes. Schienkiewitz, who had been captured by US forces in June 1944, was convicted and handed a sentence of life imprisonment based on the testimony of a German soldier, Gerhard Schild, who had deserted to the US side.[86] The 38th Regiment had also previously transmitted reports that suggested that it was perpetrating atrocities. At 20:15 hours, on 12 June 1944, the 38th Regiment reported that it had retaken Montmartin-en-Graignes. Included in the transmission was coded language suggestive of the infamous "*Nacht und Nebel*" ("Night and Fog") injunction. It was a transmission different from any other transmission recorded in the division's *Tagebuch*. The regiment reported "*In Aire[l] auf Brücke Nebel* " ("There is fog at the Airel Bridge").[87] Führer Adolf Hitler and Heinrich Himmler, the leader of the SS, used the term *Nacht und Nebel* when they wanted their perceived enemies disposed of, leaving no trace. Elements of the 17th SS *Panzergrenadier* Division perpetrated another atrocity on 25 August 1944, systematically killing 124 civilians in the village of Maillé in the Loire Valley. Forty-four of the French victims were under the age of twelve.[88] As happened in Graignes, SS officers plied their teenaged soldiers with alcohol and methamphetamines, such as Pervitin, to intensify their aggressive impulses.[89]

The story of Graignes during World War II did not end on 12 June 1944. The majority of the paratroopers who defended Graignes successfully withdrew from the village. But they had not reached safety. They would again need the help of the villagers of Graignes and French citizens in the surrounding region in order to rejoin their comrades in the 82nd and 101st Airborne Divisions. The people of Graignes would endure another trial, with the occupying German troops ordering them to abandon their homes and go into exile. The members of the 17th SS *Panzergrenadier* Division would meet a different fate, when they encountered heavily armed US troops in Normandy.

7 ESCAPE, EXILE, AND ANNIHILATION

The period from 12 June until the end of July 1944 proved a momentous time for the paratroopers of the 82nd and 101st Airborne Divisions, for the people of Graignes, and for the 17th *SS Panzergrenadier* Division. By 16 June 1944, a remarkable number of paratroopers who had defended Graignes had made it back safely to their respective division headquarters in Normandy. The men of the 82nd Airborne would continue to participate in the liberation of Normandy. Those who survived the additional three weeks of combat would not be transported back to their base in England until the middle of July. For the residents of war-torn Graignes, life would be pitiless and unrelentingly difficult. At the end of June, the German occupiers ordered them to leave their residences immediately. The people of Graignes and the surrounding countryside would be on the road for more than a month, seeking shelter and food and depending on the kindness of friends, relatives, and strangers. Some would be caught in the crossfires of war. A different fate awaited the *SS* men who had ravaged Graignes and perpetrated war crimes against US paratroopers and villagers. They would be subjected to Allied air attacks, naval gunfire, artillery bombardment, tank assaults, and infantry fire. By September, the 1st Battalion of the 37th Regiment, the group responsible for death and destruction in Graignes, was a military unit in name only.

The Great Escape

Approximately 110 out of the 164 uniformed personnel who defended Graignes on 11–12 June 1944 managed to elude the enemy and reach relative safety within a few days. Some men moved in groups and others traveled toward Carentan alone. And one paratrooper hid for more than a month and waited until US forces liberated the village in the middle of July. That so many US soldiers survived Graignes can be ascribed to outstanding leadership, the skill and dedication of the paratroopers, the bravery of the Norman citizens, and the inept and distracted military performance of the enemy. The paratroopers who stayed alive subsequently contributed to Allied victory, participating in combat in Normandy, the Battle of the Bulge, the jump over the Rhine River in March 1945, and the postwar occupation of the German capital, Berlin.

Captain David Brummitt led the largest group to Carentan. Brummitt would garner the Silver Star for his leadership from his superior officers in the 82nd Airborne Division. Sgt. Major Robert Salewski had relayed to him late on the night of 11 June that "Major [Charles] Johnston gave the order to abandon the position and attempt to return individually to friendly lines." The captain confirmed the order and further concluded that Major Johnston had been killed. There was a lull in the fighting in the last hours of 11 June. Brummitt saw an opportunity for a decision. Without ammunition, Brummitt surmised that "our chances of survival would be slim if we continued to defend the position." He ordered Salewski and Lt. Harry Wagner, the S-1 or administrative officer of the battalion, to round up people and head for the pre-arranged assembly point. The captain's idea was to implement the withdrawal plan he proposed to Major Johnston on 6 June.[1] The paratroopers would move into the *marais* and try to reach the 101st Airborne Division, which was battling for control of Carentan. Via a direct route, Carentan was about ten kilometers away from Graignes.

From the assembly area, Brummitt led a group that was initially about fifty to sixty individuals. This included the two French-speaking Spanish citizens who aided the paratroopers. Moving northward, the group walked until just past midnight and ended up in a section of hedgerows bordering the wet areas. At 4:30 a.m., the resting group arose and moved a couple of hundred yards to a new position amidst the hedgerows, because, in Salewski's words, "of being observed in our first location."[2] There were numerous German troops and *Ostbataillone* in the area who were fleeing the battlefield in Carentan. The best course of action would be to rest during the day and move at night. The two Spaniards were dispatched to find food from countryside homes, and they returned with some bean soup and milk. They were given French francs to pay for the food. The francs had been supplied to the paratroopers in England before D-Day. Also bringing milk and cider to the paratroopers was "our French friend Joe." This was almost certainly Joseph Folliot. Folliot also secured two flat boats for the paratroopers to cross deep, wide streams. During the day, the paratroopers cleaned weapons and redistributed scarce ammunition. Beyond rifles, carbines, and pistols, the paratroopers carried two machine guns and a Browning Automatic Rifle that one of the men from the 29th Infantry had carried to Graignes. The Brummitt group also received reports from friendly French country folk of more enemy movements in the area.[3]

Before resuming their journey on Monday, 12 June at 11:30 p.m., the Brummitt group encountered other, smaller groups led by Lt. Earcle Reed and Lt. George Murn and a larger group led by Lt. Frank Naughton. Paratroopers withdrawing from Graignes had a tactical advantage that aided their escape. As Madame S. Pezerin pointed out, "they had been living in the commune for a week and became familiar with all the little paths."[4] Lt. Naughton chose, however, a wet route, leading twenty-three men through the *marais*. Most of the time, they were moving through manageable depths of water. But they had to cross five or six drainage ditches that were deep. As Naughton remembered, the paratroopers "devised a system to help each other across the drainage ditches." Lt. Naughton crossed first, with S/Sgt. Edward A. Cannon, a native of Canada, bringing up the rear. By daybreak of Monday, 12 June, they were two miles behind the town and near Le Port St. Pierre. A lead scout met a girl, presumably Odette Rigault, who led the paratroopers to a hayloft in a barn. There they rested, intending to head for Carentan when dusk arrived. Lt. Naughton almost accidentally shot Gustave Rigault, when he opened the barn door. Naughton, who had not met the family patriarch, instantly trusted him. Rigault offered water, milk, cheese, and bread to the men. Naughton's group spotted a man moving in the bushes, who turned out to be a scout for the Brummitt group.[5]

Captain Brummitt now counted eighty-seven paratroopers and the two Spaniards in his group, and possibly one French citizen. They moved out at about 11:30 p.m. on Monday night, 12 June, using the flat boats to ferry themselves across large streams, the drainage ditches, and ultimately the canals that led to Carentan. Captain Brummitt took the "point" or lead position, because the paratrooper that he had commanded to lead the group became confused using the compass.[6] Sgt. John Hinchliff related that the most exciting incident of the journey occurred when a bull charged, and Captain Brummitt shot it.[7] The paratroopers reached their objective on Tuesday, 13 June, when they spotted a reconnaissance unit of the 2nd Armored Division. This was fortuitous. The 2nd Armored Division had been dispatched to Carentan that day to support the 101st Airborne's defense of Carentan from the attacking 17th *SS Panzergrenadier* Division. While the men rested, French civilians came around with milk, boiled gourds, and butter. The Spaniards again successfully "cooked up a deal" for stew, gourds, and butter. The men of the 2nd Armored shared their rations. Fifty-nine years after the event, Sgt. Hinchliff could still recall how hungry he was that day.[8] Accompanied by Lt. Murn and the men from the 101st Airborne in the group, Captain Brummitt made his way to the command post of the 101st in Carentan. He requested safe passage for the two Spaniards. He called the headquarters of the 82nd in Sainte-Mère-Église and soon trucks were dispatched to bring about eighty men from Headquarters Company back to the 3rd Battalion of the 507th Regiment. Brummitt reported directly to General Matthew Ridgway, the commanding officer of the 82nd, and to Lt. Colonel Arthur Maloney, the acting commander of the 507th Regiment. Not a man had been lost during the perilous journey. Naughton, a career military officer who served throughout World War II and in Korea and Vietnam and rose to the rank of colonel, concluded that "the battle of Graignes, the departure after the battle, and the link-up and the subsequent move through the swamps and overland will stand out in my mind as one of the most disciplined operations I have ever been witness to or associated with."[9]

The next largest group to make it back to Carentan hid in the Rigault barn for several days. Some paratroopers withdrew from Graignes in small groups of two to four men, whereas others left on their own. The mortar men who operated the two 81 mm mortars, like Fredric Boyle, Arthur "Rip" Granlund, Marion Hatton, Carlos Hurtado, and Rene Rabe, seemed to have moved out together and were among those who spent three days hiding in the Rigault barn. Beyond having knowledge of local paths, these men had the experience of having landed near the Rigault farm at Le Port St. Pierre on D-Day.

Marthe Rigault thought that 100 paratroopers had been in the house-hold yard on D-Day. The paratroopers who found safety in the barn probably spent Monday, 12 June, hiding in the hedgerows and bushes near the *marais*.

Odette and Marthe Rigault, backed by their worried but indom-itable parents, saved the lives of twenty-one paratroopers. The twelve-year-old Marthe encountered a "tall" paratrooper without a helmet or weapons who requested that he be escorted to the barn. Marthe went to the nearby home of her grandfather, seeking advice. Her grandfather rejected the idea of helping the beleaguered paratrooper, saying: "We will all be shot." Her grandfather had previously told a paratrooper that he could not help him for fear of retaliation. Nevertheless, Marthe disobeyed and brought the man to the barn. When he entered, he found four other paratroopers. Marthe's sister, Odette, had been busy rounding up the defenders of Graignes. When the number in the barn reached ten paratroopers, the sisters decided to inform their parents of what they had done. They feared upsetting their father because of his recent coronary incident. But Gustave Rigault saw two paratroopers emerging from the *marais*.[10] The occupancy rate in the barn grew.

The last three paratroopers to make it to the barn were Charlie Buscek, Frank Costa, and Eddie Page. They had been guarding the village in the six × six × six-foot foxhole down the hill from Graignes and facing north and toward the *marais*. They were aware of the battle behind them, but stayed at their post, when relative calm ensued in the dark hours of 12 June. Frank Costa, who was on watch, clambered out of the foxhole at daylight, and took a deep stretch to squeeze out the sleep and tiredness. He noticed three Germans digging a foxhole. He awoke his colleagues and simultaneously hushed them.[11] Eddie Page investigated by walking along a hedgerow toward town. He saw two soldiers behind a US machine gun and was going to walk up to them. He noticed, however, a third soldier who appeared to be eating a US "K-ration." When the man turned, he could see that he was wearing German gear on his back. In Page's words, "I ran like a son of a bitch" back to the foxhole. The three paratroopers debated what to do but apparently spent much of 12 June in their foxhole. When they moved out, they encountered a farmer who led them to one house, where they received advice and a bit of food from a farm couple, and then were led to the Rigault barn. Jean Rigault, a teenaged cousin of Odette and Marthe, aided in leading the men to the barn.[12]

Figure 7.1 This is the Rigault family barn as it appeared in 2019. The barn was approximately fourteen feet wide and thirty-six feet in length. The loft had a clearance of five to six feet. Author's photograph.

What happened in and near the barn over the next couple of days was filled with more tension than an Alfred Hitchcock movie. The family tried to feed their guests with what little they had. Fearing observation, one of the girls would act like she was doing farm chores and bring a container of food inside the barn. She would cough, as a signal, and one of the famished paratroopers would climb down from the loft and retrieve the food. S/Sgt. Rabe would forever proclaim that his portion of boiled cabbage with melting butter was the best meal of his life.[13] The paratroopers ran out of cigarettes. Frank Costa, a non-smoker, recalled the last shared cigarette. "It was just like the movies only real. It was sad and at the same time funny to see eleven men taking a deep drag, holding the smoke in their mouths, reluctant to let it out. It was like taking their last breath, hanging on for dear life."[14] The nicotine-deprived men had a near encounter with the German occupiers. Two of the enemy, searching for US soldiers, walked into the barn but did not climb into the hayloft. The paratroopers trained their rifles on the intruders. Eddie Page pulled the pin on a hand grenade. After a cursory search, the two Germans walked out of the barn. As Page later remarked, "it's a good thing that the Krauts goldbrick sometimes;

Figure 7.2 T/5 Edward "Eddie" Page served in Normandy, then at the Battle of the Bulge, participated in the jump over the Rhine River, and volunteered for occupation duty in Berlin. Page was wounded three times, including being shot in the chest. Photograph courtesy of his daughter, Cheryl Page.

just like we do." One of his buddies had to help the shaken Page put the pin back into the spoon of the grenade.[15]

An outbreak of violence in the barn would have been catastrophic for the Rigault family. The Germans would have killed them for being collaborators. The shrewd Madame Marthe Rigault, the family matriarch, averted another potential disaster. A unit of thirty German soldiers moved toward the barn. Madame Rigault posed as a friendly civilian and gave directions to the Germans that took them away from the barn. A man working for the family then led the Germans to the end of the road. "We were all so afraid once more," said the young Marthe.[16] The anxiety and pressure continued to mount. As Odette noted, "We were living, but we no longer had any notion of the passage of time. We lived only to save these people and wondered what would become of them." But a point came when the family would have to decide to save themselves. This was a family with a young girl and a toddler. As for the paratroopers, "they [also] wanted to leave."[17]

The first escape plan of Thursday, 14 June, went awry. Madame Rigault drew up a map for the paratroopers to find the canals that would lead them to liberated Carentan. The family offered a shot of Calvados to the men. The paratroopers also apparently were given small flat boats. The troopers quickly became lost and the boats filled with water. The paratroopers shocked the family by returning to the barn. The family developed a better plan. A large flat boat, of seven to eight meters in length, was anchored on the water. The local name for a boat of this type was *gabare*, and it was normally used to transport heavy

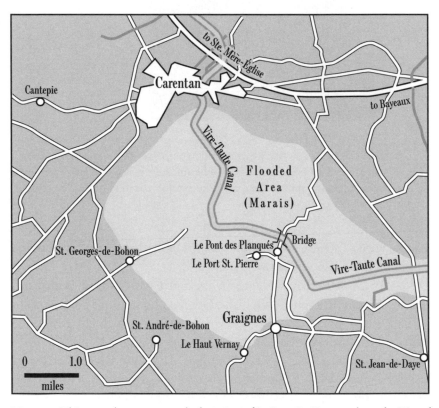

Map 7.1 This map demonstrates the location of Le Port St. Pierre, where the Rigault family barn was located. Le Port St. Pierre is approximately three to four kilometers north of Graignes. The paratroopers, who hid in the barn, made it to safety near Carentan via the Vire-Taute Canal. The map also locates the bridge, which the paratroopers blew up on 9 June, at Le Port des Planqués. Map by Joe LeMonnier, https://mapartist.com/.

loads, like bags of sand. The family further recruited the redoubtable Joseph Folliot to punt the *gabare*. Marthe placed a white flower in the lapels of each of the paratroopers. Before they departed, the paratroopers all signed a letter commending the Rigault family to the US military authorities. The paratroopers clambered into the boat, with some of them lying in the bottom. The number of paratroopers who had hid in the barn has usually been listed as twenty-one men. Gustave and his two girls formed a human chain to push the *gabare* through the *marais* until it reached the current of a river.[18]

The perilous voyage proved to be remarkably unremarkable. The men left when it became dark and arrived before midnight on Thursday, 15 June. Folliot guided the *gabare* through the canals, arriving at St. Hilaire, a hamlet just 300 meters south of Carentan. The voyagers did not encounter any hostile forces. They did see some flares lighting the sky. Pvt. Carlos Hurtado complained he was getting soaked lying at the bottom of the *gabare*. He was told to hush. The paratroopers pressed Folliot to take some of their French francs. The French patriot returned safely, but the Germans discovered that the *gabare* had been moved. Once on land, the paratroopers were challenged by patrolling US forces and soon thereafter were transported by truck back to the command post of the 82nd Airborne. On Saturday, 16 June, the men, all of whom were enlisted personnel, enjoyed a meal of pork and beans. Mortar men Durward Biggerstaff, Stephen E. Liberty, and Rene Rabe received battlefield promotions on that day. The three men would eventually achieve the rank of staff sergeant. Another mortar man, Fredric Boyle, took advantage of the relative safety of the command post at Sainte-Mère-Église to reassure his wife, Charla. When Boyle landed in Graignes, he used his jump knife to cut off a piece of his camouflaged parachute. He stuffed the fabric in his pocket with his grenades and kept it until he had the opportunity to mail it to Charla in Iowa. Because of military censorship, Boyle attached no explanation to the piece of parachute. But Charla Boyle understood that her Fred had jumped and "he was still among us."[19]

A handful of the defenders of Graignes survived on their own. Glider pilot Lt. Irwin Morales found a flat boat and made it to Carentan. Lt. Morales apparently was able to transfer the navigational skills of flying to boating.[20] Pfc. Frank Juliano of the 101st Airborne waited out the Germans until the liberation of Graignes, which took place in the middle of July 1944. Juliano spent a month concealed in a large oven in an outbuilding on a farm. He scavenged for food at night. Villagers thought rabbits were eating their hearts of cabbage.[21] It was probably Pfc. Juliano. Villagers have also recounted how they assisted paratroopers to hide for a time in schools, homes, and the wreckage of the church. Paratroopers jumped out of windows, when Germans searched rooms in homes. School teacher Renée Meunier escorted one paratrooper to Le Port des Planqués and pointed him toward Carentan. The Decaumont family hid a paratrooper in their home for a week.[22] Fifty uniformed personnel are listed as dying at Graignes. Between 110 and 112 of the liberators survived to fight another day. Two men from the 101st Airborne, Cpl. George Faukner of Brooklyn, New York and Pfc. John Piotrowicz from Indiana, apparently were captured by regular German troops while fleeing and spent the duration of the war as prisoners.[23] The withdrawal was successful, because the citizens of Graignes and the surrounding countryside continued to risk everything for their *paras* and for *liberté*.

Analyzing enemy actions also helps to explain the great escape from Graignes. Standard military practice mandated certain steps once the 1st Battalion of the 17th *SS Panzergrenadier* Division took control of Graignes. Officers and senior enlisted men would order soldiers to form a strong perimeter to guard against a counterattack. Once having secured the unit's defense, officers would then organize patrols to seek out and rout the retreating paratroopers. Instead, the Nazi soldiers engaged in a drunken rampage, looting, pillaging, and burning, and murdering prisoners of war and civilians. This gave the paratroopers critical time to get off the hill and conceal themselves in the hedgerows and *marais*. The SS soldiers probably could have readily located the paratroopers during the daylight hours of Monday, 12 June. But the central mission of the 17th *SS Panzergrenadier* Division was to capture Carentan. As early as 8 June 1944, *Oberführer* Werner Ostendorff had received orders to hold Carentan and split the invading forces at Utah and Omaha Beaches. Once Ostendorff's forces finally arrived near Carentan, after enduring the aerial attacks from P-51 Mustangs, he and his command staff constantly, on 11–12 June, pressed the 37th Regiment to move on from Graignes and be in a position to launch the German counterattack on Carentan.[24] These German military priorities gave the paratroopers the time and space to escape.

Fighting Another Day

T/5 Eddie Page anticipated that, when he and his buddies reached Carentan, US military authorities would say: "Oh, these guys are heroes." Page and friends would then be sent home. Prior to D-Day, it had been implied to the paratroopers of the 82nd Airborne that they would spend one tough week in Normandy. In fact, the 82nd accomplished all of its assigned missions during its first days in Normandy. General Ridgway thought his paratroopers should be rotated back to England, because they had taken grievous losses. The 82nd had already far surpassed the conventional military standard that a unit should be withdrawn from combat after it exceeded a 25 percent casualty rate. But officers at the highest levels – General Omar Bradley and Major General Lawton Collins – could not let superb, aggressive troops return to England. Regular infantry units were bogging down in Normandy. The hedgerows provided excellent defensive cover for German troops. Page elaborated: "Instead, they fed us, gave us clean clothes, new weapons and off we went . . . We just kept on going."[25]

When the men of Headquarters Company rejoined their comrades in the 3rd Battalion of the 507th Regiment, they promptly returned to combat. In the middle of June 1944, the three paratrooper regiments of the 82nd Airborne and the 325th Glider Regiment had been deployed to a region south and west of Sainte-Mère-Église and somewhat north and west of Carentan. They would be there until the beginning of July. Towns, villages, and hamlets – Saint-Sauveur-le-Vicomte, Étienville, Vindefontaine and Baupte – would be among the places where the paratroopers would see action. The mission of the 82nd was to serve as a blocking force to prevent the Germans from reinforcing their beleaguered forces in the northern sections of the Cotentin Peninsula.[26] The immediate goal of Allied forces was to seize the port of Cherbourg at the top of the peninsula. Three infantry divisions, under the leadership of General Collins, drove northward and liberated the port city at the end of June. The Germans wrecked and mined the port. But, by the middle of July, some Allied ships were landing supplies, and by August the port of Cherbourg was in fair operation.

Between 14 and 16 June, the 507th lost almost 200 men, facing fierce resistance and German artillery and armor along the road to Saint-Sauveur-le-Vicomte. The regiment had passed through the more heavily armed 90th Infantry Division of the US Army, which was not performing efficiently. By the time those who had defended Graignes reached their battalion, the unit had been deployed a bit farther south toward Baupte and just east of Vindefontaine.[27] Although it was ostensibly in a blocking or defensive position, the 3rd Battalion patrolled endlessly and was, as revealed in Sgt. Major Salewski's diary, in constant combat and under shelling from German mortars and artillery. On 20 June, US artillery mistakenly dropped shells on the battalion's position. As Salewski exclaimed in writing, "this shit must cease." Fortunately, the "friendly fire" did not cause any casualties. As had happened in Graignes, the paratroopers encountered *Ostbataillon* forces. They captured Russian and Polish soldiers.[28] The regiment and battalion also took on a new commander, Colonel Edson Raff. Raff had a reputation as a fierce warrior, but one who was also reckless.

Casualties, both physical and mental, began to mount in June. Pfc. Bruno A. Dauglea of Illinois, who defended Graignes with his machine gun, was killed by an artillery shell blast on 19 June. On 28 June, Lt. Harry Wagner, another veteran of Graignes, also died from artillery fire. He was in a wooded area, and the Germans exploded ordnance in tree tops, thereby driving wood fragments downward with the speed of bullets. Pennsylvania State University would subsequently name a Reserve Officers' Training Corps (ROTC) building on its University Park campus after Lt. Wagner.[29] On the other hand, S/Sgt. Charles W. Penchard earned the Silver Star for gallantry in action on the day that Lt. Wagner died. Penchard was the paratrooper rescued by John Hinchliff at Graignes, when he shot two Germans who were about to bayonet Penchard. Penchard would thereafter rise to the rank of 1st sergeant.

The paratroopers confronted one appalling experience after another in Normandy during the second half of June. Between 19 and 22 June, a terrible storm raged through Normandy. The storm destroyed the artificial "Mulberry Harbor" that had been constructed at Omaha Beach. It remained cold and wet for the rest of the month. Amidst the dampness, the paratroopers smelled the stench of death emitted by decaying bodies and animal carcasses. Rene Rabe remembered the process of digging a deep foxhole to spend the night. He and his comrades would then realize that there was a dead enemy soldier nearby and that sleep would be impossible. A new foxhole in a different location would have to be dug. As paratrooper John McKenzie observed, the impact of the "odor of death" was as much psychological as physical. He elaborated: "Although the odor would not hurt us, the message of death was threatening because one could easily imagine his own body giving up a similar odor."[30] What especially bothered the paratroopers in rural Normandy was the presence of dead horses and cows. Dr. J. Glenn Gray, who earned a Ph.D. in philosophy before the war and taught in the postwar period at Colorado College, served as an officer in counterintelligence for the US Army in Italy and France. Gray noted that soldiers could not look at dead horses without a shudder, noting that "little imagination was required to see what death was like, for the eyes of those thoroughbred animals contained its image in painful clarity."[31] Sgt. William H. Tucker of the 505th Regiment observed that the paratroopers "hated the smell of dead cows even more than dead men." Tucker added that the uniforms of German soldiers "reeked of dead cows," leading paratroopers to believe they could smell enemy soldiers before they saw them.[32] Dr. Gray contributed to that insight. He found that "the butchering of each other was almost easier to endure than the violation of animals, crops, farms, homes, bridges, and all other things that bind man to his natural environment and help to provide him with a spiritual home."[33] In the postwar period, the veterans of Graignes would have to try to cope with such unsettling experiences and memories.

One last dreadful combat mission awaited the paratroopers of Headquarters Company, 3rd Battalion of the 507th Regiment. Having seized Cherbourg, Allied commanders wanted to seal off the Cotentin Peninsula. US armored forces would thereafter be free to drive southward toward Lessay, Coutance, and Avranches, hastening the liberation of France. The mission was to force German units out of the steep hills that overlooked the town of La Haye-du-Puits, which was situated on the main highway for the western coast of the Cotentin Peninsula. Allied commanders would again ask the 82nd to pass through US infantry divisions and take Hills 95 and 131. The commanders of the 507th and 508th Regiments, Colonel Edson Raff and Colonel Roy Lindquist, protested and submitted their objections to General James Gavin. The men of the 82nd had already been bled white. In Colonel Raff's words, "if we attack anymore, we won't have a cadre to make a regiment when we get back to England. I think we ought to be withdrawn." Gavin agreed with his regimental commanders and submitted their objections to General Matthew Ridgway.[34] Although sympathetic to the suffering of the paratroopers, Ridgway rejected Raff and Lundquist's arguments, answering that "though they were weak, their fighting spirit was still unimpaired." Raff would subsequently retort that Ridgway was a "glory-seeker," who "didn't give a damn about the men fighting for him."[35]

The assaults on the two hills, which were the highest points in Normandy, began on 3 July 1944, and combat lasted until 7–8 July. The 507th Regiment stayed in the region of La Haye-du-Puits until 11 July. The battle involved all three paratrooper regiments of the 82nd Airborne and the 325th Glider Regiment. The paratroopers and glider men had air and artillery support. But the battle tactics seemed borrowed from the US Civil War, with mad charges up the hills. Lt. Colonel Louis G. Mendez, Jr., a decorated battalion commander in the 508th Regiment, protested that the charge up the hill would be too costly. General Gavin ordered him to lead the charge.[36] The 82nd succeeded in its mission, but the casualties were staggering. One paratrooper recalled that "so many were killed or wounded. It was terrible!" He added: "I remember looking at the scene in the morning after the battle, and there were trucks loaded high with piles of bodies, just like sacks of potatoes."[37] An officer told Sgt. John Hinchliff and his fellow machine gunners that "we're going to blow the whistle and we're going to go in at a dead run, and we're going to take the hill." Enemy fire went through Hinchliff's equipment but spared his body. On the top of Hill 95, Hinchliff witnessed "carnage," with "guts and brains and heads and limbs on the trees and the bushes." The four regiments of the 82nd Airborne Division had killed or wounded 500 of the enemy and taken 772 as prisoners during the operation to take the two hills.[38]

After thirty-three days of combat in Normandy, the 82nd Airborne Division had suffered overall a 46 percent casualty rate. Sixteen of the division's original twenty-one regimental or battalion commanders had been killed, wounded, or captured.[39] Of the three paratrooper regiments, the 507th Regiment took the hardest blow in Normandy, with a casualty rate of 61 percent. The 507th Regiment had a strength of 2,004 paratroopers on the evening before D-Day. When, on 13 July 1944, the men assembled on Utah Beach to return to England on a Landing Ship, Tank (LST), somewhere between 700 and 800 paratroopers boarded the ship. Battalions looked like companies; companies looked like platoons. The majority of the men who escaped from Graignes made it back to England. The LST arrived at Southampton. The paratroopers were met by military bands and cheering crowds. The Red Cross served coffee and doughnuts. Trains took the paratroopers back to Nottingham near their training base at Tollerton. The

Figure 7.3 Depicted here is one of the stained-glass windows of the church at Sainte-Mère-Église. Paul Renaud, the son of Mayor Alexandre Renaud, designed the image and Gabriel Loire from Chartres made the window. Author's photograph.

paratroopers of the 82nd Airborne had become "the stuff of instant legend."[40] In the postwar period, a new stained-glass window at the medieval church at Sainte-Mère-Église depicted the paratroopers as coming to the rescue of the Blessed Mary, the infant Jesus, and the people of Normandy.

There was, however, a sad side to the return to England. Chaplains told of paratroopers kneeling down and kissing the ground.

Returning to their tents at their respective training bases meant paratroopers had to contemplate the empty bunks of their fallen comrades. Edith Phillips Steiger of the Red Cross greeted the men of the 325th Glider Regiment at the railway station, when they returned to Leicester. As she recorded in her diary, "the soldiers got off the train slowly and walked up the stairs like tired old men." At the mess hall, Steiger poured coffee for the men, who stayed silent, did not eat, and fell asleep at the table. She noticed that "the GIs sat here, there, and everywhere in the hall as returning to a place where they had sat before. I dared not ask where this or that boy was. I knew."[41] After a short period tending to their weapons and equipment, the surviving paratroopers and glider troops of the 82nd Airborne were given ten-day passes. Drinking and carousing characterized that time. Such frolicking, while understandable, probably did not help the paratroopers start the process of coming to terms with the traumas they had experienced. More challenges – the Battle of the Bulge, the jump over the Rhine River, street fighting in Germany – awaited the warriors of Headquarters Company of the 3rd Battalion of the 507th Parachute Infantry Regiment.

Exiles in Their Own Country

As it was for the defenders of Graignes, life became hard for the citizens of Graignes and the surrounding countryside in late June and July 1944. Without warning, the German occupiers ordered the French people to leave their homes. They were given only a brief time to gather their things and were threatened with execution, if they did not leave immediately. Weeks of life on French roads awaited the people of the Graignes region. They had to scramble to find food and shelter. Despite these new hardships, the French kept faith with "our *paras*," the liberators of Graignes.

After the twenty-one paratroopers escaped from the Rigault barn, the German occupiers became intensely suspicious of the French in the area. Joseph Folliot, who had navigated the *gabare* toward Carentan, made a mistake upon returning. He docked the boat in a place different from where it had previously been. The Germans apparently took notice and began to watch the marshlands carefully. They issued an order banning boat traffic on the canals. Isidore Folliot was subsequently hit by machine-gun bullets when he ventured out on the *marais* to retrieve a parapack that had landed on D-Day and contained rations. Madame Marthe Rigault tried to tend to Folliot's wounds through the night, but he died from blood loss. He was wrapped in a parachute and buried.[42] Beyond murdering Isidore, the Germans apprehended Joseph Folliot and executed the young man. Joseph may have been carrying some of the French francs that the paratroopers gave him in gratitude for his help. As the citation for his service notes, "very little reliable information has been discovered concerning the last days of his life."[43] Perhaps news of Folliot's fearless exploits had circulated throughout the region. Mayor Alphonse Voydie had worried that a handful of people in the Graignes area were not to be fully trusted.

A new German penalty was imposed on the French near the end of June 1944. Without warning, the German occupiers ordered all to leave Graignes and the surrounding hamlets. A German officer accompanied by soldiers arrived at the Rigault household at Le Port St. Pierre at 6:00 a.m. The officer ordered the family to leave within twenty minutes. Waving a pistol, the German threatened the Rigault family with execution, if the family did not comply with his order.[44] The same scenario played out for others. Denise Boursier remembered that "one day, we were obliged to announce our departure by order of the Germans, otherwise we would be shot."[45] The evacuation order undoubtedly reflected the Germans' anger at the support that the French had offered to the paratroopers. Allied forces were also looming, and the Germans wanted to clear the area. The evacuation order did not reflect any concern for the safety of civilians, as they would encounter extreme danger during their exile. The French gathered up "their babies and cattle" and generally fled southward.[46]

The Boursier family first sought shelter with a farm family in Le Dézert, only a few kilometers south of Graignes. But, after "a long time," the Germans forced them to move again to Amigny, "where we stayed a fortnight under bombing."[47] Military bombardment also afflicted the Palla family, who lived in the village of La Barre du Pré. Désiré and Madeleine Palla had married in 1928; children followed. The family was on the road by 10:00 a.m. on 30 June to avoid the "danger of death" from the Germans. Madeleine Palla gathered blankets, clothes, and food for a few days, including "a big pot of salty bacon." With neighbors, they headed south through Le Hommet-d'Arthenay and then to La Chapelle-en-Juger, finding a small, isolated farm in a lovely valley. The Quinette family welcomed the refugees with kindness and provided the Palla family with a barn, where they could eat and sleep. They stayed there from 30 June to 20 July. The son, Daniel Palla, testified that "we thought we would be safe from bombardments."[48]

German perfidy caused a tragedy for the Palla family. At 11:00 p.m., on 16 July, a German officer entered the barn and illuminated the family with a flashlight. The officer then left the farm with his soldiers and tanks. Two hours later, an artillery shell fell on the main beam of the barn. Shrapnel bursts instantly killed four people, including father Désiré Palla, in the barn. One more refugee died from shrapnel wounds at 10:00 a.m. the next day. Five other people had shrapnel wounds. What can likely be surmised was that the Germans were illuminating the barn to attract a retaliation from Allied forces. US soldiers and Germans had been in combat in the past days. Baiting Allied artillery to fire on the barn would help the Germans to locate the position of the artillery. On 18 July, the survivors of the barn buried the dead, "the martyrs," in the farmer's garden. As they were finishing their grim but respectful work, a shell fell in the garden killing the father of the teenaged daughter he had just buried. A sixteen-year-old daughter was now the only survivor of this family of three. Those who lived headed back to Graignes on 20 July, for word had reached them that the village had been cleared of the enemy by US forces. Despite the awful loss of his father, Daniel Palla still characterized US forces as "the liberators."[49]

The Rigault family also fled southward. The family headed toward Villedieu, stopping in Percy. The family's final destination was Rouffigny, a distance of about eighty kilometers from Graignes. Madame Marthe Rigault had in her possession a letter signed by the twenty-one paratroopers who hid in the barn, commending the family to US military authorities. Rigault decided to hide the letter in the house. She hid in her sock the French francs the paratroopers had given her. The family's long journey was perilous. They traveled in horse-drawn carts that were used to carry manure among other things. Young Marthe, Jean Claude, and their grandfather sat in one cart, with the older Marthe and Gustave in another. Odette walked alongside the carts. During their exodus, the family witnessed US warplanes bombing German positions and the Germans returning fire with machine guns. Madame Rigault once exclaimed "oh, my God, my children will be killed." Another time, near Percy, Germans were leading the caravan of refugees, with young Marthe, Jean Claude, a cousin, and grandfather riding in an automobile. A German soldier jumped on the running board of the automobile and started firing at US warplanes.[50]

Beyond avoiding being caught in the crossfire, the family had other challenges. Some households provided shelter, straw to sleep on,

Figure 7.4 The Rigault family returned home in August 1944. Despite numerous brushes with disaster and death, the family survived the war, as did the eldest daughter, Marie-Jean. Near them are liberating soldiers standing in a flat boat. Photograph courtesy of the Rigault/His family.

and food, whereas other French families declined to help the refugees. While in Rouffigny, a woman who was providing shelter informed the family that Graignes had been liberated. But the family could not return to Le Port St. Pierre until August because the surrounding destruction impeded travel. When the Rigaults returned home, the family found that their home had been looted, and not by the Germans. The Rigault family subsequently found some of their possessions in surrounding neighborhoods. Fortunately, from the perspective of Odette and Marthe, some of the silk parachutes they had hidden had not been discovered. Madame Rigault could not locate, however, the letter signed by the paratroopers.[51]

Life in Graignes and the surrounding region gradually returned to normal, albeit with problems. Unexploded ordnance remained in the area and tragedies ensued, with two children being killed and a third hurt, when they played with a mine. Marthe Rigault once innocently picked up a hand grenade. The best news for the Rigault family was that their eldest daughter, Marie-Jean, had not died in the bombing of the hospital in Saint-Lô where she worked. In September 1945, Marthe made her First Communion. In early October 1945, a few months after Victory in

Europe (VE) Day, Marie-Jean and Odette married. They wore wedding dresses made from parachute silk. The family had no idea, however, whether the paratroopers who had brought the "silk from the sky" had survived. It would be four decades later before they had an answer. Gustave and Marthe Rigault did not live long enough to learn that their courage bore results. As their daughter Marthe wrote, "I regret that my parents Gustave and Marthe Rigault did not have any news of the Americans to know if they were safe or not. They were never sure of it."[52]

Figure 7.5 The "silk from the sky" remains a treasure within the Rigault family. Emmanuelle Barbey, granddaughter of Marthe Rigault His, models a dress fashioned out of parachute silk from 1944. Photograph courtesy of the Rigault/His family.

The village slowly recovered from the German bombardment and arson. Initially, Ireland and Sweden donated money for rebuilding. After 1948 and until 1951–1952, France had available to it foreign aid through the Marshall Plan. The United States provided $12 billion in direct aid to Western European countries to help them recover from the physical devastation of World War II. Temporary wooden structures to house people and a wooden church were built in Graignes to help with immediate issues. Village planners and architects decided to relocate Graignes. They moved the center of the village from the windswept mound overlooking the *marais* and created a new village designed around a protected crossroads 600 meters away. A new modern-looking church built of stone was created. A smart village hall, which housed the mayor's office, was built next to the church. The bell tower of the ruined church, which was within the walled graveyard, was preserved to commemorate the civilians and paratroopers who had died. It took about fifteen years for the village to recover fully. Reconstruction in the regional center of Saint-Lô did not end until 1964. Fortunately, livestock numbers and grain production in Normandy reached 1940 numbers by 1950 and thereafter increased.[53]

Figure 7.6 This photo depicts some of the temporary buildings constructed during the immediate postwar period in Graignes. Photograph courtesy of the Mayor's Office of Graignes.

A Gethsemane

The US paratroopers and the citizens of Graignes and surrounding regions experienced tumultuous, harrowing times in Normandy during the summer of 1944. Both the paratroopers and the French endured, and for the most part survived. The third group of actors in the tragedy of Graignes were the members of the 1st Battalion of the 37th Regiment of the 17th *SS Panzergrenadier* Division. The summer of 1944 would prove fatal for the *Panzergrenadiers* of the 37th and 38th Regiments, the heart of the division. The *SS* men would fail to achieve their central mission – establishing control over Carentan and splitting US forces on Utah and Omaha Beaches. Thereafter, they would be subjected to the combined fury of US land, air, and naval forces. The men who perpetrated war crimes against prisoners and civilians in Graignes would be annihilated.

By the dawn of 13 June 1944, the 37th Regiment was finally in position to attack Carentan. The attack had been delayed for three to four days. The aerial attacks from US fighter-bombers had impeded the northward movement of the 17th *SS Panzergrenadier* Division from the Thouars region. The determined resistance of the US paratroopers at Graignes had further delayed the attack on Carentan. This delay had given the 101st Airborne Division the time to liberate Carentan and begin to consolidate the Allied position in the town. More US forces, including the 2nd Armored Division with Sherman tanks, were moving inland from Omaha Beach. The *Panzergrenadiers* of the 1st Battalion arrived in position in the late afternoon of 12 June to join the 2nd Battalion for the upcoming assault. The 3rd Battalion, without motorized transport, was still making its way toward Carentan and would not arrive in the region until the later part of June. Two battalions of the 38th Regiment were positioned further westward near Montmartin-en-Graignes. This regiment was also awaiting the arrival of its 3rd Battalion.[54]

Despite the delays, the *SS* men of the 37th Regiment were in high spirits on the evening of 12 June. The regiment would have the support of reconnaissance forces, artillery, *Panzerjägers* (anti-tank forces), and *StuG* IV assault guns. Commanders also told their men that the *Luftwaffe* would provide air cover and would attack US ground forces. *Oberführer* Werner Ostendorff issued an ambitious order. The 37th Regiment would not only recapture Carentan but also seize the village of Saint-Côme-du-Mont, which the 101st Airborne had previously liberated. Controlling Saint-Côme-du-Mont would give the Germans a pathway toward moving on to Sainte-Mère-Église.[55] *Oberleutnant* (1st Lt.) Pöppel, a member of the 6th *Fallschirmjäger* Regiment, recorded in his diary that there was "a lot of joy" among the troops when they received the order. Pöppel was attached to the 17th *SS Panzergrenadier* Division to serve as liaison between the *SS* troops and the German paratroopers. He attended a reception on the evening of 12 June for the conquerors of Graignes, the officers of the 1st Battalion of the 37th Regiment. He dubbed the officers "consistently flawless men, totally fabulous." The battalion commander, *SS-Sturmbannführer* Christian Reinhardt, "is also magnificent."[56] These "fabulous" men were in command when the 1st Battalion of the 37th Regiment perpetrated atrocities in Graignes.

Some realism tempered the enthusiasm of the *SS* troops. *Oberführer* Ostendorff had conferred with the German commander of the 6th Parachute Infantry and had heard of the fighting spirit of the 101st Airborne. Ostendorff told his officers that they could expect naval gunfire and tank assaults from US forces. The 101st Airborne paratroopers "were crafty and astute" and they possessed a "nasty combat spirit."[57] Ostendorff should have also known that the outnumbered paratroopers from the 82nd Airborne had inflicted casualties on his men at Graignes. His senior officers, who were combat veterans, thought that the mission plans were too "rosy." Logistical problems would also bedevil the Germans. Less than 20 percent of their equipment and supplies in Thouars had reached the staging point in Baupte. Ostendorff would issue a revealing report, early in the morning of 13 June, when he observed that assault guns had arrived on the battlefield and then asked: "Where is the ammunition?"[58] The march toward Carentan and the battle for Graignes had also wearied the Germans. *SS-Rottenführer* (Senior Lance-Corporal) Arnold Hoffmann recalled that "my men and I were totally exhausted" on the morning of 13 June 1944.[59]

Oberführer Ostendorff reported that the two battalions of the 37th Regiment combined with the 6th Parachute Infantry launched their attack on Carentan at 5:20 a.m. on 13 June. By 10:15 a.m., the German attack had stalled. By the afternoon, the Germans were in retreat and being routed by combined US air, naval, artillery, armored, and ground forces. As early as 4:30 a.m., the artillery regiment of the 17th *SS Panzergrenadier* Division reported "during the night strong and harassing enemy fire." Nonetheless, the initial assault seemed to start well, with Ostendorff labeling it "good progress on the attack today."[60] Elements of the 37th Regiment reached the southern outskirts of Carentan, just 400 meters from the railroad station. The 101st Airborne fell back but did not break, stabilizing a line of defense along railroad embankments. The paratroopers used bazookas and deadly rifle fire. *SS-Rottenführer* Hoffmann labeled it as "murderous US infantry fire," and he witnessed Germans slumped over their machine guns near the railroad embankments. *Oberführer* Ostendorff wondered where the Luftwaffe was.[61] Then, beginning in the middle of the morning and lasting through the afternoon, sixty Sherman tanks from the 2nd Armored Division combined with infantry from the 29th Infantry Division and howitzers from the 14th Armored Field Battalion came to the rescue and forced the Germans to withdraw. The North American B-25 Mitchells, medium bombers, dropped bombs on the retreating *Panzergrenadiers* and German paratroopers. The supporting forces of an *Ostbataillon* broke and ran, when its German commander was killed. US tanks confronted the *StuG* IV assault guns and destroyed two of them on the road, Highway 171, from Périers to Carentan.[62] Assessing the military debacle, the German Chief of Staff in Saint-Lô pointed to the critical lack of air support for the 37th Regiment, noting that the lack of promised support damaged "the fighting morale of the not yet battle-hardened troops."[63] Businesses in Carentan began to reopen on 14 June 1944.

The 17th *SS Panzergrenadier* Division retreated into defensive positions away from Carentan. But disaster and death awaited them. In the words of a staff officer captured on 1 November 1944, "no human account ever could describe the hardship, the sacrifice, the misery [of] the men of this division." Those who survived "will never forget this Gethsemane." The officer estimated, for example, that 2,000 Allied bombers pounded the division on 26 July 1944.[64] It was inappropriate to compare a military unit that committed war crimes to the Christian symbol of anguish and suffering. But the 17th *SS Panzergrenadier* Division and especially the 37th Regiment took unimaginable casualties in the summer of 1944. The seizure of Cherbourg and the capture of La Haye-du-Puits region by the 82nd Airborne paved the way for the Allied push southward through Normandy. Allied forces also now had more mobility, for US engineers opened the flood gates at La Barquette and the *marais* began to drain. For example, by 7 July, the water level at Graignes had dropped by 70 centimeters (27.5 inches).[65]

Allied forces, whose numbers were increasing exponentially, relentlessly attacked German forces, including the 17th *SS Panzergrenadier* Division, during the summer of 1944. US forces badly wounded *Oberführer* Ostendorff and captured *SS-Sturmbannführer* Christian Reinhardt, the commander of the 1st Battalion of the 37th Regiment. During the second week of July, battles included clashes between US forces and *SS* men of the 38th Regiment in the Graignes–Tribehou area. On 20 July, US artillery forces obliterated the 3rd Battalion of the 38th Regiment. The 37th and 38th Regiments, who numbered 7,000–8,000 on D-Day, had been reduced by the end of July to 5 officers, 40 noncommissioned officers, and 800 enlisted personnel, a 90 percent casualty rate. The 17th *SS Panzergrenadier* Division consolidated the remaining *Panzergrenadiers* into one *Kampfgruppe* (combat group) under the leadership of Jacob Fick, the former commander of the 37th Regiment. The *Kampfgruppe* rapidly lost strength. By September 1944, the 1st Battalion of the 37th Regiment, the unit that had overwhelmed Graignes and murdered civilians and US prisoners, consisted of 76 *SS* men out of an original force of approximately 950 troops.[66] The captured staff officer of the 17th *SS Panzergrenadier* Division observed that the German soldiers had walked "the way of the cross."[67] Another way to characterize what happened would be to say that, as in a nineteenth-century novel, the war criminals of Graignes had received their "just deserts."

What had happened in the village of Graignes had been momentous. The villagers had displayed uncommon courage in supporting the paratroopers of the 82nd and 101st Airborne Divisions and upholding the eternal ideals of the French Revolution. For their part, the paratroopers did their best to preserve the liberty of their new-found French friends. Although they could not keep the enemy out of Graignes, their efforts had contributed significantly to the liberation of the vital town of Carentan and all of Normandy. But more than four decades would pass before there would be the beginnings of public understanding of the meaning of Graignes.

8 GRAIGNES IN HISTORICAL MEMORY

What happened in the village of Graignes between 6 and 16 June 1944 is a compelling and inspiring story. The defense of Graignes by paratroopers and villagers also was militarily and strategically significant, contributing to victory by Allied forces in Normandy. Nonetheless, it would take more than four decades before the public in both Europe and the United States would begin to grasp the meaning of what happened in a small Norman village. Before they could reminisce, the paratroopers of Headquarters Company, 3rd Battalion, of the 507th Regiment had to first survive further combat in Normandy, the rigors of winter warfare at the Battle of the Bulge, a combat jump over the Rhine River on 24 March 1945, and six weeks of fighting in the Rhineland area. The veterans also had to manage the challenges of blending back into civilian life and coping with their personal wartime traumas. The people of Graignes had similar challenges, enduring their exile in the summer of 1944 and then rebuilding their village and livelihoods. They commemorated each June what had happened in Graignes, but villagers could only wonder what had happened to their beloved *paras*. They received no help from the chroniclers of the 17th *SS Panzergrenadier* Division. These purported scholars denied that war crimes took place in Graignes.

From Normandy to Berlin

The paratroopers who survived Graignes would have been the natural candidates to tell the story of their alliance with the villagers and their fight against Nazi tyranny. Led by Colonel Frank Naughton, Lt. Colonel Earcle Reed, and T/5 Eddie Page, the paratroopers would eventually speak about the meaning of their eleven-day sojourn in Graignes. Sgt. John Hinchliff, who lived to be ninety-nine years of age, would get to the point that he could not stop talking about his adventures in France. But it would not be until the 1980s that the veterans of Graignes began to seek public forums to express their admiration for their French comrades. Wartime traumas and postwar imperatives played roles in delaying public discussion of the meaning of Graignes.

Soon after returning in the middle of July 1944 to their tent cities in Tollerton, England, the paratroopers of the 507th Regiment were jolted by unsettling, unwelcome news. The 507th had been detached from the now storied 82nd Airborne and reassigned to the new 17th Airborne Division. General Matthew Ridgway would be the commander of the XVIII Airborne Corps, consisting of the 17th, 82nd, and 101st Airborne Divisions. Major General James Gavin would now be the commander of the 82nd Airborne Division. The reorganization seemed to make sense. The 507th, with a 61 percent casualty rate from Normandy, needed time to rebuild its forces. The 507th would not have been ready to participate with the 82nd in "Operation Market Garden," an unsuccessful attempt in the middle of September 1944 to land in the Netherlands, seize nine bridges and create a bridgehead over the Rhine River. It further seemed reasonable to transfer the 507th to ensure that the new 17th Airborne Division would have one combat-experienced regiment. But personal grievances affected this decision. Regimental commander Edson Raff rubbed General Ridgway the wrong way, as General Gavin pointed out to his daughter in a letter.[1] Raff was both brave and reckless and a self-promoter. In the words of a prominent historian of the 82nd Airborne, "Raff was flashy, abrasive, and an insufferable egomaniac," but "a *terrific* combat leader."[2] Raff was proud of being the first paratrooper to hit German land in "Operation Varsity," the jump over the Rhine River on 24 March 1945. Raff mocked Ridgway for crossing the Rhine in a boat. Raff sneered that Ridgway was "not a real paratrooper who would jump with his men."[3]

Colonel Raff was the only paratrooper in the 507th pleased about the reorganization. He thought that his new commander in the 17th, General William "Bud" Miley, would listen to him. General Miley, who was a veteran of World War I, came from a military family, with several generations of his ancestors having attended West Point.

But the veterans of Normandy were outraged and would feel, as described by Major Paul F. Smith of the 1st Battalion, "great bitterness" about the transfer. Sgt. Hinchliff added "we didn't like it," because the 82nd "had quite a reputation and we were proud of the fact that we were in the 82nd." That reputation was enhanced when the 82nd Airborne was selected to represent all US military units with a victory march through New York City in January 1946. Four million people watched the parade.[4]

Beyond causing hurt feelings, the transfer to the 17th Airborne had a real impact on the ability of the paratroopers to tell their stories in the postwar world. In May 1944, every man in the 507th contributed $10 (UK 2 pounds, 10 shillings) to found the 82nd Association for the postwar period. The association became very active, under the leadership of Robert M. "Bob" Murphy (1925–2008), a pathfinder in the 505th Regiment. After the war, Murphy finished high school, attended law school, and worked for Representative and then Senator John F. Kennedy. President Kennedy appointed General Gavin to be ambassador to France. Starting in the early 1960s, Murphy went to Normandy, became friends with Mayor Alexander Renaud of Sainte-Mère-Église and his wife, Simone, and organized annual reenactment jumps of veterans each year on 6 June.[5] These developments contributed to the legend of the 82nd Airborne.

By contrast, the paratroopers of the 507th lost not only their beloved division but also their regiment. At the end of the war, many of the paratroopers were shipped home, arriving in Boston on 15 September 1945. The next day, the 507th Regiment was abruptly disbanded. Major Smith, who served thirty years in the military and achieved the rank of major general, related that "nobody called the men together and proclaimed, 'guys you did a great job – thank-you.' Nothing." Instead, the authorities said: "here's your ticket – goodbye."[6] Veterans of the 507th Regiment would eventually form their own association, with newsletters and reunions. Historians Dominique François and Martin Morgan rescued the regiment from obscurity. But, for decades, the paratroopers felt like military orphans, lacking a venue and the prestige to tell their stories about their experiences in World War II.

Another key explanation for the initial lack of attention to Graignes was that it was difficult for the paratroopers to process everything that happened to them in 1944–1945. For the veterans of

Graignes, the traumatic experiences in the village had been followed by weeks of bloody fighting in the hedgerows, endless encounters with dead people and animals, and then the mad charge up Hill 95 near La Haye-du-Puits. Almost universally, the paratroopers judged the next challenge – the Battle of the Bulge – the hardest and most damaging to their bodies and psyches. Captain David Brummitt, who was wounded in the shoulder, typified the reaction of paratroopers when he labeled the experience in Belgium "the worst."[7] The deep snow, sub-zero temperatures, and the savage nature of the fighting made the Battle of the Bulge haunting. In the middle of December 1944, the Germans launched a major offensive spearheaded by *Panzers* in the Ardennes Forest in Belgium. The rebuilding 507th Regiment, which now trained at Camp Barton Stacey in southern England, was put on alert. There were initial plans to drop the paratroopers into Belgium. But bad weather in Western Europe kept planes grounded and provided excellent cover for the rapidly advancing Germans. On Christmas Eve, the regiment flew from England to Chartres, southwest of Paris. Truck convoys took them into Belgium on Christmas Day. The paratroopers would subsequently joke that they made a "tailgate jump" into the thigh-deep snow. One trooper from South Carolina asked Sgt. Hinchliff, a native of Minnesota, "Johnny, how the hell do you fight in this stuff?"[8]

The 507th fought in the snow and cold for forty-five days, not returning to France until February. A book-length study could be devoted to analyzing what happened on a daily basis. Casualties would again be high for the regiment, approaching 40 percent. Amputations became common, with paratroopers losing toes and feet to frostbite. Rene Rabe, for example, lost part of a toe. Others would find for the rest of their lives that they had no feeling on the bottom of their feet and that their hands would crack open and bleed in cold weather.[9] At night, paratroopers had to lie down in the snow rather than in foxholes, because their entrenching tools could not penetrate the frozen ground. In his memoir, one paratrooper noted that the fiercest battles in January between the US and German forces were over hamlets, shacks, and barns in order to gain protection from the bitter cold.[10] Sgt. Hinchliff used his Minnesota experience to instruct his men to take off their socks at every opportunity and wring them out to prevent trench foot and frostbite. He and his fellow machine gunners would periodically run-in-place in the middle of the night to stimulate blood circulation. The children of David Brummitt and Frank Naughton observed that their fathers abhorred cold weather and chose in postwar life to live in warm states like Florida and Georgia.[11]

The "Battle of Cake Hill," also known as the "Battle of Dead Man's Ridge," captured the difficulties the veterans of Graignes encountered during their sojourn in Belgium and Luxembourg. The battle would become in 1948–1949 a study topic on faulty tactics in an Advanced Infantry Officers Course at Ft. Benning, Georgia. The central conclusion of the lesson was that "no commander should order a unit out on a mission, without carefully weighing the importance of the mission, and the effect it will have on the unit."[12] Colonel Raff ordered the 3rd Battalion to move on to the top of a hill that was heavily wooded in the vicinity of the villages of Laval and Chisogne in Belgium. Raff understood that German *Panzer* IV medium tanks were operating in the area. Sgt. Hinchliff overheard Raff say that "I'd almost sacrifice my gallant 3rd Battalion to see what's over in that woods."[13] The 3rd Battalion Commander, Major John T. Davis, a West Point graduate, objected to the order, arguing he needed to conduct a full reconnaissance of the region before advancing. Raff reiterated his order and instructed Davis to relay the code, "Cake is cut," when he accomplished his mission. At 2:00 a.m., on 8 January 1945, the 3rd Battalion headed up the hill, lacking communication with supporting forces such as US artillery, and with no accompanying tanks. Blizzard conditions soon developed, with snow drifts thirty-six inches deep. Visibility was less than fifty feet. The paratroopers had still not been issued winter uniforms.[14]

The Germans anticipated the attack. At daybreak, Major Davis and his staff reached the top of the hill and were immediately bombarded by German artillery shells. Davis was killed and thirty others were killed or wounded. Communication equipment was also destroyed. For a time, Captain Brummitt took command of the battalion. German artillery, mortar, and tank fire pounded the entire battalion, killing the beloved Roman Catholic Chaplain, Captain John J. Verrett, who was loading wounded on to trucks. The paratroopers feared that the *Panzer* IV tanks would charge them. The 3rd Battalion stabilized the situation. The infantry companies dug in in the woods and returned intense fire. Communication personnel managed to direct US artillery fire on the Germans. Most important, in the words of Captain John Marr, the 81 mm mortar platoon, most of whom had been in Graignes, "rained down tons of rounds in protective fires to help hold the tanks at bay and repulse the probing attacks." The new leader of the mortar platoon was 1st Lt. Auten Chitwood from Osceola, Arkansas. One of Lt. Chitwood's mortar teams, which included Rene Rabe and Homer Poss, accomplished the spectacular feat of dropping a white phosphorus round down the open turret hatch of a *Panzer* IV, incinerating the tank. The battalion withdrew from Cake Hill early on January 9. The burning *Panzer* IV illuminated the dark sky. The 3rd Battalion continued to fight through January and approached the German frontier. The paratroopers particularly distinguished themselves on 9 February, repulsing German attacks along the Our River in Luxembourg.[15]

Forty percent of the 507th Regiment, 741 paratroopers, were wounded, killed, or listed as missing during the Battle of the Bulge campaign.[16] Among those receiving Purple Hearts were veterans of Graignes, such as Brummitt, Page, and Rabe. Two veterans of Graignes, Sgt. Edward Barnes and Pfc. Charles Hammer, were so badly wounded that they would see no further combat. The pattern would repeat itself in the regiment's next combat assignment, Operation Varsity, the jump over the Rhine River. For example, on 28 March 1945, a German mortar shell exploded near an 81 mm mortar emplacement of the 3rd Battalion's Headquarters Company. Shrapnel sprayed S/Sgt. Rabe's face, and part of the mortar shell embedded itself in Cpl. Poss's head. Rabe returned to duty within a couple of days, but Poss woke up several days later in a US Army hospital in the Netherlands. The survival of all but a handful of the veterans of Graignes pointed to a military truism often repeated by General Gavin – "the definition of a replacement is someone who replaces a replacement." Those who died at the Battle of the Bulge and during the invasion of Germany tended to be newcomers to the regiment. The harsh lessons of combat had taught veteran paratroopers how to limit their exposure to enemy fire, while still carrying out their assignments, or, as Gavin put it, "if they are lucky to live thru their apprenticeship from then on with a bit of luck they are OK."[17] To be sure, an element of chance or perhaps divine grace determined who avoided becoming a casualty. During the winter of 1944–1945, an artillery shell landed in the foxhole of Sgt. Hinchliff. The shell did not explode. To the amusement of his buddies, Hinchliff emerged from the foxhole covered with dirt but unscathed. Hinchliff survived the entire war without a wound or being "clipped," as the paratroopers would say. He attributed his good fortune to imbibing the lessons of his devout grandmother to pray often.[18]

After about two months of rest, rebuilding, and training in Chalons, France, the 507th Regiment returned to combat, spearheading the Allied jump over the Rhine River on 24 March 1945. The war in the European theater lasted until 8 May 1945, with "VE Day." Operating in the Rhineland area, the regiment took an additional 380 casualties in killed, wounded, and missing. Another book-length study could be similarly written about these six weeks of combat.[19] Beyond the rigors of combat, what was a special new burden for the paratroopers was their constant contact with German civilians, European slave laborers, and German prisoners of war. Headquarters Company of the 3rd Battalion engaged in difficult house-to-house fighting in towns as they approached the city of Essen. Civilian casualties predictably occurred. On their first night in Germany, machine gunners of Headquarters Company opened up when they heard noises in a field in front of them. At daybreak the paratroopers found dead civilians – the elderly, mothers, and children. As Hinchliff noted, "they were trying to get out of the way of the war, and we killed them. It almost broke my heart." Disputes broke out among paratroopers over the protection of German property. Hinchliff and S/Sgt. Rabe castigated their buddies for trashing and looting civilian homes. What often provoked the men was that a paratrooper, while searching a home, might be injured or killed when they encountered an object that had been "booby-trapped." Rabe recalled a device exploding, when a paratrooper tried to straighten a picture frame that was askew on a wall in a German home.[20]

In the spring of 1945, the paratroopers were operating in the industrial Ruhr region of Germany, the home of war factories, including the Krupp armaments complex. Nazi Germany dragooned citizens of captive regions to work in these war factories. The 17th Airborne, which consisted of the 507th and the 513th Regiments, liberated 200,000 slave laborers, many of them from Poland and the Soviet Union.[21] To use General Gavin's description of the terrible plight of the slaves, "they are all thin and hungry and most of them dirty and lousy [lice-ridden] and many quite ill."[22] They were also filled with vengeance. The paratroopers of Headquarters Company had to use armed force to keep Russians from murdering Germans and raping German women and teenaged girls.[23] One of the 507th's prize captives was Alfred Krupp von Bohlen und Halbach, the head of the Krupp arms empire. The Allied Military Government would subsequently sentence Alfred Krupp to twelve years in prison for crimes against humanity for

Figure 8.1 Polish citizens, who were forced to work in the Rhineland region, posed for this photograph for their liberators, the paratroopers, at the end of the war. Photograph courtesy of Sherry Fletcher, daughter of Cpl. Homer Poss.

his treatment of slave labourers. The 17th Airborne also liberated 5,639 Allied prisoners. And the paratroopers took the surrender of 160,000 German soldiers, including 25 generals. The ordinary German soldier was in a miserable mental and physical state, invoking some feelings of pity from the paratroopers.[24]

Although most of Headquarters Company went home with the rest of the 507th Regiment in September 1945, a handful of them – Fredric Boyle, Page, Rabe, and others – continued the epic journey to Berlin. They rejoined the 82nd Airborne and General Gavin and participated in the Allied occupation of Berlin in the second half of 1945. Although less rigorous than combat, occupation duty presented physical and mental challenges. The paratroopers clashed with occupying troops of the Soviet Union and killed some, when they resisted US military commands to cease abusing civilians and displaced persons.[25] The soldiers of the Soviet Union considered it their right to rape German women. The paratroopers were also living in a devastated city, with widespread hunger and malnutrition. In postwar life, Rabe would speak with sadness of seeing German children looking for scraps of food to eat, scouring

Figure 8.2 The reviewing stand of the Allied Victory Parade in Berlin on 7 September 1945. In the foreground are General George S. Patton and the bemedaled Marshal Georgy Zhukov. Rene Rabe and Eddie Page marched in the parade with the 82nd Airborne. Photograph taken by Rene Rabe.

through the garbage of US soldiers.[26] On 7 September 1945, the paratroopers of the 504th Regiment of the 82nd Airborne joined soldiers from France, the Soviet Union, and the United Kingdom in an Allied Victory Parade through the *Brandenburger Tor* (Brandenburg Gate) and down *Unter den Linden*, the main boulevard in the eastern section of Berlin. The paratroopers wore scarves and gloves fashioned from their white silk parachutes. Military commanders, including Marshal of the Soviet Union Georgy Zhukov and General George S. Patton, reviewed the parade.[27]

After the War

The postwar culture in the United States and Allied countries like the United Kingdom discouraged discussion by veterans of the traumatic experiences of World War II. Looking back, Queen Elizabeth II, who was in uniform during the war as a lorry (truck) driver and mechanic, regretfully said that "the war had been so devastating that many people who had lived through it decided that keeping quiet about the traumas was the best way to deal with them."[28] The quiet approach reigned in the United States also. As one journalist observed, "the Greatest Generation might just as easily be called the Quietest." Children of veterans of World War II, now in their sixties and seventies, feel frustrated that they know so little about the experience of their parents and have turned to independent researchers and archivists at repositories like the National World War II Museum in New Orleans for help. One independent historian who works with children of veterans has testified that "sometimes they cry on the phone about how much they loved their dad, and how he had horrible nightmares, but would never talk about it."[29] The author's discussion with the children of the US veterans of Graignes supports that observation. For example, Georgene Heaney and her son Michael Heaney, a US Marine Corps veteran, had no knowledge of what their father and grandfather, Charles Penchard, did to earn his prestigious Silver Star. The veterans' children universally report that their fathers did not reminisce about their lives as paratroopers. In some cases, when their fathers entered their retirement years, they opened up a bit about the war. There were exceptions. The author's father would watch documentaries like *Victory at Sea* (1952–1954) and *The World at War* (1973–1974) and answer questions. S/Sgt. Rabe would also permit the author to listen when he discussed the war with fellow veterans, which included three uncles. More typical, however, was Eddie Page, who would punctuate the day with the cry of "Airborne," but not tell his daughters, Doris and Cheryl, much about his time as a paratrooper or what led to his being awarded three Purple Hearts. His daughters did know that Page fulfilled his pledge to Dr. Fodiman, the family dentist, that he would remunerate the dentist in the postwar period for the dentistry work that allowed Page to enlist with the paratroopers. Dr. Fodiman remarked to his office staff: "See, I told you he'd be back."[30]

US military and civilian leaders did not encourage the veterans of Graignes to process what had happened to them between 5 June 1944 and the end of 1945. John Hinchliff recalled that the 507th regiment spent three days at Camp Miles Standish after they arrived in Boston in September 1945. The bulk of the regiment had departed from Marseilles on the luxury liner *Mariposa* and arrived seven days later in Boston Harbor. The paratroopers had a three-day orientation to civilian life. No counseling services were offered to the veterans. Hinchliff remembered that the instructors in the classes that they attended emphasized the need to be non-violent. An example offered to the veterans was that if a man sat down in front of you in a movie theater with a hat on, the veteran should not to proceed to hit the man in the back of the head. After such dubious classes, the veterans of the 507th were issued train tickets for home. Hinchliff headed home to Minnesota and his wife, Muriel, whom he had not seen since he left Alliance, Nebraska in November 1943. He confessed that Muriel was now a stranger to him. Hinchliff's two-year-old daughter did not respond to him. The last time that he had held her she was two months old.[31]

General and President Dwight D. Eisenhower set the tone for not discussing and dealing with wartime experiences. During the 1952 presidential campaign, Eisenhower spoke to a veterans' group about the Normandy invasion. Eisenhower was visibly pained by the memories of soldiers and paratroopers dying as a direct result of his command decisions. During his talk, his grief overwhelmed him, and Eisenhower covered his face with a handkerchief.[32] What undoubtedly contributed to a reluctance to talk about World War II was that over 400,000 US men and women had died during the war. Six million European Jews had perished during the Nazi-perpetrated Holocaust. In view of these catastrophic losses, it was thought unseemly for a veteran to discuss personal traumas. A veteran's difficulties with sleeping and enduring "flashback" episodes might seem inconsequential compared with knowing that your paratrooper buddy had his frostbitten foot amputated during the Battle of the Bulge. Former President Eisenhower implicitly made that point when he toured Normandy with esteemed journalist Walter Cronkite in 1964, on the twentieth anniversary of D-Day. Eisenhower was most poignant when he walked among the over 9,000 Christian crosses and Stars of David at the American Cemetery in Colleville-sur-Mer near Omaha Beach. Eisenhower rejected any notion of personal accomplishment or triumph, simply adding that the men who had sacrificed for Normandy's liberation had provided a chance for contemporary Americans to achieve global peace. He noted that his son, Brigadier General John Eisenhower, had graduated from West Point on D-Day. His son and daughter-in-law had given birth to four children, which were of great comfort and joy to Eisenhower and his wife, Mamie. Eisenhower lamented that the men who rested at the American Cemetery never had the chance to live life and bring happiness to their parents.

The veterans of Graignes seemingly reentered American life seamlessly. Officers, like David Brummitt, Frank Naughton, and

Earcle Reed, continued in the US Army. They had high-school degrees and some college. The effects of the Great Depression had stymied their educational aspirations. The Army provided them with the opportunity to finish their university degrees and obtain graduate degrees. Colonel Brummitt earned an M.A. in international relations from George Washington University. Colonel Naughton also finished his college degree and subsequently graduated from law school and served as a judge in Gwinnett County, Georgia. As was the case with the enlisted men, the officers married and stayed married. The year 1947 was a popular year to get married. Naughton met his wife, Ruth T. Carlson, on a double date with another soldier from Ft. Benning, Georgia in the postwar period. They were married for over sixty years. Colonel Naughton and Ruth Carlson are both buried in Arlington National Cemetery. Brummitt married Mary O'Connor, whose picture he had carried with him through the war. They were married for fifty years.[33]

The US economy boomed in the postwar period from 1947 to the oil crisis of 1973–1974. Most enlisted men who fought at Graignes lacked a high-school diploma, and entered the working class. But many working-class jobs provided a good income, for they were union jobs. In the mid 1950s, one-third of US workers belonged to the organized labor movement. Stephen E. Liberty (1916–1978), the Native American who was a miner before the war, was a miner for another thirty years in Butte, Montana. He chose to be buried in the Flathead Indian Reservation in western Montana. John Hinchliff felt pressured to find a job quickly to support Muriel and his daughter. The Hinchliff family would grow to five children. He started driving a milk truck and delivered bottles of milk to homes. He moved up to driving a milk transport truck. He also became vice president of Local 471 of the Teamsters union. Muriel Hinchliff entered politics and served on the Minneapolis City Council.[34] Eddie Page and Homer Poss both worked in the meat-cutting trade, and both married soon after the war. Poss married Colleen Sackett on 16 May 1946. In later life, he received an honorary diploma from his high school in Lebanon, Illinois. Page married Betty King of Atlanta, to whom he had written faithfully during the war. Poss and Fredric Boyle remarkably became mayors of their respective towns in Illinois and Iowa. Boyle extended his education and became a chiropractor. Charles Penchard owned a painting company. Unfortunately, his spouse, 1st Lt. Olga Campbell Penchard, died prematurely in 1980. Rene Rabe became a cable splicer for the Southern

New England Telephone Company and a member of the Communication Workers of America labor union. In his forties, he attended school at night to achieve his high school diploma. In 1947, he married Genevieve Dreher of Manhattan. He dated Genevieve before the war, but wrote his mother from Berlin that he was uncommitted and might marry a German woman.[35] Dreher outflanked the battle-hardened paratrooper. She was waiting for him at the dock in New York City harbor, when, at the end of 1945, the *Queen Mary* delivered him home. Ever the comedian, Rene later claimed that Genevieve grabbed the liner's ropes and helped pull the *Queen Mary* into port.

Although the veterans of Graignes did not discuss the war with their loved ones, their families understood that the traumas of war were ever present with them. In January 1980, the American Psychiatric Association defined as a legitimate disease what became popularly known as "Post-Traumatic Stress Disorder" (PTSD). Others prefer to label it as Post-Traumatic Stress Syndrome, believing that the word "disorder" unfairly stigmatizes victims. In the words of the American Psychiatric Association, people with the syndrome "have intense, disturbing thoughts and feelings related to their experience that last long after the traumatic event has ended. They may relive the event through flashbacks or nightmares; they may feel sadness, fear or anger; and they may feel detached or estranged from other people. People with PTSD may avoid situations or people that remind them of the traumatic event, and they may have strong negative reactions to something as ordinary as a loud noise or an accidental touch."[36] Doctors long understood that war experiences could trouble veterans. In World War I, the popular term was "shell shock," and, in World War II, the term was "battle fatigue." The presumption was that the syndrome was short-lived or easily curable. PTSD was thought to be a unique experience and the term "post-Vietnam syndrome" was associated with the syndrome. The argument was made that veterans of Vietnam had unique difficulties reentering civilian life, because the war was unpopular and Vietnam veterans did not have a parade down New York City's 5th Avenue. Travis Bickle (Robert De Niro) in *Taxi Driver* (1976) and Ron Kovic (Tom Cruise) in *Born on the Fourth of July* came to epitomize the distinctive struggles of Vietnam veterans. Memoirs and the oral histories of paratroopers, and interviews with the children of the paratroopers who fought at Graignes, demonstrate, however, that post-traumatic stress also affected veterans of World War II.

John Hinchliff suppressed memories of World War II and avoided all talk of war from 1945 until 1979. But he had bouts of "uncontrollable anger." At the insistence of Muriel, he attended a reunion of the 507th Regiment in Denver. His wife assured him that they could leave, if John found the gathering unsettled him. After 1979, John opened up, did interviews and oral histories, appeared on television, and spoke at public schools. Hinchliff's interviews left journalists, however, "both amazed and shocked." He spared nothing about the horrors of the battlefield. But talk did not cure him. After Muriel passed in 2001, John decided to manage his anger by moving to the country and living alone. He built a log cabin near a pond in Webster, Wisconsin, where he lived with his Siberian Husky, "Chinook."[37] To be sure, not just the death and destruction of World War II troubled Hinchliff. He had a hard time coping with the pain caused by his birth parents playing no role in his life. Sgt. John J. Hinchliff of Headquarters Company, 3rd Battalion died in November 2020 at the age of ninety-nine, the last surviving veteran of the 2,004 paratroopers of the 507th Regiment who jumped into Normandy on D-Day.

A few other examples of the postwar mental struggles of the veterans of Graignes can illustrate why they were reluctant to discuss their wartime experiences. Excessive drinking characterized the lives of too many of them. Both the children of the veterans and the villagers of Graignes, who met them from 1984 on, raised the alcoholism issue. They believed that veterans drank in response to disturbing memories. Others expressed their discontent in various ways. Charla Boyle told her son Jonathan that the Fred who came home from the war was not the man she married. She did not elaborate. Jonathan Boyle remembered that his father could be "ancy" and that he always preferred to sit at the very back of a theater. Dr. Boyle also rebuked anyone who downplayed the reality of combat.[38] Captain Brummitt had nightmares. He preferred not to talk about World War II, and he avoided reunions, limiting contact to his annual D-Day anniversary conversations with two fellow career military officers, Lt. Colonel Reed and Colonel John Marr.[39] Sherry Fletcher recalled taking her father to see the film *Saving Private Ryan* (1998), which has been lauded for realistically recreating the sounds of war. Homer Poss, who was beginning to show symptoms of dementia, cried as he watched and listened to the film.[40] In the last years of his life, Charles Penchard (1918–2000) was especially bothered by nightmares. In the assisted living home, Penchard raced around, warning staff that "the Germans are coming."[41] In his forties, Rene Rabe, who had been an avid swimmer, became afraid to put his head under water. He told his youngest son, Richard, that, whenever he saw a body of water, a drowning paratrooper now appeared in his mind's eye.[42] Rabe took swimming lessons, trying to overcome his new-found fear of water. But he never regained the ability to be comfortable in the water.

Until the 1980s, the US citizens who focused on Graignes were the families of those paratroopers who died there. The US military had confused the families in 1944–1945. It had initially reported in the summer of 1944 to the Sophian, Premo, and Martinez families that their loved ones were missing. This news left the families in dreadful suspense, hoping their paratrooper would be found or had been taken as a prisoner by the Germans. At the end of 1944, the Premo and Martinez families received the news that their paratroopers had died in Normandy. The circumstances of death were not offered to families. The Sophian family did not receive official notice of Captain Abraham Sophian's death until April 1945 and were further told that his remains were buried in "Eastern France." After repeated letters to military authorities, Dr. Abraham Sophian learned, in September 1945, that his son had been buried in the US Military Cemetery #1 in Marigny, France. For more than three years thereafter, Dr. Sophian sent polite letters, expressing his wish for his son's remains to be sent home. On 3 January 1949, Captain Sophian's remains were laid to rest at Leavenworth National Cemetery in Kansas. In December 1945, Captain Sophian's widow married a Navy veteran who was a colleague of a brother-in-law. Her new spouse adopted Captain Sophian's two-year-old child.[43] In 2011, members of the extended Sophian family would publish an account of Captain Sophian's time in Graignes.

Mrs. Betty Harwood Premo, the widow of Pfc. Harold Premo of Malone in upstate New York, went on a different journey in the aftermath of reports of her husband's death. She held on to the initial "missing in action" report. In January 1946, she contacted US military authorities and told them that she saw her husband in a newsreel "showing American soldiers taken prisoner by the Germans." She obtained a cut of the film from the manager of the theater that had shown the newsreel and enclosed it in her letter. She added that she had never received any proof of her Harold's death, such as his dog tags. Military officers would subsequently send a series of kind letters to Betty Premo, informing her that they had investigated but that the sad conclusion was that Pfc. Premo had died on D-Day.[44] Burial records, which were not forwarded to his widow, confirmed Premo's death. He had been properly buried at Graignes by his fellow paratroopers on or shortly after D-Day. His body was wrapped in a blanket, and money and trinkets were found in his pockets. The *Waffen-SS* men who overran Graignes stripped the paratroopers they killed or murdered of their possessions. The Graves Registration team that moved Premo's body to the temporary cemetery at Blosville reported that shrapnel wounds appeared on his shoulder/neck region.[45] By 1951, Betty Premo had remarried and become Mrs. George E. Green of Malone, New York.

The Martinez family always wanted to know the details of Pvt. Arnold Martinez's death at Graignes. The family received only the notification of his death in 1944 and nothing of his papers, orders, or medals. The US military did not forward to the family his burial records. Graves Registration had located Martinez's body in the center of Graignes and discovered that the mandible and clavicle were missing, indicating death from a catastrophic blast. The family agreed that their Arnold's final resting place should be at the American Cemetery in

Figure 8.3 Pvt. Arnold J. Martinez's burial place at the American Cemetery in Normandy. Author's photograph.

Colleville-sur-Mer. The family apparently made contact with the leaders of Graignes. On 17 July 1952, Mayor Alphonse Voydie wrote to Samuel Martinez, the father of Arnold. In a beautiful letter, the mayor confirmed that Arnold Martinez had fought for the liberty of the villagers and that "the inhabitants of Graignes bow before your sorrow, and beg you to accept their sympathy and their assurance that they shared and even now share the sentiment of your loss."[46] Three decades later, in 1984, the family would launch a campaign to learn more about Pvt. Martinez's time in Graignes. Their leader would be Samuel Martinez, Jr., one of Arnold's eleven siblings. He was five years old when his parents told him of Arnold's death.

Memories in Graignes

As indicated by Mayor Voydie's letter to the father of Pvt. Arnold Martinez, the immediate past was very much with the citizens of Normandy. They addressed the issues of occupation, liberation, and wartime destruction in the decades after World War II. Normans also focused on reconciliation, the memorialization of the past, and reaching out to the US and British veterans who had freed them. For the villagers in Graignes, it would take four decades before they learned that their intrepid efforts to shelter their *paras* from the marauding *Waffen-SS* had been largely successful.

Once Normandy and then France was cleared of the German occupiers, General Charles de Gaulle created a mythical past to assist with domestic reconciliation. Scholars have dubbed it the "myth of resistance" or "*résistancialisme.*" The German occupation of France between 1940 and 1944 was "a glorious page of national history." Obliterated villages, like Oradour-sur-Glane with over 600 people executed, became "sites of national martyrdom." Everyone was brave. The Vichy regime had no popular support. On 3 March 1945, de Gaulle signed legislation transforming citizens into "soldiers" who "contributed toward saving the nation." To be sure, there were tribunals, with 128,000 cases, leading to 38,000 prison sentences, 767 executions, and 50,000 French citizens being labeled people of "national indignity." Automobile mogul Louis Renault (1877–1944), for example, died in prison for committing the crime of making vehicles for the Germans.[47] The reality was that authoritarian Vichy had substantial popular support. Many French people had aided the persecution of Jews. Non-political people made everyday compromises trying to survive under occupation. Nonetheless, de Gaulle's edict had the salubrious effect of helping traumatized citizens rebuild their lives and their country.

As the twentieth century proceeded, however, France had to confront the uncomfortable past. Documents from 1940 to 1944 began to be declassified. The death of de Gaulle in 1969 seemed to prompt an examination of the occupied past. The government finally released all wartime records in 2015. The declassified records marred the reputations of formidable people such as former President François Mitterrand (1981–1995), who had once been thought totally committed to the resistance. Symbolic of this change was the commercial success of the seven-year television series *Un village français (A French Village)* (2009–2017). Compromise with the German occupiers was a daily necessity.

But, in the aftermath of the war, the French preferred to read Mayor Alexandre Renaud's book *Sainte Mère Église: First American Bridgehead in France*, a runaway best seller in postwar France. His account is the dramatic retelling of the 82nd Airborne's landing in the central square of his town. Renaud wrote: "in the wake of these great night birds, other paratroopers, like the seeds of the maple tree, were silently descending; and soon the domes of bright-colored silk, silvery in the moonlight, rested on the meadow grass." The mayor admired the confidence and nonchalance of the *paras*. When out of ammunition, one smiling paratrooper said to Renaud, "oh well ... we still have our knives." The US soldiers naturally passed out sweets to the children. The people of *Sainte Mère Église* were uniformly brave. They hid paratroopers and informed them where the Germans were hiding.[48] The mayor's wife, Simone Renaud, also became a revered national and international figure. For decades, she communicated with the parents of the fallen paratroopers, placing flowers on their sons' graves.[49]

Medals were handed out like candy. Over 1,000 French citizens received the *Ordre de la Libération* for an outstanding contribution to the liberation of occupied France. Only six of the medal winners were women.[50] Women like Germaine Boursier and the Rigault sisters were, of course, inveterate freedom fighters. But, in 1944, de Gaulle announced that he supported the enfranchisement of French women. In 1945, women voted for the first time in France. Graignes received its due. In 1948, the government awarded the village the *Croix de Guerre* with Silver Star in honor of the collective bravery of the people. The next year, Ambassador to France David K. E. Bruce attended a ceremony to establish a Franco-American memorial in the ruins of the church.

Recovery and rebuilding were the first orders of business for the French, including the villagers in Graignes. Graignes was the most thoroughly destroyed locale in the Cotentin Peninsula. Major urban areas like Caen and Saint-Lô were extensively damaged during the invasion and subsequent fighting. Ten thousand of 18,000 homes had been destroyed in Caen. With innovative urban planning and significant international help, including the Marshall Plan, Caen recovered and had doubled its size by the 1960s. Saint-Lô, which had a population of 6,012 in 1946, had grown to 20,700 in 1964. Charles-Édouard Jeanneret, known as Le Corbusier, a pioneer in modern architecture, inspired some of the building in Saint-Lô. On 6 June 1986, Caen commemorated the invasion by opening an impressive War Memorial Museum (*Mémorial de Caen*).[51] The museum has interviewed Normans who lived through the summer of 1944, including villagers from Graignes. In the recent past, French archaeologists have become active in finding and preserving what the Allied liberators left behind in Normandy and assessing the impact that the invasion had on the environment of Normandy.[52]

Beyond restoring their lives and homes, the most pressing question for the people of Graignes was finding out the fate of the paratroopers who defended their village during the momentous days of 6–16 June 1944. For forty years, officials and villagers gathered only a modicum of information. Shortly after the war ended, Irwin Morales, the glider pilot, returned to the village. His mission was to find out what happened to his co-pilot, Thomas Ahmad. Morales concluded that Ahmad had been one of the men executed at Le Mesnil-Angot. But Sgt. Ed Barnes has testified that Ahmad was hit by a bullet, when Ahmad popped his head out of his foxhole in the cemetery. Frank Juliano, a police officer from Staten Island, New York, and one of the paratroopers from the 101st who fought at Graignes, came often and met with Mayor Alphonse Voydie. In gratitude for the aid the villagers gave to the paratroopers, Juliano set up an annual $1,000 scholarship to the best student in Graignes. But Juliano was not in a position to provide information. He could not remember what unit the men from the 82nd Airborne belonged to, and he confessed he never understood why the paratroopers stayed in Graignes.

Some veterans may have been reluctant to return to Graignes. Captain Dave Brummitt wondered if the villagers believed the paratroopers had let them down, when they retreated from the village. In fact, the villagers had semi-deified the *paras*, linking them to God "and that of all your Holy Church." Lt. Colonel Brummitt intended to come to Graignes in the early 2000s, but for the first time in his life he lost a battle – a fight against cancer.[53] But most of the *paras* had not forgotten the first perilous days of their combat careers. Eddie Page told his spouse, Betty, that, when they retired, the first location they would visit in Europe would be Graignes.[54] Whenever any form of cabbage was served in the Rabe household, whether it be boiled white or sweet red, Rene would dig in and remind all that the cabbage with melting butter that he had in the loft of "a farm family's barn" was the "best" meal he ever had.

French veterans of the battle of Graignes began to pass in the 1970s and 1980s. Voydie, who served as mayor from 1944 to 1977, died in 1980. Gustave Rigault died in 1975 at the age of seventy-six. He and his wife Marthe never found out what happened to the men they protected in their barn. Their daughter Marthe has lamented that "I often regret that my parents Gustave and Marthe Rigault did not have any news of the Americans to know if they were safe or not. They were never sure of it."[55] Each year, usually on 8 June, the village commemorated what had happened. Special ceremonies were held on anniversaries, such as the twentieth

Figure 8.4 The Memorial at Graignes. Abbé Le Blastier is buried near the plaque containing the names of citizens and paratroopers who defended the village. Author's photograph.

anniversary in 1964. A memorial was constructed at the top of the hill, with one arch of the church. The beloved Abbé Albert Le Blastier is buried there.

Memories Connect

The surviving villagers and paratroopers initially connected in a most unusual and hilarious way. Colonel Frank Naughton, who had served in Korea and Vietnam, was given, in 1968, a short-term assignment in England. He decided that he wanted to stop in Normandy, before boarding the channel ferry. He was accompanied by his teenaged daughter, Patricia, who had proudly mastered "high-school French." She knew nothing about Graignes, as her father did not discuss his combat experiences. At the village's café, the colonel introduced himself to a group of older men as a paratrooper who had been in the village in the early days of June 1944 and who commanded the team that destroyed the bridge at Le Port des Planqués. Mayor Voydie was in the group. High-school French was not up to the task. The word "Boom" finally conveyed meaning. Mayor Voydie apparently did not inform Colonel Naughton of the war crimes that had been perpetrated by the 17th *SS Panzergrenadier* Division, in the aftermath of the withdrawal of the *paras*. Naughton probably noticed that many buildings were missing. But Naughton was familiar with wartime destruction. As Pat remembered, "The meeting didn't last long. It was a tragic waste of an opportunity, as Marthe has said, her parents were still alive then."[56] Nonetheless, the meeting set the colonel to thinking. He would be vital in restoring the memory of the Franco-American alliance in Graignes. His daughter Patricia had the opportunity to live in Paris for two years and markedly improved her French.

Other veterans, such as Frank Costa, stopped at Graignes in the 1970s and met with the aging mayor. Members of Headquarters Company, 3rd Battalion also began to attend reunions of the 507th Regiment. They surely reminisced about the first fateful days in occupied Normandy. But the big breakthrough came in 1984, at the fortieth-anniversary celebration of D-Day. The event was heavily attended, and President Ronald Reagan arguably delivered the most moving speech of his career at the American Cemetery near Omaha Beach. On 8 June, Graignes held its memorial ceremony. In attendance were Colonel Naughton, Lt. Colonel Earcle "Pip" Reed, Frank Costa, Eddie Page, and Ed Shapert and Charlie Buscek from Pennsylvania, accompanied by their wives. Shapert and Buscek had been attending summer picnics at Eddie Page's house in

Stamford, Connecticut since the late 1950s. Eddie had been keeping the memory of Graignes alive for his fellow enlisted paratroopers. At one picnic, he described how he escaped from his foxhole on the outskirts of Graignes and eventually made it to the Rigault barn. For the first time in June 1984, the veterans learned what happened to the wounded and prisoners of war, to villagers, and to the village itself.

In June 1984, the Americans also met the Rigault sisters, and Marthe cooked a big meal for all. Her feasts often amounted to ten courses. The eating and toasting went on until the next morning. Ever generous, the heroines of Graignes saluted the liberators, with Marthe noting that she would "always thank them and I will always be grateful for saving us and especially those who lost [died] for us." For the rest of the century, numerous veterans visited with the Rigault sisters and, in turn, the sisters came to the United States and attended a reunion of the 507th Regiment. Children of the veterans also made the pilgrimage to the Carentan region. When Cheryl Page, the youngest daughter of Eddie, met the Rigault family, she confessed that she cried frequently, realizing that the Rigaults had made her life possible. Odette remembered that Pat Naughton attested: "You know, if I am here, it's thanks to you. Because my father wouldn't have come back from the war, and I wouldn't be here." A visit to her home in May 2019, as the seventy-fifth anniversary of D-Day approached, prompted Marthe, who was now in her late eighties, to write: "All my family to have very happy to see the son of the *soldat* comes for our liberty. It is a beautiful moment and remembrance." The direct descendants of S/Sgt. Rabe, who passed in 1982, number fifteen (and counting). Baby Ethan Emil Woodard, who entered the world on 12 February 2021, bears the middle name of his great-grandfather, the paratrooper who was served the "best" meal he ever had in the Rigault barn.[57]

The historical record was established by Naughton and Reed, the career military men. They spent ten "fact-finding" days in 1985, interviewing people at the café-bar *Le Rata* in Montmartin-en-Graignes. Members of the Folliot family assisted their efforts. Odette Rigault's son-in-law, Gérard, translated for the colonels. They videotaped their interviews and cross-checked the stories. Knowing the proper military channels to pursue, Naughton and Reed submitted, on 13 February 1986, an extensive report to the Department of the Army, requesting honors be extended to eleven villagers, six of them women. Mayor Voydie, the two executed clerics, their two murdered housekeepers, and resistance fighter Joseph Folliot received their awards posthumously.[58] Secretary of the Army John O. Marsh approved the petition. On 6 July 1986, Secretary Marsh and US Ambassador Joe M. Rodgers presided over the awarding of Distinguished Civilian Service medals. Samuel Martinez, Jr., a younger brother of Arnold Martinez, attended the ceremony. His employer, Coors Brewing Company, commissioned a painting of the battle at Graignes. In attendance to receive their awards were the Rigault sisters, resistance fighter Charles Gosselin, Renée Meunier, "Mess Sergeant" Boursier's co-conspirator, and the forever formidable Madame Germaine Boursier. Boursier, who was ninety years of age, walked with a cane and was supported by her two daughters. Boursier remarked that "I am very happy to see this day." Odette Rigault characterized her medal as "the most beautiful honor I have ever received."[59]

Figure 8.5 The Distinguished Service Medal that Marthe Rigault His received on 6 July 1986 is proudly displayed on her mantel. Also on her mantel are a commendation to her father, Gustave, from General Dwight D. Eisenhower and commendations to the family from Presidents Ronald Reagan and Barack Obama. Author's photograph.

German Historical Memories

German cemeteries in Normandy are the most visible sign of Germany's role and its remembrance of occupation and the subsequent Allied invasion. Approximately 80,000 German soldiers are buried in six cemeteries. The fallen presumably include the 500 men in German uniforms who died at Graignes. The largest cemetery, with over 21,000 buried there, is at La Cambe, near Omaha Beach. The German cemeteries are very somber places and give off a strong anti-war impression. There are 1,200 maple trees in a peace garden at La Cambe. The cemeteries are maintained by the German War Graves Commission, which is a voluntary organization. The commission raises money to further its work and organizes international school children to tend to the graves and grounds during the summer. Respectful German tourists visit the cemeteries.

The theme of reconciliation does not, however, characterize scholarship on the German role at Graignes, whether by Germans or other nationals. The most cursory search of the Internet will reveal that there is popular interest in all things related to the Third Reich, Adolf Hitler, the *Waffen-SS*, and Nazi ideology. Interest in the Nazi movement

Figure 8.6 The German cemetery at La Cambe, near Omaha Beach, is the largest German cemetery in Normandy. Under each cross and plaque, several German soldiers are buried. Author's photograph.

has grown with the rise of right-wing extremism and "white national-ism" in Europe and the United States. There are three major studies of the 17th *Waffen-SS Panzergrenadier* Division "Götz von Berlichingen." All glorify the unit and deny that it perpetrated war crimes. Antonio J. Munoz focused on the combat history of the division. He emphasized that it was the only SS unit to fight entirely on the Western front. In Munoz's telling, the 17th SS *Panzergrenadier* Division fought bravely over a seventeen-month period, eleven months of which were in combat. It was virtually destroyed several times and then rebuilt. Munoz even suggested that the SS men were subjected to Allied war crimes near Nuremberg. He does not provide a source for his allegation.[60]

Massimiliano Afiero, an Italian, released his study in 2018 in English. Afiero offered useful biographical information on the key officers in the unit. He also provided comprehensive analyses of the division's training in France and the quantity and quality of their weapons. Like Munoz's tome, Afiero's book lavishes praise on his subject, noting that the 17th SS *Panzergrenadier* Division "always fought valorously on every battlefield, incurring very heavy losses, especially amongst the officer corps." He further claimed that "throughout its history, the division was never involved in any war crimes against civilians, as witness of its character as a strictly military unit."[61] Neither Afiero nor Munoz men-tioned Graignes and what happened on 11–12 June 1944.

Hans Stöber was too good a chronicler of the 17th SS *Panzergrenadier* Division to gloss over Graignes. But he hid the war crimes in a fictional event. Stöber served in the division. After the war, he spent two decades collecting information. He conducted research in US and German archives. He interviewed survivors of the unit and had access to many of their diaries. On one level, his three-volume combat history of the unit, which was released in Germany in 1975, is a model of scholarship. The first volume, which covered the period from the cre-ation of the division in 1943 until it suffered devastating defeats in July–August 1944, was translated into English in 2017 by a Canadian pub-lisher. Stöber's main theme was that the SS men faced hopeless military assignments in Western Europe and that they took grievous losses when they encountered well-equipped Allied forces, who controlled the skies with their bombers and P-51 Mustangs. Stöber signaled, without being explicit, that the 1st Battalion of the 37th Regiment engaged in military conflict in Graignes on 11–12 June 1944. He noted that the 1st Battalion arrived late in the day on 12 June to the staging area for the assault on

Carentan on 13 June. He further noted that the soldiers of the 1st Battalion were already "exhausted" when they attacked Carentan. But the author then deluded the reader. He claimed that on 12 June the 1st Company of the 1st Battalion attacked the small village of Auvers, which is about ten miles northwest of Graignes. (Stöber spells Auvers various ways in the text.) Like Graignes, Auvers had an impressive, large church. The 1st Company allegedly took prisoners, including paratroopers who were six feet tall. Stöber's alleged source was *Rottenführer* (Senior Lance-Corporal) Hoffman. Hoffman stated that a US doctor was allowed to do his work in the church. Later in the afternoon, according to Hoffman, the 2nd Company of the 1st Battalion relieved the 1st Company.[62]

A historian does not need superior detective skills to unpack the author's lie. Stöber is referring to Captain and Doctor Abraham Sophian, Jr., who was tending to the wounded in what remained of the Romanesque church in Graignes on 11–12 June 1944. The *SS* men of the 1st Battalion captured Dr. Sophian and then murdered him. They also executed the wounded paratroopers and paratroopers who were prisoners of war. Three decades after these atrocities were committed, the 17th *SS Panzergrenadier* Division continued to cover up the unit's war crimes.

Despite the effort to hide the truth about Graignes by those devoted to Nazi Germany, the villagers of Graignes and their beloved *paras* were able to tell their stories. It took four decades for them to connect and share their experiences. But their steadfastness, courage, and devotion to the shared ideals of *liberté, égalité et fraternité* serve as examples for all.

AFTERWORD

The story of Graignes is a dramatic war story and a compelling tale of civilian courage and loyalty. Paratroopers from the 82nd and 101st Airborne Divisions landed hopelessly off target in the early, dark hours of 6 June 1944, D-Day. The small Norman village held no strategic significance and had been spared physical occupation by German troops. Although it was situated only about ten kilometers from the town of Carentan, the village seemed isolated, because the surrounding area was flooded. The ranking military officer made the defensible, albeit perilous, decision to keep the paratroopers in the village and to wait for Allied troops who were storming the beaches of Normandy to reach them. The decision to defend Graignes pleased the villagers, who had pledged to serve the paratroopers. From 6 to 11 June, villagers – men, women, and children – gathered intelligence, conducted reconnaissance missions, went into flooded areas to retrieve the equipment of the paratroopers, and organized a notable feeding campaign that delivered hot meals twice a day to the paratroopers. During this time, the paratroopers and the villagers became not just allies but also friends.

The village's harmony was shattered, beginning on Sunday morning, 11 June, when German forces launched three separate attacks on the village. The paratroopers repulsed the first two attacks, but were overwhelmed by the superior forces of the 17th *SS Panzergrenadier* Division, whose main mission was to capture Carentan and split US forces at Utah and Omaha Beaches. During the evening of 11–12 June, the paratroopers began to withdraw from Graignes, because they had exhausted their ammunition, and because they had no defense against the German artillery bombardment of the village. By 15–16 June, over 100 paratroopers, perhaps two-thirds of the original defenders of Graignes, had made it back to the safety of the headquarters in Normandy of the 82nd and 101st Airborne Divisions. Their successful withdrawal had been facilitated by the villagers of Graignes, who provided intelligence, food, and safehouses. Although they were unaware of it at the time, the paratroopers had contributed to the defense of Carentan by delaying the progress and disrupting the fitness of the 17th *SS Panzergrenadier* Division. The paratroopers subsequently contributed to the Allied victory in Europe by participating in further fighting in Normandy and at the Battle of the Bulge, and by leading, in March 1945, the full-scale invasion of Germany with a combat jump over the Rhine River. While in the Rhineland area, the paratroopers of Headquarters Company, 3rd Battalion of the 507th Regiment liberated Eastern European slave laborers.

The people of Graignes suffered for their fidelity to the US paratroopers. When they took control of the village, the *SS* troops executed religious men and their housekeepers for aiding the US wounded. The *SS* also executed all captured US personnel, including unarmed medical staff – a doctor and medics. The *SS* further lined up prominent citizens and threatened to execute them. German soldiers subsequently burned much of the village to the ground and, by the end of June 1944, had forced people to leave the village and go into exile. Despite these travails, the people of Graignes never disclosed information about their beloved *paras* to the German occupiers. For forty years thereafter, until the mid 1980s, they remained uncertain about the fate of the paratroopers they had saved. But the women of Graignes continued to exhibit the village's devotion to their liberators by marrying in wedding dresses fashioned from parachute silk.

The story of Graignes has a "they lived happily ever after" conclusion. The paratroopers who survived a year of combat in Europe returned to the United States and built middle-class, domestic lives in prosperous postwar America. Some officers continued their military service, achieving both postgraduate educations and high military ranks. To be sure, the veterans of Graignes had to cope with the traumas created by their horrific, battlefield experiences in Europe. The people of Graignes similarly triumphed in postwar life, rebuilding their town and economic life. Rebuilding took more than a decade and was aided, in part, by US economic assistance. Today, Graignes is a tidy town, filled with neat cottages, an impressive Roman Catholic Church, a fine town hall, and a nearby horse-race track. The veterans and the villagers celebrated the past together. The US government recognized the gallantry of the people of Graignes with commendations and medals. The veterans took pride in bringing their children and grandchildren to meet villagers. The obvious fact was that these children and grandchildren owed their very existences to the unwavering commitments made by the villagers to the paratroopers from the 6 to the 16 June 1944.

The story of the paratroopers and Graignes is indeed a compelling tale of resistance, courage, and solidarity. A scholar who reviewed the manuscript concluded that "this book is interdisciplinary and will appeal to a broad audience – undergraduate and graduate student, History professors, WW II enthusiasts, the armed forces, D-Day specialists, and I suspect a more general audience as well." Most everyone enjoys reading about ordinary citizens who accomplish extraordinary things. A second referee agreed with the first, adding that the story of Graignes would attract "those in search of tales of American courage and improvisation."[1] The referee should have broadened the characterization and spoken also of French "courage and improvisation." It would be hard to think of a more intrepid duo than Madame Germaine Boursier and her associate, Mademoiselle Renée Meunier, who clandestinely entered occupied Norman villages to hunt for food to cook for their *paras* and then drove their loaded, horse-drawn wagons through German checkpoints. Historians too infrequently highlight the roles that European women played in facilitating their liberation during World War II.

Evidence about what happened in Graignes was everywhere – in archives, oral histories, autobiographies, interviews, local newspapers, and local libraries, and in the memories of the veterans and their children. The evidence was in France, Germany, and the United States. The abundance of historical evidence from the three countries needed to be assembled and collated. What was also required to tell properly the story of Graignes was a recognition that the Allied invasion of France was not just about the decisions made by male elites – President Franklin Roosevelt, Prime Minister Winston Churchill, General Charles de Gaulle, and General Dwight D. Eisenhower. The paratroopers and the villagers took actions that affected US foreign and military policies. The Allies would have succeeded in Normandy and defeated Nazi Germany without the lost paratroopers of the 82nd and 101st Airborne Divisions or the women of Graignes. But the story of Graignes is not just a curious local event, deserving of a footnote in a general history of the Normandy campaign. The *paras* and the villagers disrupted German plans to recapture Carentan. The village and farm families protected and guided over 100 paratroopers to safety. These men played their part in Normandy, the Battle of the Bulge, the invasion of Germany, and the occupation of Berlin. Who knows what momentous feats their great-grandchildren will accomplish in the future?

ACKNOWLEDGMENTS

I am most grateful to the numerous people in France and the United States who have assisted my research. John Brummitt, Dominique François, Marthe Rigault His, Doris Martinez, Martin K. A. Morgan, Patricia Naughton, Cheryl Page, Mayor Denis Small, and Sandra Smith sent me primary source documents. In particular, Mayor Small, the mayor of Graignes and Le Mesnil-Angot, provided invaluable German military documents that he had collected over the years. My wife, Genice A. G. Rabe, translated these documents. This was exceedingly difficult and time-consuming work, for the German documents were filled with obscure military acronyms and abbreviations.

Martin Morgan sent me two key documents about Graignes – Captain David Brummitt's account of his odyssey in Graignes and Sergeant Major Robert Salewski's diary of his time in Normandy. Morgan had worked on the story of Graignes for more than two decades and had expressed frustration that he had not been able to reach a wide audience. I hope that my effort will help fulfill Morgan's aspirations.

I interviewed the children and relatives of the paratroopers. All contributed to the making of this book. But I would like to highlight the efforts of four people – Sherry Poss Fletcher, Cheryl Page, Patricia Naughton, and Doris Martinez. I had a connection with Fletcher and Page. Staff Sergeant Rene Rabe's "best buddies" in the paratroopers were Corporal Homer Poss and Technician Fifth Class Edward "Eddie" Page. My father and Page kept in touch and exchanged visits in our state of Connecticut. As a child, I met Cheryl and her older sister, Doreen. At reunions sponsored by Eddie Page, I also met Sherry (we think). But a good fifty years would pass before we renewed our acquaintances.

Beginning in 2018, I devoted my research and writing to Graignes. My first contact was with Keith Poss of Highland, Illinois, whose name I found in his father's obituary. Keith immediately put me in touch with his sister, Sherry, who proved to be a fountainhead of information about Graignes, the 507th Regiment, and the children of the paratroopers. Sherry put me in touch with Cheryl, who had accompanied her father to Graignes, had met the Rigault family, and had ideas on people that I should contact.

Doris Martinez of Lakewood, Colorado never met her brother-in-law, paratrooper Arnold Martinez, who died at Graignes. Arnold is buried at the American Cemetery at Colleville-sur-Mer in Normandy. But, for decades, the extended Martinez family wondered about the circumstances of Arnold's death and conducted independent research. Doris kindly sent me documents that the family had collected. Doris also encouraged me with her inspiring letters. We converse now about our grandchildren.

Patricia Naughton of Seattle, Washington had been to Graignes as a teenager. She accompanied her father, Colonel Francis "Frank" Naughton, a career military officer and a veteran of Graignes. Her father would be instrumental in initiating the process of reuniting the veterans of Graignes and the villagers and persuading US political and military leaders that the people of Graignes were owed a debt of gratitude from the United States. Patricia, who studied in France, became friends with villagers and provided introductions for me.

My greatest debt is to the Rigault/His family and especially to Marthe His and her daughters, Gabrielle and Danielle. Marthe has tirelessly answered questions and offered me invaluable insights. Unfortunately, Marthe's older sister, Odette, passed just a few months before I traveled to Normandy. It is an overwhelming experience to meet a family that saved your father's life and made your grandchildren's lives possible.

NOTES

Introduction

1. Dr. Eric Groce, a professor of elementary education at Appalachian State University, coined the term "silk from the sky." Groce has written an unpublished novel about Graignes for young adults.
2. Olivier Wieviorka, *Normandy: The Landings to the Liberation of Paris*, translated by M. B. DeBevoise (Cambridge, MA and London: Belknap Press of Harvard University Press, 2008), 1.
3. President Reagan's speech can be viewed at: www.youtube.com/watch?v=eEIqdcHbc8I.
4. Homily by Graignes Village Priest Louis Binet, 8 June 1964. In the author's possession through courtesy of the Martinez family.
5. Tom Brokaw, *The Greatest Generation* (New York: Random House, 1998).
6. Letter, Lieutenant M. Pontinier, Secretary of Mayor of Graignes Alphonse Voydie, to Samuel Martinez, Sr., 17 July 1952. In the author's possession through courtesy of the Martinez family.
7. Gary N. Fox, *Graignes: The Franco-American Memorial* (Fostoria, OH: Gray Printing, 1990).
8. Dominique François, *La bataille de Graignes: Les paras perdus, 5–12 juin 1944* (Valognes: Le Révérend, 2012).
9. Martin K. A. Morgan, *Down to Earth: The 507th Parachute Infantry Regiment in Normandy, June 6–July 15, 1944* (Atglen, PA: Schiffer Military History, 2004), 232–62; Martin K. A. Morgan, *D-Day: A Photographic History of the Normandy Invasion* (Minneapolis, MN: Zoom Press, 2014), 185–209. In a December 2020 interview, Morgan surprisingly renounced his previous two decades of research. He stated that he had been "sucked into" presenting a false narrative, because he had not kept his scholarly distance from the villagers. He admitted that he had developed a close personal relationship with a woman in the village. Even though Morgan had violated scholarly ethics and compromised his credibility, his repudiation of his work seems bizarre and illogical. Morgan, for example, now questions whether SS forces perpetrated war crimes in Graignes. But in *Down to Earth* (p. 258), he presented four affidavits by villagers who testified to US military investigators in 1947 about the atrocities

committed in Graignes in June 1944 by the Germans. In his 2020 interview, he makes similarly dubious statements about other critical issues. For the interview, see "Graignes – Challenging a Legend: Interview of Martin Morgan by Paul Woodadge," 12 December 2020, www.youtube.com/watch?v=_y8xA74Zy7I.

10. Georgia Public Broadcasting, *Papa Said: We Should Never Forget*, DVD (Warner Robins, GA: Salute America, Inc.; Museum of Aviation, 2008).

11. Morgan quoted in Robert Venditti, Kevin Maurer, and Andrea Mutti, *Six Days: The Incredible Story of D-Day's Lost Chapter* (Burbank, CA: DC Comics, 2019), v.

12. For innovative approaches to the study of US foreign relations, see essays in *America in the World: The Historiography of American Foreign Relations since 1941*, 2nd edition, edited by Frank Costigliola and Michael J. Hogan (New York: Cambridge University Press, 2014).

13. Mary Louise Roberts, *D-Day through French Eyes: Normandy, 1944* (Chicago, IL: University of Chicago Press, 2014), 4–5.

14. Ronald C. Rosbottom, *Sudden Courage: Youth in France Confront the Germans, 1940–1945* (New York: HarperCollins, 2019).

15. Massimiliano Afiero, *The 17th Waffen-SS Panzergrenadier Division Götz von Berlichingen*, translated by Ralph Riccio (Atglen, PA: Schiffer Publishing, 2018), 6.

1 Paratrooper

1. Scott Garrett, "Airborne through the Ages," in *U.S.A. Airborne: 50th Anniversary*, edited by Bart Hagerman (Paducah, KY: Turner Publishing, 1990), 25–27.

2. Ibid., 25–26; Guy LoFaro, *The Sword of St. Michael: The 82nd Airborne Division in World War II* (Cambridge, MA: Da Capo Press, 2011), 8–9.

3. Ibid., 9–12; Garrett, "Airborne through the Ages," 29.

4. Ibid., 29; LoFaro, *Sword of St. Michael*, 12–13.

5. Gavin quoted in ibid., 13.

6. Ibid., 17–19; Garrett, "Airborne through the Ages," 32–34.

7. US Army, *Official History of the 82nd Division American Expeditionary Forces, "All American" Division, 1917–1919* (Indianapolis, IN: Bobbs-Merrill, 1919); Deryk Wills, *Put on Your Boots and Parachutes! A Collection of Personal Stories from the Veterans of the 82nd Airborne Division* (Leicester: AB Printers Limited, 1992), 9–11.

8. Martha Gellhorn, "Rough and Tumble," *Colliers Weekly*, 2 December 1944, 12, 70.

9. LoFaro, *Sword of St. Michael*, 19.

10. John Hinchliff oral history (OH), 2005. Interviewed by Douglas Bekke. Minnesota Historical Society, Minneapolis, Minnesota; John Dunn OH, 1994. Interviewed by Mark Van Ells. Wisconsin Veterans Museum Research Center, Madison, Wisconsin; Bob Bearden, *To D-Day and Back: Adventures with the 507th Parachute Infantry Regiment and Life as a World War II POW* (St. Paul, MN: Zenith Press, 2007), 20–21.

11. LoFaro, *Sword of St. Michael*, 39–40.

12. Jones quoted in Gerald Astor, *June 6, 1944: The Voices of D-Day* (New York: Dell Publishing, 1994), 3. See also John McKenzie, *On Time, on Target: The World War II Memoir of a Paratrooper in the 82nd Airborne* (Novato, CA: Presidio Press, 2000), 38–39.

13. Mark J. Alexander and John Sparry, *Jump Commander: In Combat with the 505th and 508th Parachute Infantry Regiments, 82nd Airborne Division in World War II* (Philadelphia, PA and Oxford: Casemate Publishers, 2010), 50–53; LoFaro, *Sword of St. Michael*, 46–51.

14. Miller's athletic prowess was described in an obituary notice: www.findagrave.com /memorial/90081444/robert-r-miller.
15. Gavin quoted in Astor, *June 6, 1944*, 61.
16. James P. James OH, 2005. Interviewed by James Kurtz. Wisconsin Veterans Museum Research Center, Madison, Wisconsin; Kurt Gabel, *The Making of a Paratrooper: Airborne Training and Combat in World War II*, edited and with an introduction and epilogue by William C. Mitchell, foreword by Theodore A. Wilson (Lawrence, KA: University Press of Kansas, 1990), 29–32; Rene E. Rabe as told to author.
17. James Megellas, *All the Way to Berlin: A Paratrooper at War in Europe* (New York: Presidio Press, 2003), 12–16.
18. Isbell quoted in John P. McCann, *Passing Through: The 82nd Airborne Division in Northern Ireland, 1943–1944* (Newtownards, Northern Ireland: Colourpoint Books, 2005), 22; Bearden, *To D-Day and Back*, 26–27.
19. Hinchliff OH, 2005; Isbell quoted in McCann, *Passing Through*, 22; Alexander and Sparry, *Jump Commander*, 56; introduction by Gerald M. Devlin in Barbara Gavin Fauntleroy, *The General and His Daughter: The Wartime Letters of General James M. Gavin to His Daughter Barbara*, edited by Gayle Wurst (New York: Fordham University Press, 2007), xvii–xxii; Astor, *June 6, 1944*, 63.
20. Telephone interview with Jonathan Boyle of Springfield, MO, 6 June 2020; "Keosauqua Man Observes 50th Anniversary of D-Day," *Van Buren County Register* (Iowa), 5 May 1994.
21. Bearden, *To D-Day and Back*, 21, 53; Gavin quoted in LoFaro, *Sword of St. Michael*, 26–27.
22. Matthew B. Ridgway, *Soldier: The Memoirs of Matthew B. Ridgway* (New York: Harper & Brothers, 1956), 5–6; Robert M. Murphy OH, Digital Collections of World War II Museum, New Orleans, LA, www.ww2online.org/view/robert-murphy.
23. T. Michael Booth and Duncan Spencer, *Paratrooper: The Life of General James M. Gavin* (New York: Simon & Schuster1994), 17–34; introduction by Devlin in Fauntleroy, *The General and His Daughter*, xvii–xxii.
24. Ibid., 1–6, 111.
25. Booth and Spencer, *Paratrooper*, 64.
26. Gavin quoted in ibid., 242.
27. Gellhorn, "Rough and Tumble," 12, 70.
28. Booth and Spencer, *Paratrooper*, 15.
29. Ibid., 157–58; Fauntleroy, *The General and His Daughter*, xiv; Clay Blair, *Ridgway's Paratroopers: The American Airborne in World War II* (Garden City, NY: The Dial Press, 1985), 193–97; LoFaro, *Sword of St. Michael*, 46–51.
30. Fauntleroy, *The General and His Daughter*, 112.
31. LoFaro, *Sword of St. Michael*, 17; Fauntleroy, *The General and His Daughter*, 111.
32. Gavin quoted in Booth and Spencer, *Paratrooper*, 169–70.
33. Page quoted in Tony Pavia, *An American Town Goes to War* (Paducah, KY: Turner Publishing, 2013), Chapter 11; LoFaro, *Sword of St. Michael*, 46.
34. Ibid., 243–44, 257–61; Ridgway, *Soldier*, 15–16; Blair, *Ridgway's Paratroopers*, 282; Booth and Spencer, *Paratrooper*, 189, 199–202; Wills, *Put on Your Boots*, 228–29.
35. Ridgway, *Soldier*, 15–16.
36. Gavin quoted in Astor, *June 6, 1944*, 60.
37. Letter of 5 June 1944 in Fauntleroy, *The General and His Daughter*, 107–8.
38. Gavin quoted in Astor, *June 6, 1944*, 61.

39. Gavin quoted in Booth and Spencer, *Paratrooper*, 157–59.
40. Graham quoted in Astor, *June 6, 1944*, 167–69; McNally quoted in LoFaro, *Sword of St. Michael*, 202.
41. Gavin quoted in Astor, *June 6, 1944*, 154–55.
42. Murphy OH; LoFaro, *Sword of St. Michael*, 257; McKenzie, *On Time, on Target*, 98–99; Wills, *Put on Your Boots*, 180.
43. Booth and Spencer, *Paratrooper*, 300.
44. Ridgway and Eaton quoted in Blair, *Ridgway's Paratroopers*, 202.
45. Quoted in Booth and Spencer, *Paratrooper*, 266.
46. Gavin quoted in LoFaro, *Sword of St. Michael*, 572, footnote 21; Alexander, *Jump Commander*, 53.
47. Letter of 5 June 1944 in Fauntleroy, *The General and His Daughter*, 107–8.
48. G. St. J. Perrott, "Selective Service Rejection Statistics and Some of Their Implications," *American Journal of Public Health* 34 (April 1946): 336–42.
49. Letter of Cheryl Page of Burlington, VT to author, 25 May 2020.
50. Telephone interview with John Brummitt of Hilton Head, SC, 6 June 2020.
51. John W. Marr OH, Digital Collections of World War II Museum, www .ww2online.org/view/john-w-marr#d-day-objectives.
52. Interview with John Brummitt.
53. Margaret R. O'Leary and Dennis S. O'Leary, *Tragedy at Graignes: The Bud Sophian Story* (Bloomington, IN: Universe, Inc., 2011), 12–165.
54. Letter, Patricia Naughton of Seattle, WA, to author, 1 June 2020; Curt Yeomans, "Ex-Gwinnett Judge, WW II Vet Buried at Arlington National Cemetery," *Gwinnett Daily Post*, 17 May 2015, www.gwinnettdailypost.com/news/2015/may14; Frank Naughton OH, interviewed by Martin Morgan in Cherbourg, France, 21 July 2002, National World War II Museum.
55. Al Zdon, "For $50 a Month More Pay, You Could Join the Paratroopers," *Minnesota Legionnaire* (April 2013), 8–10; John Hinchliff OH, 2005; John Joseph Hinchliff OH, interviewed by Martin Morgan in Cherbourg, France, 22 July 2002, World War II Museum.
56. Elaine Tyler May, *Homeward Bound: American Families in the Cold War Era* (New York: Basic Books, 1982), 58–91.
57. Hospital Admissions Card for Rene E. Rabe (Service #31325488), 28 March 1945, National Personnel Records Center (NPRC), St. Louis, Missouri.
58. Letter, Rene E. Rabe, Berlin, to Maria Rabe, New York City, 1 September 1945, in the author's possession.
59. Headquarters Company Morning Report, 24 July 1944, Tollerton, Nottingham, England, NPRC. The report lists promotions made in Normandy on 16 June 1944.
60. Letters, Sherry (Poss) Fletcher of Highland, IL to author, 11 July 2018, 14 June 2019, and 28 May 2020; Roland Harris, "Highland Man Fought from D-Day to the Battle of the Bulge," *Highland News Leader*, 4 July 2018, 4A.
61. Cheryl Page to author, 14 April 2020; Pavia, *An American Town Goes to War*, Chapter 11.
62. Ridgway, *Soldier*, 99–100; Blair, *Ridgway's Paratroopers*, 201; Booth and Spencer, *Paratrooper*, 161.
63. Garrett, "Airborne through the Ages," 42.
64. Sherry Fletcher to author, 14 August 2018.
65. Letter and accompanying material, Doris Martinez of Lakewood, Colorado to author, 15 September 2018; news clipping in scrapbook of Mrs. Miguel Martinez of Del Norte, Colorado posted at www.findagrave.com/memorial/56647320/ arnold-j-martinez.

66. Astor, *June 6, 1944*, 197, 404, 441; US Army Air Forces, "Album: 74th Troop Carrier Squadron" (1945), *World War Regimental Histories*, 126, https://digi com.bpl.lib.me.us/ww_reg_his/126/?utm_source=digicom.bpl.lib.me.us%2Fww_reg_his%2F126&utm_medium=PDF&utm_campaign=PDFCoverPages.
67. Zdon, "For $50 a Month More Pay," 8.

2 Overseas

1. John Marr, "507th Parachute Infantry Regiment," in *U.S.A. Airborne: 50th Anniversary*, edited by Bart Hagerman (Paducah, KY: Turner Publishing, 1990), 264.
2. Martin K. A. Morgan, "Battle of Graignes: An HQ Company's Heroic Last Stand in Normandy," *Warfare History Network* (31 December 2018), https://warfarehistory network.com/2018/12/31/battle-of-graignes-an-hq-companys-heroic-last-stand-in-normandy/; James OH; Harold J. Premo, Service Record, NPRC.
3. Morgan, "Battle of Graignes."
4. Marthe Rigault Testimony, "4 Days in June" ("*4 Jours en juin*"), https://quatrejour senjuin.com/76eme-live/marthe-rigault-temoigne-episode-1/.
5. Bearden, *To D-Day and Back*, 57.
6. US Army, "507th Parachute Infantry," (1943), *World War Regimental Histories*, https://core.ac.uk/download/pdf/234781347.pdf; Marr, "507th Parachute Infantry Regiment," 265; Bearden, *To D-Day and Back*, 61.
7. Ibid., 79.
8. Headquarters Company Morning Report, 22 November 1943, NPRC.
9. Ibid., 29 November 1943.
10. Wieviorka, *Normandy*, 5.
11. John W. Dower, *War without Mercy: Race and Power in the Pacific War* (New York: Pantheon, 1986).
12. Page quoted in Pavia, *An American Town Goes to War*, Chapter 11.
13. Hinchliff OH, 2005.
14. Davis and Carl Letson of 507th Regiment quoted in McCann, *Passing Through*, 42–43.
15. Ibid., 42–44.
16. O'Leary and O'Leary, *Tragedy at Graignes*, 185.
17. Ibid., 188–89.
18. McCann, *Passing Through*, 69, 85–87.
19. Ibid., 53–56; Harris, "Highland Man Fought from D-Day," 4A; James OH.
20. O'Leary and O'Leary, *Tragedy at Graignes*, 188–89.
21. McCann, *Passing Through*, 61–66.
22. Letter of 2 December 1943, in Fauntleroy, *The General and His Daughter*, 79.
23. Nelson quoted in Astor, *June 6, 1944*, 118; McCann, *Passing Through*, 85.
24. Ibid., 78–80; Clinton "Clint" Riddle OH, Digital Collection of National World War II Museum, www.ww2online.org/view/clinton-clint-riddle#entering-the-service.
25. McCann, *Passing Through*, 85.
26. Mary Louise Roberts, *What Soldiers Do: Sex and the American GI in World War II France* (Chicago, IL: University of Chicago Press, 2013), 258.
27. Harold J. Premo, Service Record, NPRC.
28. Dunn OH; McCann, *Passing Through*, 58; Bearden, *To D-Day and Back*, 90–91.
29. Riddle quoted in McCann, *Passing Through*, 99; J. Glenn Gray, *The Warriors: Reflections on Men in Battle* (New York: Harcourt, Brace and Company, 1959), 61–63.

30. McCann, *Passing Through*, 90–91.
31. Ibid., 80–81.
32. Hinchliff OH, 2005; Bearden, *To D-Day and Back*, 96.
33. Isbell quoted in McCann, *Passing Through*, 94.
34. Ibid., 95–97; Bearden, *To D-Day and Back*, 95–96.
35. Booth and Spencer, *Paratrooper*, 159.
36. Gavin quoted in ibid., 161; Blair, *Ridgway's Paratroopers*, 201.
37. Wills, *Put on Your Boots and Parachutes*, 41–42.
38. Ridgway, *Soldier*, 99–100.
39. Gavin quoted in Booth and Spencer, *Paratrooper*, 159.
40. Blair, *Ridgway's Paratroopers*, 194.
41. Letter of 11 May 1944, in Fauntleroy, *The General and His Daughter*, 103.
42. Marr, "507th Parachute Infantry Regiment," 265; O'Leary and O'Leary, *Tragedy at Graignes*, 194.
43. James OH; on Boyle see "Keosauqua Man Observes 50th Anniversary of D-Day," *Van Buren County Register* (Iowa), 5 May 1994.
44. Bearden, *To D-Day and Back*, 99–100; O'Leary and O'Leary, *Tragedy at Graignes*, 196; LoFaro, *Sword of St. Michael*, 187; George Koskimaki, *D-Day with the Screaming Eagles* (Haverton, PA: Casemate, 1970), 1–12.
45. T/5 Davis quoted in McCann, *Passing Through*, 98.
46. Wills, *Put on Your Boots and Parachutes*, 44, 58, 85, 175.
47. Millett quoted in McCann, *Passing Through*, 100.
48. Alexander and Sparry, *Jump Commander*, 172; James OH.
49. Letters of 19 April 1944 and 2 June 1944 in Fauntleroy, *The General and His Daughter*, 100–1, 106.
50. Marr OH.
51. Davis quote in McCann, *Passing Through*, 100.
52. LoFaro, *Sword of St. Michael*, 33–38.
53. Alexander S. Cochran, "ULTRA, FORTITUDE, and D-Day Planning: The Missing Dimension," in *D-Day 1944*, edited by Theodore Wilson (Lawrence, KS: University Press of Kansas, 1994), 63–79; Don Whitehead, "A Correspondent's View of D-Day," in *D-Day 1944*, edited by Theodore Wilson (Lawrence, KS: University Press of Kansas, 1994), 203–12; Wieviorka, *Normandy*, 69; Joshua Levine, *Operation Fortitude: The Greatest Hoax of the Second World War* (New York: HarperCollins, 2012).
54. Koskimaki, *D-Day with the Screaming Eagles*, 9.
55. Devlin, *Paratrooper*, 372; Robert M. Murphy, *No Better Place to Die: The Battle for La Fière Bridge* (Philadelphia, PA and Oxford: Casement Publishers, 2009), 23–25.
56. Devlin, *Paratrooper*, 355.
57. Forrest C. Pogue, "D-Day 1944," in *D-Day 1944*, edited by Theodore Wilson (Lawrence, KS: University Press of Kansas, 1994), 189; Wieviorka, *Normandy*, 89–90.
58. Dwight D. Eisenhower, *Crusade in Europe* (Garden City, NY: Doubleday, 1948), 239–47.
59. Gerhard L. Weinberg, "D-Day: Analysis of Costs and Benefits," in *D-Day 1944*, edited by Theodore Wilson (Lawrence, KS: University Press of Kansas, 1994), 326.
60. Eisenhower quoted in Pogue, "D-Day 1944," 189.
61. Leigh-Mallory quoted in LoFaro, *Sword of St. Michael*, 193.
62. Charles Houghton, "82nd Airborne's Stunning 1-Day KIA at Normandy," 5 November 2018, *Real Clear History*, www.realclearhistory.com/2018/11/06/82nd_airborne039s_stunning_1-day_kia_at_normandy_9424.html.

63. Weinberg, "D-Day: Analysis of Costs and Benefits," 331.
64. Houghton, "82nd Airborne's Stunning 1-Day KIA at Normandy."
65. Eisenhower, *Crusade in Europe*, 239. For the debate about Eisenhower's actual words to launch the invasion, see Tim Rives, "'OK, We'll Go': Just What Did Ike Say When He Launched the D-Day Invasion 70 Years Ago," *Prologue* (Spring 2014), www.archives.gov/files/publications/prologue/2014/spring/d-day.pdf.
66. Blair, *Ridgway's Paratroopers*, 208; Murphy, *No Better Place to Die*, 23–25; Marr OH.
67. LoFaro, *Sword of St. Michael*, 195; Bearden, *To D-Day and Back*, 107; Jeziorski quoted in Astor, *June 6, 1944*, 144.
68. Ridgway and Gavin quoted in Wills, *Put on Your Boots and Parachutes*, 62; Booth and Spencer, *Paratrooper*, 170. Eisenhower's letter can be found at www.archives .gov/global-pages/larger-image.html?i=/historical-docs/doc-content/images/ww2-eisenhower-d-day-order-l.jpg&c=/historical-docs/doc-content/images/ww2-eisenhower-d-day-order.caption.html.
69. Letter, 30 May 1944, in Fauntleroy, *The General and His Daughter*, 105–6.
70. Isbell quoted in McCann, *Passing Through*, 101–2.
71. Pogue, "D-Day 1944," 197–98.
72. McCann, *Passing Through*, 101–3; Koskimaki, *D-Day with the Screaming Eagles*, 11.
73. Colonel (Ret.) Francis E. Naughton "Account of Graignes," 1998. In the author's possession, through courtesy of the Naughton family.

3 Occupied France

1. Mark Mazower, *Hitler's Empire: How the Nazis Ruled Europe* (New York: Penguin, 2008), 108–10; Matthew Adam Kocher, Adria K. Lawrence, and Nino P. Monteiro, "Nationalism, Collaboration, and Resistance: France under Nazi Occupation," *International Security* 43 (Fall 2018): 128.
2. Robert O. Paxton, *Vichy France: Old Guard and New Order, 1940–1944* (New York: Alfred K. Knopf, 1972), 3; Charles Sowerwine, *France since 1870*, 3rd edition (London: Red Globe Press, 2018), 168; Philip Nord, *France 1940: Defending the Republic* (New Haven, CT: Yale University Press, 2015), 86.
3. Pétain quoted in Mazower, *Hitler's Empire*, 417. See also Paxton, *Vichy France*, 173–84.
4. The text of the 18 June 1940 speech can be found at https://abmceducation.org/sites/default/files/activity/DeGaulle-Appeal.pdf; the text of the 22 June 1940 speech can be found at https://franceintheus.org/IMG/pdf/General_de_Gaulles_Address_-_June_22_1940.pdf.
5. Kocher, Lawrence, and Monteiro, "Nationalism, Collaboration, and Resistance," 140, footnote 79; French General Maxim Weygand quoted in Sowerwine, *France since 1870*, 176; Olivier Wieviorka, *The French Resistance*, translated by Jean Marie Todd (Cambridge, MA and London: Belknap Press of Harvard University Press, 2016), 1.
6. Ibid., 208–20; Paxton, *Vichy France*, 173–84.
7. Rosbottom, *Sudden Courage*, 112, 155–58, 185; Paxton, *Vichy France*, 374–75.
8. Caroline Moorehead, *A Train in Winter: An Extraordinary Story of Women, Friendship, and Resistance in Occupied France* (New York: HarperCollins, 2011), 23–24.

9. Kocher, Lawrence, and Monteiro, "Nationalism, Collaboration, and Resistance," 140, footnote 79; Wieviorka, *The French Resistance*, 359; testimony of Jean Nallit of Resistance movement in Eric Touya de Marenne, *French–American Relations: Remembering D-Day after September 11* (Lanham, MD: University Press of America, 2008), 81–89.

10. Hans Stöber, *Combat History of the 17. SS-Panzer-Grenadier-Division "Götz von Berlichingen,"* vol. 1, translated by Klaus Scharley (Winnipeg: J. J. Fedorowicz, 2017), 13–14.

11. Lynne Olson, *Madam Fourcade's Secret War* (New York: Random House, 2019), 295.

12. Wieviorka, *The French Resistance*, 410–12.

13. Rosbottom, *Sudden Courage*, 274, 280.

14. Wieviorka, *The French Resistance*, 454–58; Rosbottom, *Sudden Courage*, 242. For a fictional account that glorifies the Resistance, see Romain Gary, *The Kites*, translated by Miranda Richmond Mouillot (New York: New Directions, 2017). Gary participated in the resistance to German occupation.

15. Mazower, *Hitler's Empire*, 517.

16. Wieviorka, *The French Resistance*, 369.

17. Eisenhower, *Crusade in Europe*, 232–33.

18. Hugh Clout, "Reconstruction in the Manche *département* after the Normandy Landings," *Modern & Contemporary France* 16 (February 2008): 3–21; Arthur Layton Funk, "Caught in the Middle: The French Population in Normandy," in *D-Day 1944*, edited by Theodore Wilson (Lawrence, KS: University Press of Kansas, 1994), 249; Vice-Mayor Joret quoted in Denis Van Den Brink, *Carentan: The Battle – June 1944* (Paris: Régi'arm, 2016), 92.

19. S. L. A. Marshall, *Night Drop: The American Airborne Invasion of Normandy* (Boston, MA: Little, Brown and Company, 1962), 244–46.

20. Layton Funk, "Caught in the Middle," 238.

21. Sowerwine, *France since 1870*, 139, 175–90.

22. Alexandre Renaud, *Sainte Mère Église: First American Bridgehead in France* (Saint Lô: Éditions Odile Pathé, 1964), 1–17; Van Den Brink, *Carentan*, 92; letter, Patricia Naughton, Seattle, to author on discussion with Marthe Rigault His about Gustave Rigault, 19 January 2020, in the author's possession.

23. Odette Lelavechef and Marthe His OH, 16 May 2003, interview conducted by Martin Morgan, National World War II Museum; notes from interview with Marthe Rigault His, 16 May 2019, conducted by author in Carentan, in the author's possession.

24. Renaud, *Sainte Mère Église*, 24, 34–37.

25. Lelavechef and His OH; Odette also quoted in NBC News, *The Greatest Generation with Tom Brokaw*, DVD, Disc 2: *D-Day: A Leap into History* (Eugene, OR: Timeless Media Group, 2005).

26. Renaud, *Sainte Mère Église*, 25–26.

27. François, *La bataille de Graignes*, 18–23; Lelavechef and His OH.

28. Notes from interview with Marthe Rigault His conducted by author in Carentan, 20 May 2019.

29. Clout, "Reconstruction in the Manche *département*," 8.

30. Testimony of Fortification Development Officer Gert Hoffman in Holger Eckhertz, *D Day through German Eyes* (San Bernadino, CA: DTZ History Publications, 2016), 254–60.

31. Layton Funk, "Caught in the Middle," 239.

32. Renaud, *Sainte Mère Église*, 28–44.

33. Voydie quoted in Koskimaki, *D-Day with the Screaming Eagles*, 315.
34. Marshall, *Night Drop*, 246; Dominique François, *The 507th Parachute Infantry Regiment* (Bayeux: Éditions Heimdal, 2000), 55.
35. Lelavechef and His OH; Layton Funk, "Caught in the Middle," 239.
36. Christmas cancellation announcement quoted in ibid., 240.
37. Olson, *Madam Fourcade's Secret War*, 302–3.
38. Renaud, *Sainte Mère Église*, 28–44.
39. French farmer cited in Koskimaki, *D-Day with the Screaming Eagles*, 315.
40. Marthe Rigault His, "Madam Marthe His Presents Her Child's Eye View: 1944 Graignes, Normandy from D-Day," translated to English from her diary, in the author's possession, courtesy of the Page family; Lelavechef and His OH; Colin Beavan, *Operation Jedburgh: D-Day and America's First Shadow War* (New York: Viking, 2016), 116.
41. Booth and Spenser, *Paratrooper*, 173; Layton Funk, "Caught in the Middle," 240; Wieviorka, *Normandy*, 171–72.
42. Ibid., 139, 153–66.
43. Weinberg, "D-Day," 326.
44. Wieviorka, *French Resistance*, 422–32; Mazower, *Hitler's Empire*, 517; Olson, *Madam Fourcade's Secret War*, 302–7.
45. Devlin, *Paratrooper*, 368–72; Chef des Stabes (Chief of Staff) Military History Blog, *LXXXIV Armee-Korps on the Cotentin Peninsula – 6th to 9th June 1944*, https://chefdesstabes.wordpress.com/the-response-of-lxxxiv-armee-korps-to-the-allied-amphibious-landings-at-7-armee-kva-kusten-verteidigung-abschnitt.
46. Devlin, *Paratrooper*, 387–88; Bearden, *To D-Day and Back*, 174.
47. Eckhertz, *D Day through German Eyes*, 4–26, 44–62, 254–60.
48. LoFaro, *Sword of St. Michael*, 188.
49. General von Schlieben quoted in Chef des Stabes, *LXXXIV Armee-Korps*; Stöber, *Combat History of the 17. SS-Panzer-Grenadier-Division*, 84.
50. Murphy, *No Better Place to Die*, 23–25; Chef des Stabes, *LXXXIV Armee-Korps*; Van Den Brink, *Carentan*, 51–85.
51. Koskimaki, *D-Day with the Screaming Eagles*, 126, 284–302; Alexander and Sparry, *Jump Commander*, 195.
52. Bearden, *To D-Day and Back*, 174–248; Henry Langrehr and Jim DeFelice, *Whatever It Took: An American Paratrooper's Extraordinary Memoir of Escape, Survival and Heroism in the Last Days of World War II* (New York: William Morrow, 2020), 135–84; James OH.
53. Eckhertz, *D Day through German Eyes*, 33.
54. Stöber, *Combat History of the 17. SS-Panzer-Grenadier-Division*, 11, 491–96; Antonio J. Munoz, *Iron Fist: A Combat History of the 17. SS Panzergrenadier Division "Goetz von Berlichingen," 1943–1945* (Bayside, NY: Axis Europa Books, 1999), 5.
55. Afiero, *The 17th Waffen-SS Panzergrenadier Division*, 204.
56. Ibid., 10–21; Stöber, *Combat History of the 17. SS-Panzer-Grenadier-Division*, 3–13; Richard Hargreaves, *The Germans in Normandy* (Mechanicsburg, PA: Stackpole Books, 2006), 15–16.
57. Afiero, *The 17th Waffen-SS Panzergrenadier Division*, 204–5.
58. Stöber, *Combat History of the 17. SS-Panzer-Grenadier-Division*, 70–72.
59. Ibid., 9–13; Afiero, *The 17th Waffen-SS Panzergrenadier Division*, 10, 17.
60. Stöber, *Combat History of the 17. SS-Panzer-Grenadier-Division*, 19, 65.
61. Ibid., 491–96; Afiero, *The 17th Waffen-SS Panzergrenadier Division*, 17, 199.
62. Ibid., 17; Stöber, *Combat History of the 17. SS-Panzer-Grenadier-Division*, 19–45.

63. Hargreaves, *The Germans in Normandy*, 68–69; Stöber, *Combat History of the 17. SS-Panzer-Grenadier-Division*, 25–26, 47–49.

64. Transmissions of 6 and 7 June 1944 in *Tagebuch* (Daily Record) of the 17th SS Panzergrenadier Division "Götz von Berlichingen," translated by Genice A. G. Rabe, in the author's possession, courtesy of Mayor Denis Small of Graignes; Afiero, *The 17th Waffen-SS Panzergrenadier Division*, 17, 27–28.

4 Liberators and Friends

1. Eisenhower, *Crusade in Europe*, 251–52.
2. For a display of the equipment paratroopers carried, see Morgan, *Down to Earth*, 106–69.
3. François, *La bataille de Graignes*, 93.
4. Bearden, *To D-Day and Back*, 110–16; obituary of Thomas P. Woodward in *Courier-Post*, Camden, NJ, 20 March 2000, 14.
5. Verret quoted in McCann, *Passing Through*, 102.
6. Ridgway, *Soldier*, 3.
7. Gavin quoted in Langrehr and DeFelice, *Whatever It Took*, 77; Gunning remembered in Hinchliff OH, 2005; Morales and Ahmad quoted in Astor, *June 6, 1944*, 197.
8. McCann, *Passing Through*, 103; obituary of Maloney, *Hartford Courant*, 19 August 1994, www.courant.com/news/connecticut/hc-xpm-1994-08-19-9408190853-story.html.
9. Zdon, "For $50 a Month More Pay," 9; 6 June 1944 notation, diary of Sgt. Major Robert Salewski, in the author's possession, courtesy of Martin Morgan.
10. Devlin, *Paratrooper*, 379; Gavin, *On to Berlin*, 104–5; Alexander and Sparry, *Jump Commander*, 176–78.
11. LoFaro, *Sword of St. Michael*, 201.
12. Bearden, *To D-Day and Back*, 110–16; Eddie Page letter to Gary Fox, as told to Betty Fox, April 1990, in the author's possession, courtesy of the Page family; Thomas quoted in Astor, *June 6, 1944*, 186–87.
13. Ibid., 177–79; Isbell quoted in McCann, *Passing Through*, 102.
14. Ridgway, *Soldier*, 3.
15. Bearden, *To D-Day and Back*, 116; S/Sgt. Rabe quoted in conversation with author.
16. Hinchliff OH, 2005; Koskimaki, *D-Day with the Screaming Eagles*, 48; Ridgway quoted in Astor, *June 6, 1944*, 188–89.
17. Renaud, *Sainte Mère Église*, 56.
18. James OH; Isbell and Bowell quoted in McCann, *Passing Through*, 103–4; Koskimaki, *D-Day with the Screaming Eagles*, 49–68; testimony of William Tucker of the 505th Regiment in de Marenne, *French–American Relations*, 62.
19. Ibid., 49–68; Captain C. B. McCoid of the 507th Regiment quoted in Astor, *June 6, 1944*, 172–76; Gavin, *On to Berlin*, 101–2.
20. S/Sgt. Rabe as told to author; on Poss, see Harris, "Highland Man," 4A.
21. Renaud, *Sainte Mère Église*, 51; Pentecôte quoted in Roberts, *D-Day through French Eyes*, 34.
22. Davis quoted in McCann, *Passing Through*, 104.
23. Devlin, *Paratrooper*, 386; LoFaro, *Sword of St. Michael*, 200.
24. Gavin, *On to Berlin*, 104–5; Murphy, *No Better Place to Die*, 42; Langrehr and DeFelice, *Whatever It Took*, 82.
25. Bearden, *To D-Day and Back*, 121–22.
26. Von der Heydte quoted in LoFaro, *Sword of St. Michael*, 325.

27. David Kenyon Webster, *Parachute Infantry: An American Paratrooper's Memoir of D-Day and the Fall of the Third Reich*, with introduction by Stephen E. Ambrose (Baton Rouge, LA and London: Louisiana State University Press, 1994), 3–44.

28. Cornelius Ryan, *The Longest Day: June 6, 1944* (New York: Simon & Schuster, 1959), 168.

29. Norman Costa, *My Father: A Veterans Story*, 2008, https://3quarksdaily.com /3quarksdaily/2008/12/my-.html; Leroy David Brummitt, "Experiences of Captain Leroy David Brummitt during the Allied Invasion of Normandy, France, June 6, 1944," composed in 1999, in the author's possession, courtesy of Martin Morgan, p. 2. For speculation that the C-47 pilots mistakenly followed the wrong river, see Rudy Passera, "Graignes – Bloody Sunday," 13 December 2018, www .normandyamericanheroes.com/blog/graignes-bloody-sunday. One "stick" of the 508th Regiment landed forty miles off target. See LoFaro, *Sword of St. Michael*, 245.

30. Ibid.; Naughton OH, 1998; Page quoted in Pavia, *An American Town Goes to War*, Chapter 11.

31. Marr, "507th Parachute Infantry Regiment," 269; Barnes interview in NBC News, *The Greatest Generation*, Disc 2: *D-Day: A Leap into History*; Steve Shriver, "D-Day Holds a Special Memory for Keosaugua Veteran: Staff Sgt. Fredric Boyle Remembers Events from 60 Years Ago," *Van Buren County Register*, 3 June 2004; Naughton OH, 1998; Costa, "My Father"; Page quoted in Pavia, *An American Town Goes to War*, Chapter 11.

32. Hinchliff quoted in Zdon, "For $50 a Month More Pay," 9; Pezerin quoted in Roberts, *D-Day through French Eyes*, 59.

33. On Page, Pavia, *An American Town Goes to War*, Chapter 11; paratrooper Henry Langrehr quoted in Langrehr and DeFelice, *Whatever It Took*, 93; on Rabe, conversation, as related to author in 2020, between Rabe and his son, Richard E. Rabe of Willington, CT.

34. On toy metal clickers see Blair, *Ridgway's Paratroopers*, 228; Barnes quoted in G. H. Bennett, *Destination Normandy: Three American Regiments on D-Day* (Westport, CT: Stackpole Books, 2007), 105; Spencer F. Wurst and Gayle Wurst, *Descending from the Clouds: A Memoir of Combat in the 505th Parachute Infantry Regiment, 82nd Division* (Haverton, PA: Casemate, 2004), 127.

35. Page quoted in Pavia, *An American Town Goes to War*, Chapter 11; entry of 6 June 1944 at 02:38 a.m. in Diary of Sgt./Major Robert Salewski; "Statement of Private Marion Hatton," in the author's possession, courtesy of Dominique François.

36. Brummitt, "Experiences of Captain Leroy David Brummitt," 2; Naughton OH, 1998; Barnes quoted in Bennett, *Destination Normandy*, 105.

37. Morales quoted in Astor, *June 6, 1944*, 197; George "Pete" Buckley, "D-Day Experience of Flight Officer Morales, an American Glider Pilot," www .ww2gp.org/normandy/accounts/ErwinMoralesbyBuckley.php. See also Morgan, *D-Day*, 196.

38. Juliano quoted in Koskimaki, *D-Day with the Screaming Eagles*, 49, 116–17; letters of Juliano to Clarence Hughart of Arvarda, Colorado, 11 December 1982 and 23 February 1983, and letter to "Tom," 25 November 1982, all in the author's possession, courtesy of the Martinez family; Mark Bando, "Lest We Forget," www .101airborneww2.com/lestweforget.html.

39. Notes in 1964 by Pastor Louis Binet on records of Abbé Guyot, Curé in Graignes, 1944–1953, in the author's possession.

40. Voydie quoted in Koskimaki, *D-Day with the Screaming Eagles*, 324; Boursier's activities in Lt. Col. Earcle Reed (Ret.) and Col. Francis E. Naughton (Ret.) to

Secretary of the Army John O. Marsh, "Recommendations for Awards," 13 February 1986, in the author's possession, courtesy of the Naughton family; notes in 1964 by Pastor Binet on records of Abbé Guyot, Curé in Graignes.

41. Lepourry's account (translated by author) in François, *La bataille de Graignes*, 47.
42. Pezerin and Hamel-Hateu quoted in Roberts, *D-Day through French Eyes*, 54–59.
43. Marthe Rigault Testimony, "4 Days in June" ("*4 Jours en juin*"), https://quatrejour senjuin.com/76eme-live/marthe-rigault-temoigne-episode-1/.
44. Lelavechef and His OH, 2003; Rigault His, "Madam Marthe His Presents Her Child's Eye View."
45. Hinchliff OH, 2002.
46. Lelavechef and His OH, 2003; Decaumont quoted in Bennett, *Destination Normandy*, 106.
47. Reed quoted in Morgan, *Down to Earth*, 239; Naughton OH, 1998.
48. Brummitt, "Experiences of Captain Leroy David Brummitt during the Allied Invasion of Normandy," 2–3.
49. Ibid., 3.
50. Ibid., 3.
51. Van Den Brink, *Carentan*, 55.
52. Salewski Diary, entries 6 and 7 June 1944; Rigault His, "Madame Marthe Rigault His Presents Her Child's Eye View."
53. Hinchliff OH, 2005.
54. Fox, *Graignes*, 29, 68–69. Paratroopers in the 101st Airborne Division also jumped with carrier pigeons. They enclosed the birds in an 81 mm mortar shell box. Koskimaki, *D-Day with the Screaming Eagles*, 79.
55. For estimates of US troop strength in Graignes, see Hinchliff OH, 2002; Naughton OH, 1998; Brummitt, "Experiences of Captain Leroy David Brummitt during the Allied Invasion of Normandy," 2; entry, 11 June 1944, Salewski Diary; Fox, *Graignes*, 28; Morgan, *Down to Earth*, 238; Martin Morgan interview in November 2020 with Paul Woodadge in "Graignes 1944 – Challenging a Legend," www.youtube.com/watch?v=_y8xA74Zy7I. Sgt. Major Salewski lists 14 officers and 168 enlisted men. His diary entry of 11 June 1944 is a compelling piece of evidence, because the notation was presumably made the day of the battle in Graignes. In fact, there were fifteen officers, not fourteen, in Graignes on 11 June. Salewski apparently believed Lt. Morales, a glider pilot, was a non-commissioned officer or warrant officer. Salewski refers to him as "Mister Morales." Eleven officers from Headquarters Company landed near Graignes. The other four officers were the two glider pilots and the two officers from the 101st Airborne Division – the injured Captain Bogart and Lt. George Murn.

Salewski's calculation of 168 enlisted men is problematic. US military personnel listed in any history, memoir, oral history, or interview that pertains to Graignes can be traced to the nine-plane "V" that carried Headquarters Company personnel, the C-47 that carried a stick of B Company of the 101st Airborne Division, or the four men on the glider plane. Fleet Sgt. Black and two unidentified 29th Infantry men walked into Graignes. Five paratroopers from Headquarters Company and possibly one paratrooper from B Company died on D-Day. This leaves a total of 149 enlisted men defending Graignes. In addition, the fifty personnel who are listed as killed in action at the Memorial in Graignes can be identified as being with the same groups. It is possible that one additional C-47 dropped paratroopers near Graignes. If so, the stick had no officers, none of the men died, and none did anything at Graignes that caught the attention of others. Dominique François suggested that a tenth C-47 dropped Headquarters Company paratroopers near Graignes. François, *La bataille de Graignes*, 84. François no longer believes that (email to author), and the suggestion can be readily disproved. The C-47, #42–32870, carried Lt. Willard E. Chambers. Lt. Chambers received the Silver Star for his bravery on 8 June 1944 in Normandy far away from Graignes. See The Hall of Valor Project, "Willard E. Chambers: Silver Star," https://valor.militarytimes.com/hero/90425.

56. Craig Bowman, "Australian Pilot Honoured for Fighting in Graignes," 12 July 2015, www.warhistoryonline.com/war-articles/australian-pilot-honoured-for-fighting-in-graignes.html. See also Morgan, *D-Day*, 199.

57. Dunn OH, 1994.

58. Hinchliff OH, 2003.

59. Reed and Naughton to Secretary of Army on service of Alphonse Voydie in "Recommendations for Awards."

60. Boursier-Lereculey quoted in François, *La bataille de Graignes*, 66–67.

61. Morgan, *Down to Earth*, 238.

62. Brummitt, "Experiences of Captain Leroy David Brummitt during the Allied Invasion of Normandy," 1.

63. Bennett, *Destination Normandy*, 106.

64. Voydie quoted in Reed and Naughton to the Secretary of the Army on service of Alphonse Voydie in "Recommendations for Awards."

65. Rigault sisters quoted in Georgia Public Broadcasting, *Papa Said: We Should Never Forget*, DVD, and NBC News, *Greatest Generation*, Disc 2: *D-Day: A Leap into History*.

5 Days of Friendship, Hope, and Waiting

1. East Tennessee Veterans Memorial Association, https://etvma.org/veterans/charles-d-johnston-7799/.

2. Reed and Naughton to the Secretary of the Army in the narrative "Recommendations for Awards"; Brummitt, "Experiences of Captain Leroy David Brummitt during the Allied Invasion of Normandy," 2–3.

3. Ibid., 3.

4. Ibid., 3.

5. Morgan, "Battle of Graignes," *Warfare History Network*; Mark Bando, "Lest We Forget: Remembering the Fallen 101st Airborne Heroes of the Battle of Graignes, France," www.101airborneww2.com/lestweforget.html; Roberts, *D-Day through French Eyes*, 59; Page quoted in Pavia, *An American Town Goes to War*, Chapter 11; Norman Costa, "My Father: A Veterans Story," https://3quarksdaily.com/3quarksdaily/2008/12/my-.html.

6. Naughton OH, 1998; NBC News, *Greatest Generation*, Disc 2: *D-Day: A Leap into History*; Morgan, "Battle of Graignes," *Warfare History Network*; Brummitt, "Experiences of Captain Leroy David Brummitt during the Allied Invasion of Normandy," 5.

7. Fox, *Graignes*, 22; Pezerin quoted in Roberts, *D-Day through French Eyes*, 59–61; Georgia Public Broadcasting, *Papa Said: We Should Never Forget*, DVD.

8. Page quoted in Pavia, *An American Town Goes to War*, Chapter 11.

9. Diary entry, 6 June 1944, Salewski Diary; on Poss see Harris, "Highland Man," 4A; "Statement of Private Marion Hatton."

10. Diary entry, 8 June 1944, Salewski Diary.

11. Naughton OH, 1998; Costa, "My Father: A Veteran's Story."

12. Letter, Juliano to Hughart, 11 December 1982 and 23 February 1983.

13. Brummitt, "Experiences of Captain Leroy David Brummitt during the Allied Invasion of Normandy," 3.

14. Voydie quoted in François, *La bataille de Graignes*, 61.

15. Ibid., 63; diary entry, 10 June 1944, Salewski Diary.

16. Pezerin quoted in Roberts, *D-Day through French Eyes*, 59.

17. Bearden, *To D-Day and Back*, 226–27: James OH; Isbell quoted in McCann, *Passing Through*, 122; Alexander and Sparry, *Jump Commander*, 196–97.

18. Page quoted in Pavia, *An American Town Goes to War*, Chapter 11.

19. Naughton OH, 1998; Brummitt, "Experiences of Captain Leroy David Brummitt during the Allied Invasion of Normandy," 5.

20. Testimony of Madame S. Pezerin in Roberts, *D-Day through French Eyes*, 60–61.

21. Reed and Naughton to Secretary of Army, "Recommendation for Alphonse Voydie"; Breuer, *Geronimo*, 274; Fox, *Graignes*, 21.

22. Reed and Naughton to the Secretary of the Army, "Recommendation for Abbé Albert Le Blastier."

23. Breuer, *Geronimo*, 274; Reed and Naughton to the Secretary of the Army, "Recommendations for Joseph Folliot and Charles Gosselin."

24. Morgan, *Down to Earth*, 260. Unlike his father, Isidore, Joseph Folliot is not listed as a casualty on the Memorial in Graignes. The name "Georges Folliot" is listed on the Memorial.

25. Lelavechef and His OH, 2003; Morgan, *Down to Earth*, 239–40.

26. Naughton OH, 1998.

27. Entry, 7 June 1944, Salewski Diary.

28. Rigault His, "Madame Marthe His Presents Her Child's Eye View;" Marthe Rigault Testimony, "4 Days in June" ("*4 Jours en juin*"), https://quatrejoursenjuin.com /76eme-live/marthe-rigault-temoigne-episode-1/.

29. Reed and Naughton to Secretary of Army, "Recommendations for Germaine Boursier and Renée Meunier"; testimonies of Denise Boursier-Lereculey and Madame S. Pezerin in Roberts, *D-Day through French Eyes*, 57–60; Breuer, *Geronimo*, 273–74; Naughton OH, 2003.

30. Author's interview with Rigault His, 16 May 2019; Rigault His, "Madame Marthe His Presents Her Child's Eye View." For the lyrics and an English translation of *Ma Normandie*, see https://en.wikipedia.org/wiki/Ma_Normandie.

31. Testimonies of Denise Boursier-Lereculey and Madame S. Pezerin in Roberts, *D-Day through French Eyes*, 57–62.

32. Peros quoted in Dave McNamara, "Heart of Louisiana: Cajun Paratrooper," www .fox8live.com/2019/06/05/heart-louisiana-cajun-paratrooper/.

33. Roberts, *D-Day through French Eyes*, 4; Funk, "Caught in the Middle," 254–55; Robert Lynn Fuller, *After D-Day: The U.S. Army Encounters the French* (Baton Rouge, LA: Louisiana State University Press, 2021), 70–81.

34. Ibid., 249.

35. Anne's testimony in Roberts, *D-Day through French Eyes*, 18.

36. Transmissions of 6 June 1944 in *Tagebuch* of the 17th *SS Panzergrenadier* Division.

37. Corey Adwar, "This Never-Before-Seen WW II Document Offers an Inside Account of an Elite Nazi Combat Unit's Collapse," *Business Insider*, 11 July 2014, www .businessinsider.com/never-before-seen-document-reveals-nazi-soldiers-struggle-2014-7. The document is "Special IPW (Interrogation of Prisoner of War) Report: The Odyssey of Götz Von Berlichingen." The German officer is not identified.

38. Afiero, *The 17th Waffen-SS Panzergrenadier Division*, 29–30.

39. Ibid., 29–30, 41; Stöber, *Combat History of the 17. SS-Panzer-Grenadier-Division*, 33–49.

40. Ibid., 19, 21–23, 34; Afiero, *The 17th Waffen-SS Panzergrenadier Division*, 13.

41. Stöber, *Combat History of the 17. SS-Panzer-Grenadier-Division*, 41–43.

42. Adwar, "This Never-Before-Seen WW II Document."
43. Ibid.
44. Transmission of 8 June 1944 in *Tagebuch* of the 17th *SS Panzergrenadier* Division.
45. Adwar, "This Never-Before-Seen WW II Document."
46. Transmission of 9 June 1944 in *Tagebuch* of the 17th *SS Panzergrenadier* Division.
47. Adwar, "This Never-Before-Seen WW II Document."
48. Transmissions of 9, 10, 11 June 1944 in *Tagebuch* of the 17th *SS Panzergrenadier* Division.
49. Stöber, *Combat History of the 17. SS-Panzer-Grenadier-Division*, 61.
50. Transmissions of 9 June 1944 in *Tagebuch* of the 17th *SS Panzergrenadier* Division.
51. Transmission of 11 June 1944, ibid.
52. *Abschrift, Hauptsturmführer, SS Pz.Gren.Rgt. 37 an Div. Ia, "Rgt.Gef.Std., 11.6.44, 23:50 Uhr"* (Copy, Captain, *SS* 17th *Panzergrenadier Regiment* 37 to Chief of Staff of Regiment 37, "Regimental Combat Report, 11 June 1944, 11:50 p.m."). The signature of the captain is illegible. Translated by Genice A. G. Rabe. Document in the author's possession, courtesy of Mayor Denis Small of Graignes.
53. Koskimaki, *D-Day with the Screaming Eagles*, 61–112, 310.
54. Ambrose, *Band of Brothers*, 71–107; Van Den Brink, *Carentan*, 4–5, 18–33.
55. Bradley quoted in Fuller, *After D-Day*, 78; Rommel quoted in Ambrose, *Band of Brothers*, 91.
56. Van Den Brink, *Carentan*, 34–55; Transmission of 11 June 1944 in *Tagebuch* of the 17th *SS Panzergrenadier* Division.
57. Afiero, *The 17th Waffen-SS Panzergrenadier Division*, 33–35.
58. Transmissions of 11 June 1944 in *Tagebuch* of the 17th *SS Panzergrenadier* Division.
59. *Abschrift, Hauptsturmführer, SS Pz.Gren.Rgt. 37 an Div. Ia, "Rgt.Gef.Std., 11.6.44, 23:50 Uhr."*

6 The Longest Day in Graignes

1. Delacotte quoted in Roberts, *D-Day through French Eyes*, 67.
2. Ryan, *The Longest Day*.
3. Perezin quoted in Roberts, *D-Day through French Eyes*, 61.
4. Diary entry, 11 June 1944, Salewski Diary.
5. Folliot quoted in Roberts, *D-Day through French Eyes*, 62.
6. Odette Lelavechef and Marthe His OH, 2003.
7. Hinchliff OH, 2005; Morgan, *Down to Earth*, 243.
8. Reed and Naughton to the Secretary of the Army, "Recommendations for Awards," with citations of Boursier, Folliot, Gosselin, and Voydie.
9. Naughton OH, 1998.
10. Boursier-Lereculey cited in Roberts, *D-Day through French Eyes*, 57; Naughton OH, 1998.
11. Letters to author from historian Martin Morgan, 23 April 2019, and from Mayor Denis Small of Graignes, 20 April 2019, in the author's possession.
12. Naughton OH, 1998; Hinchliff OH, 2005; Zdon, "For $50 a Month More Pay"; "Statement of Private Marion Hatton."
13. Fox, *Graignes*, 38; testimony of Michel Folliot in Roberts, *D-Day through French Eyes*, 62.
14. Diary entry, 11:00 hours, 11 June 1944, Salewski Diary.

15. Diary entry, 12:30 hours, 11 June 1944, ibid.; Headquarters Company Morning Report, 24 July 1944, Tollerton, Nottingham, on promotions of Biggerstaff, Liberty, and Rabe on 16 June 1944, in the author's possession.

16. *Abschrift, Hauptsturmführer, SS Pz.Gren.Rgt. 37 an Div. Ia, "Rgt.Gef.Std., 11.6.44, 23:50 Uhr."*

17. Hinchliff OH, 2005.

18. Costa, "My Father: A Veterans Story."

19. Diary entry, 19:00 hours, 11 June 1944, Salewski Diary.

20. McNamara, "Heart of Louisiana: Cajun Paratrooper." Danielle Peros, niece of Odette, told the story.

21. Lelavechef and His OH, 2003.

22. Testimony of Denise Boursier in François, *La bataille de Graignes*, 66–67. Translated by the author.

23. Naughton OH, 1998.

24. Brummitt, "Experiences of Captain Leroy David Brummitt," 6.

25. Diary entries, from 20:00 hours on, 11 June 1944, Salewski Diary.

26. Morgan, *Down to Earth*, 246.

27. For the artillery arsenal, see Munoz, *Iron Fist*, 56; Afiero, *The 17th Waffen-SS Panzergrenadier Division*, 21.

28. Reed quoted in Fox, *Graignes*, 39; "Statement of Private Marion Hatton"; Disinterment Directive, Pvt. Arnold J. Martinez, Blosville Cemetery, Normandy, France, 15 November 1947, US Army Resources Command, Ft. Knox, Kentucky. This report provides a general autopsy. See also email, Sarah Martínez to author, 18 August 2021, in the author's possession.

29. Naughton OH, 1998; Naughton comments on Lt. Farnham in NBC News, *The Greatest Generation with Tom Brokaw*, DVD, Disc 2: *D-Day: A Leap into History*.

30. Morgan, *Down to Earth*, 246; Morgan, *D-Day*, 204; Morgan, "Battle of Graignes."

31. Pezerin quoted in Roberts, *D-Day through French Eyes*, 62.

32. Morgan, "Battle of Graignes."

33. Venditti, Maurer, and Mutti, *Six Days*.

34. Hinchliff OH, 2005.

35. Boursier cited in François, *La bataille de Graignes*, 66–67.

36. Naughton quoted in NBC News, *The Greatest Generation with Tom Brokaw*, DVD, Disc 2: *D-Day: A Leap into History*.

37. Breuer, *Geronimo*, 277.

38. Barnes quoted in NBC News, *The Greatest Generation with Tom Brokaw*, DVD, Disc 2: *D-Day: A Leap into History*. For a different view of Lt. Ahmad's fate, see Buckley, "D-Day Experience of Flight Officer Morales."

39. Page quoted in Pavia, *An American Town Goes to War*, Chapter 11.

40. Hinchliff OH, 2005.

41. Rigault's testimony in City of Carentan, "4 Days in June" ("*4 Jours en juin*"), 2020. Link to interview is no longer available. A summary of the interview is in the author's possession.

42. Voydie quoted in François, *La bataille de Graignes*, 61.

43. Naughton OH, 1998; Naughton OH, 2003.

44. Hinchliff OH, 2005.

45. Brummitt, "Experiences of Captain Leroy David Brummitt," 3–4.

46. Richig quoted in Fox, *Graignes*, 40.

47. Diary entries, 11–12 June 1944, Salewski Diary; Brummitt, "Experiences of Captain Leroy David Brummitt," 3–4.

48. Ibid., 3.

49. Zdon, "For $50 a Month More Pay," 9; Hinchliff OH, 2005.
50. Author's telephone interview with Jonathan J. Boyle of Springfield, MO, 6 June 2020; "Keosauqua Man Observes 50th Anniversary of D-Day," *Van Buren County Register* (Iowa), 5 May 1994.
51. Naughton OH, 1998; NBC News, *The Greatest Generation with Tom Brokaw*, DVD, Disc 2: *D-Day: A Leap into History*.
52. François, *La bataille de Graignes*, 66.
53. Afiero, *The 17th Waffen-SS Panzergrenadier Division*; Munoz, *Iron Fist*; Stöber, *Combat History of the 17. SS-Panzer-Grenadier-Division*.
54. Transmissions of 11 and 12 June 1944 in *Tagebuch* of the 17th *SS Panzergrenadier Division*; *Abschrift, Hauptsturmführer, SS-Pz.Gren.Rgt. 37 an Div. Ia, "Rgt.Gef. Std., 11.6.44, 23:50 Uhr."*
55. Brummitt, "Experiences of Captain Leroy David Brummitt," 4.
56. O'Leary and O'Leary, *Tragedy at Graignes*, 247.
57. Koskimaki, *D-Day with the Screaming Eagles*, 281–301.
58. Pezerin quoted in Roberts, *D-Day through French Eyes*, 64.
59. Boursier quoted in François, *La bataille de Graignes*, 66–67.
60. Ibid., 66–67.
61. Pezerin quoted in Roberts, *D-Day through French Eyes*, 65.
62. Odette Lelavechef and Marthe His OH, 2003.
63. Boursier notes in François, *La bataille de Graignes*, 66–67.
64. Voydie testimony in Morgan, *Down to Earth*, 258.
65. Baragona Cook quotation found at www.findagrave.com/memorial/10567116/george-strickle-baragona.
66. Pezerin quoted in Roberts, *D-Day through French Eyes*, 64.
67. Mayor Poullain testimony in Morgan, *Down to Earth*, 258.
68. Bando, "Lest We Forget."
69. Morgan, *D-Day*, 207–8.
70. O'Leary and O'Leary, *Tragedy at Graignes*, 260–74.
71. Morgan, *Down to Earth*, 246–48; Morgan, *D-Day*, 208.
72. Statement of Technical/Sgt. George Colli, 22 January 1946 in Adjutant General File 201, Johnston, Charles D. in Casualty Branch and Officers Branch, Adjutant General Office, in the author's possession, courtesy of Martin Morgan.
73. Disinternment Directive, Pvt. Arnold J. Martinez, Blosville Cemetery, Normandy, France, 15 November 1947, US Army Resources Command. This report provides the coordinates where Martinez's body was located.
74. Of the thirty-two citizens of Graignes who are memorialized, some may have died before or after the period between 6 and 16 June 1944.
75. Boursier quoted in François, *La bataille de Graignes*, 66–67.
76. Pezerin quoted in Roberts, *D-Day through French Eyes*, 63–66.
77. Ibid., 65.
78. Morgan, *Down to Earth*, 259.
79. Transmissions of 11 and 12 June 1944 in *Tagebuch* of the 17th *SS Panzergrenadier Division*.
80. Delacotte quoted in Roberts, *D-Day through French Eyes*, 67.
81. Morgan, *Down to Earth*, 259; Clout, "Reconstruction in the Manche *département* after the Normandy Landings," 8.
82. Page quoted in Pavia, *An American Town Goes to War*, Chapter 11.
83. Steven P. Remy, *The Malmedy Massacre: The War Crimes Trial Controversy* (Cambridge, MA and London: Harvard University Press, 2017), 11.
84. Ibid., 3, 6–9, 24.

85. Eckhertz, *D Day through German Eyes*, 33.
86. Deputy Judge Advocate's Office, 7708 War Crimes Group, European Command, *United States versus Erwin Wilhelm Konrad Schienkiewitz*, Case No. 11–18, 4 April 1947, "Review and Recommendations," www.online.uni-marburg.de /icwc/dachau/000-011-0018.pdf.
87. Transmissions from the 38th Regiment, 20:15 hours, 12 June 1944 in *Tagebuch* of the 17th *SS Panzergrenadier* Division.
88. Sébastien Chevereau and Luc Forlivesi, "Histoire et mémoire d'un massacre: Maillé, Indre & Loire" ("History and memory of a massacre, Maillé, Indre & Loire"), www .fondationresistance.org/documents/ee/Doc00004-008.pdf.
89. Remy, *Malmedy Massacre*, 25; Eckhertz, *D Day through German Eyes*, 20: Norman Ohler, *Blitzed: Drugs in Nazi Germany* (Boston, MA: Mariner Books, 2018).

7 Escape, Exile, and Annihilation

1. Brummitt, "Experiences of Captain Leroy David Brummitt," 3–4.
2. Entry, 12 June 1944, Salewski Diary.
3. Ibid.; Brummitt, "Experiences of Captain Leroy David Brummitt," 3–4.
4. Pezerin quoted in Roberts, *D-Day through French Eyes*, 66.
5. Naughton OH, 1998; Naughton testimony in NBC News, *The Greatest Generation with Tom Brokaw*, DVD, Disc 2: *D-Day: A Leap into History*.
6. Brummitt, "Experiences of Captain Leroy David Brummitt," 3–4.
7. Hinchliff OH, 2005.
8. Diary entry, 13 June 1944, Salewski Diary; Hinchliff OH, 2005.
9. Naughton quoted in Fox, *Graignes*, 42.
10. Marthe Rigault interview, "4 Days in June" ("4 *Jours en juin*"); Rigault His, "Madame Marthe His Presents Her Child's Eye View"; Lelavechef and His OH, 2003.
11. Fox, *Graignes*, 44.
12. Page quoted in Pavia, *An American Town Goes to War*, Chapter 11; Fox, *Graignes*, 44.
13. Rabe as told to author.
14. Costa quoted in Fox, *Graignes*, 44–45.
15. Page quoted in Breuer, *Geronimo*, 280–81; Pavia, *An American Town Goes to War*, Chapter 11.
16. Marthe quoted in Rigault His, "Madame Marthe His Presents Her Child's Eye View."
17. Odette quoted in Lelavechef and His OH, 2003.
18. Ibid.; author's interview with Rigault His, 20 May 2019; Rigault His, "Madame Marthe His Presents Her Child's Eye View"; Rigault interview, "4 Days in June" ("4 *Jours en juin*"); Morgan, *Down to Earth*, 256–57.
19. Fox, *Graignes*, 46–49; Shriver, "D-Day Holds a Special Memory for Keosauqua Veteran."
20. Astor, *June 6, 1944*, 404.
21. Morgan, *D-Day*, 208; testimony of Madame Odile Delacotte in Roberts, *D-Day through French Eyes*, 67–68.
22. Testimony of Denise Boursier in François, *La bataille de Graignes*, 66–67; Bennett, *Destination Normandy*, 125; testimony of S. Pezerin in Roberts, *D-Day through French Eyes*, 63.
23. Bando, "Lest We Forget."

24. Transmissions, 11–12 June 1944, in *Tagebuch* of the 17th *SS Panzergrenadier* Division.

25. Page quoted in Pavia, *An American Town Goes to War*, Chapter 11. See also Ridgway, *Soldier*, 15–16; Booth and Spencer, *Paratrooper*, 189.

26. LoFaro, *Sword of St. Michael*, 252–56; Marr, "507th Parachute Infantry Regiment," 269–70.

27. Booth and Spencer, *Paratrooper*, 199–200; Alexander and Sparry, *Jump Commander*, 199–200.

28. Entries 20 and 21 June 1944, Salewski Diary.

29. Entry 28 June 1944, ibid.; Sean Yoder, "Remembering Penn State ROTC Building's Namesake, H. Edward Wagner," www.psu.edu/news/university-park/story/remembering-penn-state-rotc-buildings-namesake-h-edward-wagner/.

30. As related to the author by S/Sgt. Rabe; McKenzie, *On Time, on Target*, 20.

31. J. Glenn Gray, *The Warriors: Reflections of Men in Battle* (New York: Harcourt, Brace and Company, 1959), 108.

32. Tucker quoted in Wills, *Put on Your Boots*, 228–29.

33. Gray, *The Warriors*, 237–38.

34. Raff quoted in Alexander, *Jump Commander*, 223; Blair, *Ridgway's Paratroopers*, 292–93.

35. Ridgway, *Soldier*, 15–16; Raff quoted in *Ridgway's Paratroopers*, 292–93.

36. Alexander and Sparry, *Jump Commander*, 232.

37. Quoted in ibid., 231.

38. Hinchliff OH, 2005; LoFaro, *Sword of St. Michael*, 257–62.

39. Ibid., 257–62; Marr, "507th Parachute Infantry Regiment," 271.

40. LoFaro, *Sword of St. Michael*, 263–64; Devlin, *Paratrooper*, 417.

41. Steiger quoted in Wills, *Put on Your Boots*, 115.

42. Lelavechef and His OH, 2003; Morgan, *Down to Earth*, 260–61.

43. Reed and Naughton to the Secretary of the Army, "Recommendation for Joseph Folliot."

44. Lelavechef and His OH, 2003; author's interview with Marthe Rigault His, 16 May 2019.

45. Boursier quoted in François, *La bataille de Graignes*, 66–67.

46. Author's interview with Mayor Denis Small of Graignes, 19 May 2019.

47. Boursier quoted in François, *La bataille de Graignes*, 66–67.

48. Palla family saga in ibid., 70–71.

49. Ibid., 70–71.

50. Author's interview with Rigault His, 16 May 2019; Lelavechef and His OH, 2003; Marthe Rigault Testimony, "4 Days in June" ("*4 Jours en juin*"), https://quatrejoursenjuin.com/76eme-live/marthe-rigault-temoigne-episode-4-les-retrouvailles/.

51. Ibid.

52. Lelavechef and His OH, 2003; Rigault His, "Madame Marthe His Presents Her Child's Eye View."

53. Clout, "Reconstruction in the Manche *département* after the Normandy Landings," 6–17; author's interview with Mayor Denis Small, 19 May 2019; Layton Funk, "Caught in the Middle," 254–55.

54. Transmissions from 03:01 to 16:15 hours, 13 June 1944, in *Tagebuch* of the 17th *SS Panzergrenadier* Division.

55. Afiero, *The 17th Waffen-SS Panzergrenadier Division*, 39–41; Stöber, *Combat History of the 17. SS Panzer-Grenadier-Division*, 70–72.

56. Ibid., 70–72.

57. Ostendorff quoted in Afiero, *The 17th Waffen-SS Panzergrenadier Division*, 41.

58. Ostendorff transmission, 06:52 hours, 13 June 1944, in *Tagebuch* of the 17th *SS Panzergrenadier* Division; Stöber, *Combat History of the 17. SS Panzer-Grenadier-Division*, 73.

59. Hoffmann quoted in ibid., 77–80.

60. Transmissions from 03:01 to 16:15 hours, 13 June 1944, in *Tagebuch* of the 17th *SS Panzergrenadier* Division.

61. Hoffman quoted in Stöber, *Combat History of the 17. SS Panzer-Grenadier-Division*, 77–80.

62. Ambrose, *Band of Brothers*, 99–107; Van Den Brink, *Carentan*, 75; Afiero, *The 17th Waffen-SS Panzergrenadier Division*, 45–50; Stöber, *Combat History of the 17. SS-Panzer-Grenadier-Division*, 80–81.

63. Quoted in ibid., 84.

64. "Special IPW (Interrogation of Prisoner of War) Report: The Odyssey of Götz Von Berlichingen."

65. Stöber, *Combat History of the 17. SS-Panzer-Grenadier-Division*, 131–32.

66. Munoz, *Iron Fist*, 7, 10–11, 31; Afiero, *The 17th Waffen-SS Panzergrenadier Division*, 73–77, 104, 112; Stöber, *Combat History of the 17. SS-Panzer Grenadier-Division*, 169, 204, 213–14, 229, 236, 481, 524.

67. "Special IPW (Interrogation of Prisoner of War) Report: The Odyssey of Götz Von Berlichingen."

8 Graignes in Historical Memory

1. Gavin's remarks in Fauntleroy, *The General and His Daughter*, 225, fn#1.

2. LoFaro, *Sword of St. Michael*, 270–71.

3. Raff quoted in Blair, *Ridgway's Paratroopers*, 441.

4. Smith quoted in ibid., 301; Hinchliff OH, 2005. For a video of the victory parade in New York City, see www.youtube.com/watch?v=7v4OMPhRDIM.

5. Murphy OH, 2015.

6. Smith quoted in Morgan, *Down to Earth*, 271–72.

7. Telephone interview with John Brummitt, son of David Brummitt, of Hilton Head, South Carolina, 6 June 2020.

8. Hinchliff OH, 2005.

9. S/Sgt. Rabe to author; Riddle OH.

10. Wurst and Wurst, *Descending from the Clouds*, 231–37.

11. Hinchliff OH, 2005; interview with John Brummitt; interview with Patricia Naughton, Seattle, Washington, 1 September 2019.

12. "Operations of the 3rd Battalion, 507th Parachute Infantry (17th Airborne Division): 'The Battle of Dead Man's Ridge,' Vicinity of Laval–Chisogne, Belgium, 7–8 January 1945 (Ardennes Campaign)." Advanced Infantry Officers Course, 1948–1949. Academic Department, The Infantry School, Fort Benning, GA. In the author's possession, courtesy of Sandra Smith, daughter of Major General Paul Smith.

13. Hinchliff OH, 2005.

14. Ibid.; Marr, "507th Parachute Infantry Regiment," 271–72.

15. Ibid.

16. Ibid., 265, 272.

17. Letter, Gavin to his daughter, 31 July 1944, Fauntleroy, *The General and His Daughter*, 118–19.

18. Hinchliff OH, 2005.

19. A good synopsis can be found in Marr, "507th Parachute Infantry Regiment," 272–76.

20. Zdon, "For $50 a Month More Pay," 10; Hinchliff, OH, 2003; S/Sgt. Rabe as told to author.

21. Blair, *Ridgway's Paratroopers*, 486.

22. Letter, Gavin to his daughter, 9 April 1945, Fauntleroy, *The General and His Daughter*, 168–69.

23. Hinchliff OH, 2005; Zdon, "For $50 a Month More Pay," 10.

24. Devlin, *Paratrooper*, 632; Breuer, *Geronimo*, 561; Blair, *Ridgway's Paratroopers*, 486; Ridgway, *Soldier*, 140; S/Sgt. Rabe to author.

25. McKenzie, *On Time, on Target*, 192–200.

26. Rabe to author.

27. For a video of the parade, see www.bing.com/videos/search?q=Allied+Victory+Parade+Berlin&docid=607996816525820903&mid=77CE86F4E7119D232B7877CE86F4E7119D232B78&view=detail&FORM=VIRE.

28. Queen Elizabeth quoted in Palko Karasz, "Prince William Urges Candor in Dealing with Trauma," *New York Times*, 25 January 2019, A7.

29. Dave Phillips, "Yellowed Records Vividly Show Valor That Veterans Concealed," *New York Times*, 5 June 2019, A1.

30. Telephone conversations with Georgene and Michael Heaney, 17 November 2020 and 22 November 2020; Cheryl Page to author, 25 May 2020. Email in the author's possession.

31. Michael Beschloss, "Why Ike Wouldn't Celebrate the D-Day Anniversary," *New York Times*, 19 May 2014.

32. www.cbsnews.com/video/eisenhower-recalls-sacrifices-of-d-day-20-years-later/.

33. Patricia Naughton to author, 4 January 2020; biographical material on Colonel Brummitt provided to author by John Brummitt.

34. Hinchliff OH, 2005.

35. Rabe in Berlin to Maria Rabe, 1 September 1945. Letter in the author's possession.

36. American Psychiatric Association, "What Is Posttraumatic Stress Disorder," www.psychiatry.org/patients-families/ptsd/what-is-ptsd.

37. Hinchliff, OH, 2003; Zdon, "For $50 a Month More Pay," 8–10.

38. Telephone interview with Jonathan Boyle of Springfield, MO, 5 June 2020.

39. Telephone interview with John Brummitt, 6 June 2020.

40. Fletcher to author, 21 June 2018.

41. Telephone interview with Georgene Penchard Heaney of Long Island, NY, 22 November 2020.

42. Richard E. Rabe to author, 17 March 2020. Post-traumatic stress was commonplace among paratroopers, see Alexander and Sparry, *Jump Commander*, 253–63; McKenzie, *On Time, on Target*, viii–ix; Wurst and Wurst, *Descending from the Clouds*, 256–57.

43. O'Leary and O'Leary, *Tragedy at Graignes*, 259–77.

44. Betty Premo's correspondence can be found in Pfc. Harold J. Premo's service record on deposit at the National Personnel Records Center, St Louis, MO.

45. Ibid.; Disinterment Directive for Harold J. Premo, 15 January 1949, deposited at US Army Human Resources Command.

46. Secretary of Mayor of Graignes, Lt. M. Pontinier, for Mayor Voydie, to Samuel Martinez, 17 July 1952.

47. Sowerine, *France since 1870*, 205–6; Wieviorka, *French Resistance*, 454–58; Mazower, *Hitler's Empire*, 521.

48. Renaud, *Sainte Mère Église*, 60, 67, 102, 118.

49. *Mother of Normandy: The Story of Simone Renaud*, DVD, World War II Museum, 2010.
50. Rosbottom, *Sudden Courage*, 242.
51. Clout, "Reconstruction in the Manche," 20; Layton Funk, "Caught in the Middle," 254–55.
52. Adam Nossiter, "'Archaeology of D-Day' Aims to Preserve What the Solders Left Behind," *New York Times*, 5 June 2019, A8.
53. Astor, *June 6, 1944*, 44; letters of Juliano to Clarence Hughart of Arvarda, CO, 11 December 1982 and 23 February 1983, and letter to "Tom," 25 November 1982; François, *La bataille de Graignes*, 73–80.
54. Pavia, *An American Town Goes to War*, Chapter 11.
55. Rigault His, "Madam Marthe Presents Her Child's Eye View."
56. Email, Patricia Naughton to author, 11 January 2021, in the author's possession.
57. Rigault His, "Madam Marthe His Presents Her Child's Eye View"; Marthe Rigault Testimony, "4 Days in June" ("*4 Jours en juin*"), https://quatrejoursenjuin.com /76eme-live/marthe-rigault-temoigne-episode-4-les-retrouvailles/; Lelavechef and His OH, 2003; telephone conversation with Cheryl Page, 15 May 2018; letter, His Rigault to author, 31 January 2020, in the author's possession.
58. Email, Patricia Naughton to author, 11 January 2021; Reed and Naughton (Ret.) to Marsh, "Recommendations for Awards," 13 February 1986, in the author's possession.
59. *Denver Post*, 8 July 1986.
60. Munoz, *Iron Fist*, 7–31, 63.
61. Afiero, *The 17th Waffen-SS Panzergrenadier Division*, 6.
62. Stöber, *Combat History of the 17. SS-Panzer-Grenadier-Division*, 70–75.

Afterword

1. Reports of Reviewers B & C for Cambridge University Press, in the author's possession.

UNPUBLISHED PRIMARY SOURCES

Archives

Mémoire & Database: Les Cimetières Provisoires (Memory & Database: Temporary Cemeteries). Normandy, France.
National Personnel Records Center. St. Louis, Missouri.
US Army Human Resources Command. Ft. Knox, Kentucky.

Interviews and Letters

Jonathan Boyle, 2020. Springfield, Missouri.
John Brummitt, 2020–2021. Hilton Head, South Carolina.
Sherry (Poss) Fletcher, 2018–2021. Highland, Illinois.
Dominique François, 2019–2021. Carentan, Normandy.
Sally A. Granlund, 2019. Belle Vernon, Pennsylvania.
Eric Groce, 2018. Boone, North Carolina.
Georgene Penchard Heaney, 2020. Manorville, New York.
Michael Heaney, 2020–2021. Long Island, New York.
Marthe Rigault His, 2019. Carentan, Normandy.
Margaret Kovach, 2019. Edison, New Jersey.
Frédéric Lavernhe, 2020. Normandy, France.
Doreen (Page) McKenna, 2019–2021. Norwalk, Connecticut.
Doris Martinez, 2018–2021. Lakewood, Colorado.
Felicia Naranjo Martinez, 2019. Boulder, Colorado.
Jim Martinez, 2019. Boulder, Colorado.

Sarah Irene Martínez, 2021. Makawao, Hawaii.
Wilbur Martinez and Anita Akerley, 2019. Denver, Colorado.
Martin K. A. Morgan, 2018–2020. Ponchatoula, Louisiana.
Patricia Naughton, 2019–2021. Seattle, Washington.
Patrick (Hinchliff) Ostergren, 2018. Minneapolis, Minnesota.
Cheryl Page, 2018–2021. Burlington, Vermont.
Rene E. Rabe, 1957–1982. Vernon, Connecticut.
Richard E. Rabe, 2020. Willington, Connecticut.
John Romeiser, 2019. Knoxville, Tennessee.
Mayor Denis Small, 2019–2021. Graignes, Normandy.

Oral Histories

John Dunn, 1994. Wisconsin Veterans Museum Research Center. Madison, Wisconsin.
John Hinchliff, 2002. World War II Museum. New Orleans. Louisiana.
John Hinchliff, 2005. Minnesota Historical Society. Minneapolis, Minnesota.
James P. James, 2005. Wisconsin Veterans Museum Research Center. Madison, Wisconsin.
Odette Lelavechef and Marthe His, 2003. World War II Museum. New Orleans. Louisiana.
John W. Marr, 2015. World War II Museum. New Orleans. Louisiana.
Robert M. Murphy, 2015. World War II Museum. New Orleans. Louisiana.
Frank Naughton, 2002. World War II Museum. New Orleans. Louisiana.
Clinton Riddle, 2015. World War II Museum. New Orleans. Louisiana.

Private Collection of Stephen G. Rabe

Key primary sources, such as German military documents, are listed in the endnotes as "in the author's possession." These are documents collected by the author or donated to him by the children of the paratroopers, by the villagers of Graignes, and by historians. Any scholar who wishes to gain access to these documents for legitimate intellectual purposes can contact me at rabe@utdallas.edu.

INDEX

Page numbers in *italics* refer to content in figures.